D0101109

THE COLONIAL

REFORMERS

AND CANADA

1830-1849

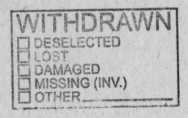

THE COLONIAL
REFORMERS
AND CANADA
1830-1849

SELECTIONS FROM DOCUMENTS

AND

PUBLICATIONS OF THE TIMES

EDITED AND WITH AN INTRODUCTION BY

PETER BURROUGHS

The Carleton Library No. 42

McClelland and Stewart Limited
Toronto / Montreal

The Canadian Publishers

McClelland and Stewart Limited

25 Hollinger Road, Toronto 16

PRINTED AND BOUND IN CANADA BY

T. H. BEST PRINTING COMPANY LIMITED

THE CARLETON LIBRARY

A series of Canadian reprints and new
collections of source material relating
to Canada, issued under the editorial
supervision of the Institute of Canadian
Studies of Carleton University, Ottawa.

1969(B-4119/X

CONTENTS

INTRODUCTION

Most writers on British imperial history have agreed that the Colonial Reformers exerted a decisive influence over colonial policy and practice in the second quarter of the nineteenth century. The distinctive views on systematic colonization and the reform of colonial government put forward by Gibbon Wakefield, Charles Buller, Sir William Molesworth, Lord Durham, and others had a profound and constructive impact on both public opinion in Britain and official policy. In the 1830's and 1840's there was a significant revival of public and parliamentary interest in colonial affairs. During these years large numbers of Englishmen emigrated to various parts of the empire; both the controversy over slavery in the West Indies and the political unrest in Canada produced parliamentary repercussions in England; advocates of economy busily denounced the financial burden imposed on the British taxpayer by colonial administration and defence; and champions of free trade successfully eroded the remaining vestiges of the old colonial system. The small but vocal group of Colonial Reformers in the House of Commons and outside parliament both stimulated and benefited from this renewed debate over colonial affairs and the reappraisal which it produced of the traditional economic and political bases of imperial relations. Indeed, the Reformers claimed, with some truth but much exaggeration, that they were principally responsible for dispelling the ignorance and indifference concerning the British empire that had prevailed in England since the loss of the American colonies, and for demonstrating to British administrators, capitalists, and emigrants alike the continued value of overseas possessions if settled and administered under a reformed system.

The Colonial Reformers constituted an important and influential group in the 1830's because they extended from the purely domestic scene to the field of colonial affairs the spirit of reform generated in Britain by the passage of the Reform Act. They applied to the government of the empire the generous impulse and salutary principles which inspired contemporary legislation on such matters as Catholic emancipation, municipal corporations, and public health. Indeed, they sustained the momentum for reform in the area of imperial relations long after its impetus in domestic politics had subsided – as the Whigs ran out of radical steam and eventually gave way to the

Tories in 1841. It is an interesting coincidence that Lord Durham should have been responsible for playing a leading part in drafting the Reform Bill of 1832 and for setting out the classic statement of the Colonial Reformers on the government of the empire in his *Report on the Affairs of British North America* in 1839. His scheme for the future of the empire was liberal, constructive, and firmly in the mainstream of English whiggism, at a time when many radicals felt that the response of Whig ministers to the Canadian crisis had shown them to be unreliable guardians of the liberal tradition.

As contemporary reactions to the Canadian crisis suggest, there existed in the 1830's a bond of friendship and political sympathy between the small body of Colonial Reformers and the wider group of English radicals, as well as an identity of opinions over many domestic issues. Demands for the secret ballot, an extended suffrage, shorter parliaments, and other measures of electoral reform, which formed major planks in the radicals' programme, were strongly supported in parliament by Buller and Molesworth, and until 1839 Lord Durham remained the putative leader of a prospective radical party. Nevertheless, while the Colonial Reformers advocated constitutional changes in Britain as a means of reforming parliament, society, and the national economy, their social rank, buttressed in some cases by substantial wealth, made them cautious reformers – gradualists rather than democrats. Although Wakefield's early political views showed traces of liberal sentiments, he in fact remained a conservative at heart and an associate of aristocrats and bishops by preference. He did not share the confidence of his radical friends that education and the ballot would adequately prepare the unpropertied masses for democracy. Unless they first showed some evidence of prudence, thrift, and a desire for self-improvement, he believed that an extension of the suffrage could only lead to confiscatory attacks on property. Similarly, Molesworth staunchly expressed radical views on the ballot and household suffrage, which were in fact too extreme for the majority of his supporters in East Cornwall, where he felt obliged in 1836 to resign his parliamentary seat in order to preserve the Whig interest. Yet he remained an aristocrat by temperament, and the reforms he advocated sought to preserve what was good in existing institutions while destroying what was bad.

Moreover, while the Colonial Reformers generally behaved as radicals in English politics, and Buller, Molesworth, and George Grote were members of the select group of Benthamites associated with J. S. Mill, the term "radical" has been loosely applied to a wide variety of their contemporaries, not all of whom can legitimately be described as Colonial Reformers. Benthamites and the parliamentary radicals in general were preoccupied in the 1830's with domestic issues and their interest in colonial affairs was aroused only intermittently, when such matters as the cost of the empire to the British taxpayer and the need for economy in government expenditure were under discussion. Many radicals viewed with scepticism the theoretical schemes of systematic colonization and the importunity of their promoters. It was not until the Canadian rebellions focused parliamentary and public attention on the unsatisfactory nature of colonial government and Whig policy that J. A. Roebuck and Joseph Hume persuaded their associates that the basic issue was a struggle between British oppression and Canadian liberty. Their consequent endorsement of rebellion was in fact a more extreme view than many of the Colonial Reformers felt able to support. The radicals' violent criticism of imperial administration naturally led them to condemn the empire as a liability and to urge the immediate grant of independence to the colonies. At first the Colonial Reformers were also advocates of separation, and they remained uncertain about the future of the empire until the publication of the Durham *Report* in 1839 gave them confidence, optimism, and a programme of reform. Thereafter, for a decade or more, the Reformers advocated with increasing success the virtues of colonial self-government and the need for a thoroughgoing reform of imperial administration. Meanwhile the parliamentary radicals of the late 1830's had long since ceased to be a force in party politics through a lack of leadership and insufficient numerical support.

During the thirties and forties the Colonial Reformers were especially significant for their distinctive and influential views on two facets of imperial activity: colonization and colonial government. The theory of systematic colonization was principally set out in the writings of Edward Gibbon Wakefield.[1]

---

[1] EDWARD GIBBON WAKEFIELD (1796-1862), b. London; educated at Westminster School and Edinburgh High School; 1814-25? minor diplomatic posts in Turin and Paris; 1816 runaway marriage with heiress and ward in chancery, Eliza Pattle, who died in 1820; 1826 abducted and married Ellen Turner; 1827 imprisoned in Newgate for three years; a leading promoter of the National Colonization Society 1830, South Australian Land Company 1831, South Australian Association 1833, New Zealand Association 1837, New

Born in 1796 into a family with a tradition of philanthropic activity, Gibbon Wakefield first captured public attention by his matrimonial adventures, which led in 1827 to three years' confinement in Newgate Prison for abducting a young heiress. Here association with criminals awaiting transportation to Australia apparently encouraged him to develop an interest in emigration and colonies, and the period of enforced leisure provided an opportunity to indulge this new interest through extensive reading in newspapers and books on various aspects of colonial affairs. It was out of this study and contemplation that the theory of systematic colonization began to take shape.

Wakefield's ideas were first introduced to the English public in a series of anonymous letters, supposedly from a settler in Sydney, New South Wales, which appeared in the *Morning Chronicle* during the autumn of 1829. The correspondence was published later that same year as *A Letter from Sydney, the principal town of Australasia*, under the editorship of Robert Gouger, subsequently a leading promoter with Wakefield of the National Colonization Society and the scheme for colonizing South Australia. The letters themselves were written in a colourful, racy style, with a wealth of illustrative detail concerning the fortunes of an Australian settler with more land than he had the labour or capital to develop. The new principles of colonization were more baldly stated in *A Sketch of a Proposal for Colonizing Australasia*, which also appeared anonymously in 1829, and were thereafter elaborated and repeated *ad nauseam* in a variety of signed and unsigned writings and in the evidence which Wakefield gave before several select committees of parliament.[2] The most concise and impressive statement of his ideas appeared in 1833 in *England and America, A Comparison of the Social and Political State of Both Nations.* His other

---

Zealand Land Company 1839, Western Australian Company 1840; unofficial adviser to Lord Durham on his Canadian mission 1838; 1841-4 twice returned to Canada as agent of the North American Colonial Association of Ireland, which owned the seigneury of Beauharnois; 1842-4 member of the assembly for Beauharnois; 1848-50 promoter of the Church of England settlement at Canterbury, New Zealand; one of the founders of the Colonial Reform Society 1850; 1852 went to New Zealand and elected to the assembly; 1854-62 lived there in retirement.

[2] Wakefield expounded his views on colonization before the select committees on colonial waste lands, *Parliamentary Papers* 1836 (512) XI, and transportation, *P.P.* 1837-8 (669) XXII. He also appeared before the select committees on South Australia, *P.P.* 1841 (394) IV, and New Zealand, *P.P.* 1840 (234) XXXIII, and *P.P.* 1844 (556) XIII.

major work, *A View of the Art of Colonization*, published in 1849, repeated these views, together with an account of various attempts to translate principles into practice.

Wakefield's theory was based on the sale of colonial land at a sufficiently restrictive price to concentrate settlement in compact agricultural communities and prevent labourers from becoming landowners too easily. In this way both economic development and civilizing values would be most effectively promoted and colonies rendered attractive to British emigrants and capitalists by becoming little Englands overseas. The proceeds from land sales would be used to finance selected emigration from the British Isles. The constituent elements of systematic colonization did not show much originality; they were drawn from a variety of contemporary sources – from the writings of Robert Torrens and Robert Gourlay, Wilmot Horton's schemes of pauper emigration in the 1820's, the sobering experiences of the Swan River settlement in Western Australia, and the much admired land administration of the United States.[3] But from this diversity Wakefield constructed a plausible and pseudo-scientific theory which possessed many merits. His writings provided a cogent analysis of the urgent domestic problems with which British politicians were then struggling, and he demonstrated to administrators and capitalists the way in which the colonies might be effectively employed to alleviate these economic and social difficulties by furnishing homes and jobs for emigrant labourers and profitable new fields for the investment of surplus British capital. His plan for using colonial funds rather than those of the British Treasury to defray the cost of English emigration offered a convenient solution to the basic financial problem which had hitherto prevented the government from adopting schemes of assisted emigration. At the

---

[3] For an analysis of Wakefield's theory, H. Merivale, *Lectures on Colonization and Colonies* (London, 1841-2, and 1861); R. C. Mills, *The Colonization of Australia, 1829-1842: The Wakefield Experiment in Empire Building* (London, 1915), ch. 5; D. Pike, *Paradise of Dissent: South Australia 1829-1857* (Adelaide, 1957), chs. 3, 4; D. N. Winch, *Classical Political Economy and Colonies* (Cambridge, Mass., 1965), chs. 6, 7.

Robert Torrens, the English economist, claimed to have anticipated the theory in a parliamentary speech in 1827. See his evidence before the Select Committee on Colonial Waste Lands, *P.P.* 1836 (512) XI, Q. 1178. The theory was adumbrated in 1822 by Robert Gourlay, the eccentric promoter of Canadian colonization, in his *General Introduction to Statistical Accounts of Upper Canada*. Robert Wilmot Horton was parliamentary under-secretary at the Colonial Office, 1821-8, and a tireless advocate of schemes of pauper emigration.

same time, Wakefield was anxious to render the colonies attractive to the English middle classes. He therefore emphasized the substantial opportunities that awaited emigrants, as well as Britain's civilizing mission, in areas of the world where the broad structure and refinements of English rural society might be successfully reproduced. While such an objective was not, and could never have been, completely achieved, Wakefieldian propaganda did effectively dissociate emigration from transportation and disgrace, and so encourage a climate of opinion more favourable to the migration of Englishmen from all ranks and occupations.

During the 1830's and 1840's Wakefield and his sympathizers attempted to introduce the main principles of systematic colonization into various parts of the empire by seeking to influence the land and emigration policies of the Colonial Office. At certain moments their propaganda and representations recognizably influenced the character and content of imperial regulations governing the disposal of crown lands in Australia and British North America and the conduct of assisted emigration. The first and most notable example was the Ripon Regulations of 1831 when the Colonial Office adopted a restrictive system of land alienation based on sale by public auction at a specified minimum upset price, and in the case of the Australian colonies earmarked the proceeds for an immigration fund.[4] Subsequent imperial practice represented a more stringent and extensive application of this system, and traces of a continuing Wakefieldian influence can be seen in such measures as the creation of the Colonial Land and Emigration Commission in 1840 and the Australian Land Sales Act of 1842.

Nevertheless, the degree of Wakefield's influence over imperial practice, and the success with which the regulations and instructions of the Colonial Office were implemented overseas, varied considerably according to the particular continent and the individual colony. His views were extensively applied in Australia, even though they were in the long run impracticable and unrealistic in a pastoral country;[5] they were of far less

---

[4] On Wakefield and the Ripon Regulations, see J. Philipp, "Wakefieldian Influence and New South Wales, 1830-1832," *Historical Studies, Australia and New Zealand*, IX, May 1960, 173-8; P. Burroughs, "Wakefield and the Ripon Land Regulations of 1831," *loc. cit.*, XI, April 1965, 452-66.
[5] Wakefield's influence over imperial land administration in Australia is discussed in P. Burroughs, *Britain and Australia 1831-1855: A Study in Imperial Relations and Crown Lands Administration* (Oxford, 1967).

importance in British North America, and certainly no more relevant to conditions in heavily forested regions.[6] The chief impact of Wakefieldian ideas in Canada can be found in the criticisms of land administration, contained principally in the Durham *Report*, which exposed the evils of the wasteful and haphazard system of alienation that had been followed in the past and underlined the need for a radical reform of existing abuses. Even in the case of British North America, however, the attitudes of imperial officials towards crown lands, and the policies which those attitudes produced, were considerably influenced by the Wakefieldians and cannot be fully understood without some reference to the views being urged in England at this time by the Colonial Reformers.

The systematic colonizers were far from satisfied, however, with the partial and unenthusiastic reception accorded their ideas at the Colonial Office, and so they sought to test the theory by establishing model settlements in South Australia and later in New Zealand, with the support of financiers and businessmen who were attracted by the opportunities for profitable land speculation which the projects appeared to offer. Although the promoters had to contend with opposition from the Colonial Office, unsatisfactory compromises in their original plans, and incompetent administrative arrangements, the Wakefieldians were responsible for founding South Australia in 1836 and a string of settlements in New Zealand, from Wellington in 1840, Nelson, New Plymouth, and Auckland, to the Otago colony formed by Scottish Presbyterians in 1848, and Canterbury by the Church of England in 1850.[7]

These colonizing ventures not only opened up new areas for British enterprise, but influenced public opinion and imperial policies through the flood of colourful propaganda which invariably publicized the projects. This propaganda was designed to convince the public that these distinctive principles of colonization would produce model colonies, and to attract the investment of capitalists and the interest of potential emigrants. Cer-

---

[6] See for example, H. I. Cowan, *British Emigration to British North America, the First Hundred Years* (Toronto, 1928, and 1961), chs. 5, 6; N. Macdonald, *Canada, 1763-1841: Immigration and Settlement* (London, 1939).

[7] For the Wakefieldians and South Australia and New Zealand, A. G. Price, *The Foundation of South Australia, 1829-1845* (Adelaide, 1924); Pike, *Paradise of Dissent*; J. S. Marais, *The Colonisation of New Zealand* (Oxford, 1927); J. Miller, *Early Victorian New Zealand, A Study of Racial Tension and Social Attitudes 1839-1852* (London, 1958).

tainly at first, in the 1830's, the colonizing ventures and the exorbitant claims made by the promoters for their self-supporting theory were greeted with considerable scepticism and much hostility in England, particularly by such newspapers as *The Times*, the *Morning Herald*, and the *Courier*. "There is nothing cheaper than a fine-spun theory," commented *The Times* in 1834, "the brains of your political economists exhibit an absolute diarrhoea of that description." As far as the South Australian project was concerned, *The Times* had no sympathy whatever for "a plan so childish and preposterous," for such "a heap of indigested absurdity."[8] The *Courier* was equally sceptical whether Wakefield's theory would eventually provide "a sovereign panacea for all the evils hitherto incident to colonization"; but meanwhile it took the opportunity to condemn "the rottenness of the principles on which the pretended new theory of colonization is founded, and the quackery and humbug of the project in question."[9] Much of this hostility to Wakefield and his ideas was to persist in England throughout the forties and beyond, though it was never as bitter or inveterate as the outraged denunciations voiced by colonists in Australia.

The Wakefieldians were hardly surprised that their novel schemes should attract as much hostility as admiration, and they were content to treat this criticism with the contempt it clearly deserved. As Charles Tennant commented,

It is the common fate of nearly all new inventions, to be called, for a time, wild and visionary. The quantity of ridicule and abuse bestowed on such inventions, is generally in proportion to the greatness of the objects, and the simplicity of the means by which it is proposed that those objects should be obtained. The suggestion of the National Colonization Society has not escaped the ordinary fate of new proposals having in view great objects; nor was it to be expected that any thing so entirely novel, and proposing to accomplish objects of such vast importance by means so very easy of application, should be received, at first, otherwise than with derision, contempt or indifference.[10]

---

[8] *The Times*, 23 and 3 July 1834.
[9] *Courier*, 1 July and 3 Oct. 1834.
[10] C. TENNANT, *Letters forming part of a correspondence with Nassau William Senior, Esq., concerning Systematic Colonization* (London, 1831), pp. 67-68. Tennant was a prominent member of the National Colonization Society and an advocate in the House of Commons of pauper emigration. He had earlier written the pam-

Nevertheless, contemporary criticism was forcefully answered through the columns of the *Spectator*, edited by Wakefield's friend, R. S. Rintoul, and after 1838 also through the *Colonial Gazette*. It was a standard technique of Wakefield and his supporters to pretend that they were being subjected to a barrage of criticism, most of it biased and ill-informed, and that they were both misunderstood and unfairly abused. This was a method of generating controversy and public interest in their schemes, and of arousing the Englishman's instinctive sympathy for the underdog. Hostility was certainly to be preferred to the indifference which the Wakefieldians had encountered in the early 1830's. "The public cared nothing about the matter," Wakefield later wrote concerning the activity of the National Colonization Society in 1830, "and could not be brought to take the slightest interest in it. If opponents had been many and much in earnest, converts would not have been wanting: the general inattention was too complete for an opposition that might have proved useful."[11]

This situation soon changed as Wakefield forced his views on the attention of a public hitherto indifferent to colonies and colonization by an adroit campaign of propaganda conducted by sympathizers at public meetings, in pamphlets, in the press, and in parliament. This success was achieved, not so much through the merits of the theory, but through Wakefield's magnetic personality, assiduous activities, flair for publicity, and shrewd but unscrupulous manipulation of individuals. According to Richard Garnett, Wakefield's earliest biographer, "No man knew better how to play upon the various human passions, from the loftiest philanthropy down to the most sordid self-seeking."[12] Samuel Sidney, a contemporary critic, grudgingly admitted Wakefield's talents and success as a propagandist.

Energetic, tenacious, indefatigable, unscrupulous, with a wonderful talent for literary agitation, for simultaneously feeding a

---

phlet, *A Letter to the Right Hon. Sir G. Murray on Systematic Colonization* (London, 1830), and was probably the author of a pamphlet usually attributed to Wakefield, *A Statement of the Principles and Objects of a Proposed National Society, for the Cure and Prevention of Pauperism, by means of Systematic Colonization* (London, 1830).

[11] E. G. Wakefield, *A View of the Art of Colonization, Letters between a Statesman and a Colonist* (London, 1849), p. 40.

[12] R. Garnett, *Edward Gibbon Wakefield: the Colonization of South Australia and New Zealand* (London, 1898), p. 80.

hundred journalists with the same idea and the same illustrations in varying language, for filling eloquent, but indolent, orators with telling speeches; at one time he had rallied round him nearly every rising man of political aspirations, and secured the support of nearly every economical writer of any celebrity.[13]

Much to his undoubted satisfaction, Wakefield became the acknowledged expert on matters of colonization, once he had deliberately destroyed the rival but tenuous reputation of an amateur like Wilmot Horton. However devious and reprehensible some of his stratagems certainly were, Wakefield exerted a significant influence over practical colonization and over the prevailing attitudes of his contemporaries to a subject which, as Wilmot Horton regretfully admitted, had been "scouted as theoretical, sneered at as visionary, and, above all, rejected as expensive."[14]

Nevertheless, the Colonial Reformers understood the processes of contemporary government sufficiently well to realize that, however much popularity their views enjoyed amongst the public at large, their adoption by the Colonial Office and incorporation into imperial practice was essentially a matter of parliamentary pressure and private representations. From its earliest days the National Colonization Society attracted the support of a number of Whig and radical members of parliament, and it was these sympathizers who were to air the new principles of colonization in the House of Commons. Because their efforts were at first preoccupied with the South Australia scheme, it was not until the mid-1830's that the Colonial Reformers began to develop their campaign of parliamentary agitation in a significant way and bring pressure to bear on successive ministries for the reform of imperial land administration. But, as Sidney critically commented, the Reformers soon showed themselves to be "adepts of the first water in the arts of puff publicity and parliamentary canvass. They knew how to get up a company, fascinate and cram the ablest writers of the press, agitate Parliament, pack a committee, manufacture a case, and bamboozle the public."[15] So effective were the Reformers in this campaign that Sidney described the group

---

[13] S. Sidney, *The Three Colonies of Australia: New South Wales, Van Diemen's Land, South Australia* (London, 1853 ed.), p. 95.
[14] R. W. Horton, *Inquiry into the Causes and Remedies of Pauperism* (London, 1830), 3rd Series, p. 22.
[15] Sidney, *op. cit.* (London, 1852 ed.), p. 103.

as "much more successful in its parliamentary tactics than in its colonizing operations."[16]

One of the leading members of the small parliamentary group of Colonial Reformers was Charles Buller,[17] who sat for the Cornish constituency of Liskeard between 1832 and 1848. He enjoyed the reputation of being an entertaining speaker, who could always be sure of a good hearing in the Commons. Although his style in debate was relaxed and conversational, a contemporary journalist referred to his "neat epigramatic mind," and continued: "His speeches abound with sharp points, apposite anecdotes, playful satire, smooth pebbly arguments, and short smart hits at the speakers who preceded him."[18] His ready wit exhibited no malice, however, for he was by nature amiable, even-tempered, and generous in his sympathies. Although his inveterate sense of humour masked more substantial qualities associated with a quick and resourceful intellect, he arrived at his opinions in a leisurely way, and his easy-going manner and indolent disposition made him a loyal follower rather than a potentially prominent and influential leader.

Buller's chief interest lay in constitutional questions. At home he advocated an extension of the principles of the Reform Act by such measures as shorter parliaments, vote by ballot, and an extended suffrage. His desire for cheap and efficient administration was reflected in colonial affairs by a belief that colonists should be allowed to govern themselves, and pay their own way without the assistance of the British Treasury but freed from the financial burden imposed by the lingering demands of British patronage. If such a programme could be instituted, Buller felt sanguine about the future of the empire, and to the attainment of this goal he devoted the larger part of his parliamentary career. On his death in 1848, a tribute was paid by Joseph Howe to Buller's efforts on behalf of colonial reform:

---

[16] *Ibid.*, 1853 ed., p. 99.
[17] CHARLES BULLER (1806-48), b. Calcutta; educated Harrow, privately by Thomas Carlyle, Edinburgh University, and Trinity College, Cambridge; B.A. 1828; called to the bar at Lincoln's Inn 1831; M.P. for West Looe, Cornwall, 1830-1, and Liskeard, Cornwall, 1832-48; member of the National Colonization Society, and the South Australian Association; presided over an inquiry into Irish electoral law and introduced subsequent reforms, 1837-40; 1838 chief secretary to the Durham Mission; 1841 secretary to the board of control of the East India Company; 1846 judge-advocate-general; 1847 chief poor law commissioner.
[18] *Weekly Dispatch*, 9 May 1841.

Contrasted with some others who take an interest in Colonial questions, there was something safe, practical, and conciliatory, in Buller's advocacy of North American interests. Unlike Hume, he never frightened or misled by counselling extreme measures – and instead of traversing boundless fields, and generalizing like Molesworth, he stuck to the matter in hand, and raised no difficulties, the facile removal of which was not proved to be as compatible with the dignity of the Parent State, as with the security of the distant Provinces of the Empire.

It was for this quality of his mind that we chiefly admired Buller. He never did violence to the antique prejudices of Parliament, or feared to give honest counsel, when they seemed to require it, to the Colonists themselves. There may be rising men in both Houses, of whom we know little – but of those we do know, there is not one, in the peculiar walks he chose, who can fill Charles Buller's place.[19]

Sir William Molesworth[20] was another leading exponent of radical measures and colonial reform. The sincerity and consistency of his views made him an effective parliamentary speaker, though the amount of reflection, research, and preparation which he invariably lavished on his speeches tended to produce elaborate treatises rather than spontaneous popular oratory. The *Spectator* typically described his contribution to the debate on colonization in June 1839 as a "striking speech, though perhaps too abstract in some parts for the floor of the House of Commons."[21] Although a young man in the 1830's, his outspoken views and energy greatly invigorated the parliamentary campaign of the radicals for the introduction of the ballot, an extension of the suffrage, the spread of national education, and the recognition of religious equality. Even though a contemporary described him as "one of Mr. Wakefield's speaking-trumpets,"[22] Molesworth was more concerned in the sphere of

---

[19] *Novascotian*, 25 Dec. 1848.
[20] SIR WILLIAM MOLESWORTH (1810-55), educated Trinity College, Cambridge, and Edinburgh University; 8th baronet 1823; M.P. for East Cornwall, 1832-7, Leeds, 1837-41, and Southwark, 1845-55; member of the South Australian Association, and later the New Zealand Company; founded the *London Review* in 1835, bought the *Westminster Review* and amalgamated the two journals, transferred to J. S. Mill in 1837; chairman of the select committee on transportation, 1837; editor of Hobbes' works, 1839-45; 1853 commissioner of the board of works, with a seat in the cabinet; colonial secretary, 2 July to 22 Oct. 1855.
[21] *Spectator*, 29 June 1839.
[22] *Sidney's Emigrant Journal*, I, No. 26, 29 Mar. 1849, p. 202.

colonial affairs with retrenchment in overseas expenditure than with the promotion of systematic colonization. His interest in colonial reform had initially been aroused by a careful and intensive study of the system of transporting convicts to the colonies, which led to his chairmanship of a parliamentary inquiry in 1837-8, and was thereafter reinforced by his hostility to Whig policy on the Canadian question. It was the Durham *Report*, however, which fully converted him to the wisdom of colonial self-government and thereafter its advocacy formed a mainspring of his parliamentary activity until his death in 1855.

One of the more outspoken and independent members of the radical group in parliament was John Arthur Roebuck.[23] Although his advanced political opinions mellowed in later years, he was in the 1830's a thoroughgoing radical in his views on electoral reform and other domestic questions. Not content with indifference to party ties, he remained strongly out of sympathy with the Whigs and never lost an opportunity to denounce them as an aristocratic faction and express his contempt for the insincerity with which they employed democratic principles and phrases as slogans in the conduct of party politics. While he addressed popular audiences with great effect, Roebuck's impassioned and intemperate speeches tended in parliament to dispel rather than arouse general sympathy for the causes he advocated. In 1835 he was appointed parliamentary agent by the assembly of Lower Canada, though he subsequently lost his Commons seat in the election of 1837. To a considerable extent his views on the Canadian question and its settlement reflected the opinions of Louis Papineau, the French Canadian leader, whose personal representative Roebuck in effect became. The constitutional revisions he recommended entailed a reform of the institutions of representative government (such as the creation of an elective legislative council) rather than a clear recognition of the principle of responsible government as the appropriate solution for Canadian problems. In some respects, therefore, Roebuck's views on colonial government were not precisely those of the Colonial Reformers generally, though he has usually been included amongst their

---

[23] JOHN ARTHUR ROEBUCK (1801-79), b. Madras; travelled to England, 1807; emigrated to Upper Canada, 1815; returned to Britain, 1824; called to the bar at the Inner Temple, 1831, and Q.C. 1843; M.P. for Bath, 1832-7, 1841-7, Sheffield, 1849-68, 1874-9; member of the South Australian Association; agent for the House of Assembly of Lower Canada, 1835-7; Privy Councillor, 1878.

ranks. Indeed, the comments of Molesworth, Buller, and Wake-field suggest that their relations with Roebuck were seldom cordial and frequently acrimonious. Nevertheless, his vigorous advocacy of colonial liberties and the wisdom of conciliation made him a fervent critic of arbitrary and coercive policies.

Amongst the lesser figures in parliament, and at one time editor of the *Weekly Chronicle*, Henry George Ward[24] became a tireless advocate of systematic colonization. He was appointed chairman of the select committee on colonial waste lands in 1836, and thereafter sought to impress upon successive minis-tries the value of Wakefield's principles as a means of rendering the colonies more effective and prosperous outlets for Britain's surplus population. William Hutt[25] was another exponent of Wakefieldian views from the early days of the National Coloni-zation Society. He was particularly impressed with the need for large-scale emigration, financed by the revenue from colonial land sales, as a remedy for domestic unemployment and dis-tress. Like most of the Colonial Reformers, he was a supporter of free trade, and argued that cheap and efficient government in both Britain and the colonies could be secured only by the abolition of restrictions and monopolies and by a vigorous attack on patronage. Henry Warburton[26] was also an ardent advocate of retrenchment in domestic and overseas expendi-ture. His support for colonial reform was reinforced by an antipathy towards Whig policy at the time of the Canadian crisis.

---

[24] HENRY GEORGE WARD (1797-1860), b. London; educated Harrow; minor diplomatic posts in Stockholm 1816, The Hague in 1818, Madrid 1819, Mexico 1823-5; retired from the diplomatic service 1827; M.P. for St. Albans, 1832-7, Sheffield, 1837-49; member of the South Australian Association; sometime editor of the *Weekly Chronicle*; secretary to the Admiralty 1846; knighted G.C.M.G. 1849; lord high commissioner of the Ionian Islands 1849-55; associated with the government of Ceylon 1855-60; appointed governor of Madras 1860.

[25] WILLIAM HUTT (1801-82), b. Lambeth; educated Trinity College, Cambridge; B.A. 1827, M.A. 1831; M.P. for Hull, 1832-41, Gates-head, 1841-74; member of the National Colonization Society, South Australian Association, and New Zealand Company; South Australian Colonization Commissioner 1835; paymaster general, vice president of the Board of Trade, and Privy Councillor 1860; negotiated commercial treaty with Austria 1865; knighted K.C.B. 1865.

[26] HENRY WARBURTON (1784?-1858), educated Trinity College, Cam-bridge, 1802-6, M.A. 1812; involved in the timber trade at Lambeth, but interested in science; F.R.S. 1809; M.P. for Bridport, 1826-41, Kendal, 1843-7; chairman of a parliamentary committee on anat-omy 1828; on the council of the University of London; member of the Political Economy Club, South Australian Association, and Anti-Corn Law League.

On the fringes of the group of Colonial Reformers from the time of his membership in the National Colonization Society was George Grote,[27] a wealthy banker, historian, classical scholar, and Benthamite. Although a man of advanced liberal and independent views, and an impressive speaker, his preoccupation with the ballot and other domestic issues meant that he was an infrequent commentator on colonial matters until the rebellions thrust the Canadian question to the forefront of English politics. In the 1830's he was generally recognized as the leader of the small group of parliamentary radicals, but his scholarly virtues ill fitted him to become a forceful and influential political figure capable of taking a strong and energetic line and thus able to overcome the prevailing disunity and timidity of the radicals.

One weapon which the Colonial Reformers found particularly effective in their publicity campaign was the appointment of select committees of parliament. Since they were able to dominate the membership of these committees,[28] and favourable witnesses might be called, the Reformers could be reasonably confident that the reports of the committees would reflect their views, even if subsequent acceptance by the ministry of the day remained in doubt. In 1836 they were able to secure the appointment of a select committee to examine the whole question of the disposal of colonial waste lands in Australia, the Cape of Good Hope, and the West Indies. The Reformers meant to include Canada within the scope of the inquiry, but this intention was apparently thwarted "by a trick of the Colonial Office." The hearings of the committee offered an ideal forum for the propaganda of the systematic colonizers; it was, according to the *Spectator*, "*England and America* dramatized and animated."[29] Of the members on the committee, H. G. Ward, William Hutt, J. A. Roebuck, Francis Baring, and Henry Bulwer were all favourably disposed towards the principles of

---

[27] GEORGE GROTE (1794-1871), b. Beckenham, Kent; educated Charterhouse; banker, historian, classical scholar, Benthamite; associated with the foundation and administration of the University of London; M.P. for the City of London, 1831-41; member of the South Australian Association.

[28] It is not clear exactly how the members of these select committees were chosen and the Reformers able to secure the appointment of sympathizers, but Molesworth nominated the members of his committee on transportation in 1837. In 1844 Lord Stanley admitted that he had been outwitted by the Reformers in the selection of the committee on New Zealand. Stanley to Peel, 17 Dec. 1844, Peel Papers, British Museum, Add. MSS. 40,468.

[29] *Spectator*, 24 Sept. 1836.

systematic colonization. Wakefield, as the chief witness, eagerly expounded his theory, and five of the other ten witnesses were sympathetic to its general principles. With so many supporters and so few critics, it is hardly surprising that the committee recommended in its report a wider application of the Wakefield system.[30]

A further opportunity for the Reformers to present their views came in 1837 with the appointment of a select committee on the transportation of convicts. Wakefield and other systematic colonizers were again called to give evidence, and the committee itself included such sympathizers as Sir William Molesworth, the chairman, Charles Buller, H. G. Ward, Francis Baring, Lord John Russell, and Benjamin Hawes. In the course of its inquiries, the committee realized that the continuation of transportation to Australia was inextricably connected, and totally incompatible, with the promotion of free emigration. "The continuance of Transportation to the Australian colonies," the committee reported, "would be inconsistent with the policy of encouraging emigration there, for Transportation has a tendency to counteract the moral benefits of emigration, while, on the other hand, emigration tends to deprive Transportation of its terrors."[31] The Wakefieldian sympathizers on the committee also took advantage of the presentation of the report to advocate once again the benefits of systematic colonization and the need for the reform of imperial land regulations.

Parliamentary concern over matters of colonization in the late 1830's reflects the renewed interest in questions of colonial policy which is apparent both in the House of Commons and amongst the public at large. The Canadian crisis and the publication of the Durham *Report* served to stimulate a growing awareness of the need for reform in all aspects of colonial administration at home and overseas. With regard to crown lands and emigration, ministers could expect to face continued attacks from the Colonial Reformers in parliament and from Wakefieldians outside the House if they failed to revise imperial regulations. Officials at the Colonial Office could no longer regard parliamentary inquiry into colonial land affairs as an impertinent interference with matters that lay exclusively within

---

[30] Report of the Select Committee on Colonial Waste Lands, *P.P.* 1836 (512) XI.
[31] Report of the Select Committee on Transportation, *P.P.* 1837-8 (669) XXII, p. XXXV.

their own private jurisdiction. This pressure was at least partly responsible for the appointment of the Colonial Land and Emigration Commission in 1840, a body whose theoretical and doctrinaire views on land administration bore a distinct similarity to those of Wakefield.[32] The Australian Land Sales Act of 1842 also owed something to the Reformers, and in many ways represented a further step, and a final one, in the extended application of Wakefield's principles in Australia. Charles Buller declared in 1843 that the "great principles of the plan of colonization which I urge have been formally but unequivocally adopted by the Government of this country."[33] Nevertheless, subsequent practice failed to fulfil this optimistic judgment, and in the case of British North America neither the Wakefieldian principles of land sales nor assisted emigration were introduced. Land administration remained the wasteful and unsatisfactory system that Lord Durham had described in his *Report*, and emigration to that part of the world was ill-regulated and inadequately supervised, since the "state exercised not the slightest control over the hordes whom it simply allowed to leave want in one part of the empire for hardship in another."[34]

In addition to their advocacy of the theory of systematic colonization, the Reformers were distinguished by enlightened views on colonial government. The existing system for administering the empire produced irresponsible authority at home and overseas. In the colonies representative government created oligarchic control by governors and councils, and the executive remained at loggerheads with assemblies torn by malevolent and factional politics. The concomitant evil in Britain was the centralized bureaucratic control exercised by the Colonial Office. With the rise of the Colonial Reformers, the battlecry of economy, used by the parliamentary radicals in the late twenties and early thirties as an excuse to attack the government of the day for its illiberal colonial policies, gave way to the charge of

---

[32] See F. H. Hitchins, *The Colonial Land and Emigration Commission* (Philadelphia, 1931).
[33] *Hansard*, 3rd Series, LXVIII, 6 April 1843, 523.
[34] C. Buller, *Systematic Colonization. Speech of Charles Buller, Esq., M.P., in the House of Commons on Thursday, April 6, 1843, etc.* (London, 1843), pp. 48-49. On the supervision of British emigration, see O. MacDonagh, *A Pattern of Government Growth, 1800-1860: The Passenger Acts and their Enforcement* (London, 1961).

bureaucracy. Administration of the empire, so the Reformers argued, was effectively centred in the hands of anonymous and irresponsible officials within the Colonial Office who were not answerable to parliament or public opinion for their conduct and were inadequately supervised by a colonial secretary who might be in office for only a short period and was sometimes incompetent. Political patronage, exorbitant expense, and other major evils flourished under this system. James Stephen, the permanent under-secretary at the Colonial Office between 1836 and 1847, became the principal target of spiteful attacks by Wakefield and others, and won contemporary renown as "Mr. Mothercountry," once it was found that civil servants could not publicly defend themselves.

The solution to these evils, as adumbrated in the Durham *Report*, was to give the colonists control over their own affairs, except for certain reserved subjects of imperial concern, and at the same time so adjust the practical operation of colonial government that the executive would become responsible to the popular voice in the legislature. The financial burden placed by the empire on the British taxpayer would be eased if under this constitutional arrangement the colonists paid their own administrative expenses and could also be persuaded to meet the cost of defending themselves. The major causes of friction in imperial relations would be eliminated, and the colonists would then be content to remain within the empire. "Responsible government" thus represented a means of preserving the British empire, because it seemed to hold out the possibility of reconciling local autonomy and imperial unity. Lord Durham's recommendations on colonial government therefore offered a potential solution to a basic imperial dilemma which had been presented some sixty years earlier at the time of the American Revolution and not then successfully resolved. Until the publication of the Durham *Report*, the proponents of colonial self-government, with very few exceptions, had been those who had expected that maturing colonies would inevitably follow the American pattern and sooner or later declare their independence of Britain; they might therefore as well be allowed to take this step without bloodshed or unnecessary bad feeling. Meanwhile, the advocates of a continuing empire had assumed that it must necessarily continue to be governed from London.

The Durham *Report* changed this alignment; it rearranged the factors in the imperial equation. From this time onwards, the proponents of self-government offered a scheme whereby the colonies might achieve their ambitions without following the American example; the advocates of a continuing empire now saw decentralization as their ally. If powers and fields of administrative responsibility were divided, a few reserved to the imperial authorities but most surrendered to the colonists, then mutual advantage would hold the two together more securely than direct rule from London. This method of reconciling autonomy with unity was one of the earliest and clearest visions of an empire based on consent. Whatever the extent of his indebtedness to the views of Robert Baldwin and the Canadian reformers, Lord Durham forcefully presented a scheme of reform that would place imperial relations on a new and more cordial footing, and the publicity subsequently given to this programme by the Colonial Reformers prevented its neglect by public or government in Britain. Admittedly, its most enthusiastic proponents remained somewhat confused over the precise meaning and operation of "responsible government" in a colonial setting, and especially over the role and position of the governor, though they were probably less bewildered than most of their contemporaries.[85]

It is also significant to note the equally radical change produced by the Durham *Report* in the attitude of the Colonial Reformers themselves to the questions of colonial government and the future of the empire. Apart from a sentence or two in *A Letter from Sydney* castigating the factional strife and virulence of colonial politics, Wakefield's early writings contain no discussion of the political arrangements he wished to see adopted in overseas settlements. Even the South Australian promoters contented themselves with the demand for the eventual concession of an elected assembly. Wakefield was a man of one idea, who took up the cause of colonial self-government only after the Canadian crisis and the Durham mission had shown the significance of this issue, its usefulness as a weapon for attacking his *bête noir*, the Colonial Office, and the assistance which its advocacy might bring to his campaign for the introduction of systematic colonization. The conversion of the other Reformers to a constructive programme of colonial constitutional reform was equally late in the day and swiftly accomplished, and again it was the publication of the Durham *Report* which formed the decisive element in this important transformation.

The opinions of Englishmen during these years on the value

---

[85] See below, pp. 145ff.

and future of the empire were often expressed in ambiguous and uncertain terms, and many public figures were far from consistent in their pronouncements. Nevertheless, as the debates on the Canadian crisis clearly demonstrate, the views of the Colonial Reformers in the late 1830's were distinctly pessimistic and despairing. Molesworth had little confidence in the possibility of preserving the empire, and if the existing oppressive and expensive system of colonial administration could not be reformed and friendly relations with the colonies thereby guaranteed, he would have preferred to give them independence. Grote was no more optimistic for the future and advocated separation. Similarly, Ward stated in 1837 that, since it would clearly be impossible to maintain the imperial connection in Canada, colonies and mother country should separate on good terms. Warburton emphasized in 1838 the positive political and commercial advantages which separation would confer on both parties.[36] At this period, therefore, the "imperialist" sentiment commonly associated with the views of the Colonial Reformers had certainly not emerged. Indeed, there was very little difference of opinion between the Reformers on the one hand, and parliamentary radicals, Benthamites, and political economists on the other – except in the degree of reluctance or enthusiasm with which the eventual and certain disruption of the British empire was contemplated. Until 1839 there is certainly no evidence of the sharp contrast subsequently discerned by most historians between the "imperialist" views of the Colonial Reformers and the prevailing "anti-imperialism" of contemporary opinion.[37] In the late thirties, such a distinction is obviously illusory.

This situation changed radically with the publication of the Durham *Report*. Thereafter the views of the Colonial Reformers were principally distinguished by a pervading confidence in the benefits of colonial possessions and in the future of the British empire once the present system of administration had been suitably reformed. Not only did their ideas point the way to a successful reconciliation of local self-government and the continued unity of the empire, but they were sanguine about the permanency of the imperial connection, at a time when many

---

[36] See below, pp. 123-7.
[37] See for example, C. A. Bodelsen, *Studies in Mid-Victorian Imperialism* (Copenhagen, 1924; London, 1960); R. L. Schuyler, *The Fall of the Old Colonial System, A Study in British Free Trade 1770-1870* (New York, 1945; Hamden, Conn., 1966).

Englishmen still thought that the separation of the colonies from the mother country was only a matter of time and occasion. After 1839 the views of the Reformers contained neither the pessimism of some contemporaries nor the indifference of others. For these reasons the importance of this small but influential group at a crucial period of imperial relations cannot be overestimated. They provided the ministries of the forties and beyond with the fundamentals of a more imaginative and constructive colonial policy that could be applied not only in British North America, but in other places and at other times. This is not to suggest, however, as some historians have done, that the Colonial Reformers were farsighted prophets or conscious architects of the modern Commonwealth.[38] They provided, not a complete solution to the recurring imperial dilemma of reconciling autonomy with unity, but only the path by which it would eventually be achieved with the coming of full dominion status.

It is hoped that the compilation of documentary material in this volume will give some insight into the views of the Colonial Reformers on Canadian questions and imperial relations. Material has been included which refers to colonial affairs in general, and not specifically to British North America or Canadian internal politics, in the firm belief that the opinions of the Reformers on these particular questions are more intelligible if they are set against the wider background of attitudes to the empire at large. This broader approach is all the more viable since the Colonial Reformers were concerned almost exclusively with the colonies of British settlement, and particularly in the late 1830's their interest was concentrated on Canadian questions. On the other hand, this collection is primarily concerned with the Canadas rather than with British North America as a whole. The Reformers were preoccupied with the crisis in Upper and Lower Canada and they commented very seldom on the seemingly peaceful and relatively contented state of the Atlantic provinces.

A substantial proportion of the material in this volume relates to matters of colonization and colonial government. This emphasis is both unavoidable and justified, since it reflects the

---

[38] See for example, H. E. Egerton, "The Colonial Reformers of 1830," in F. J. C. Hearnshaw, *King's College Lectures on Colonial Problems* (London, 1913), ch. 5; P. Bloomfield, *Edward Gibbon Wakefield, Builder of the British Commonwealth* (London, 1961).

preoccupation of the Reformers themselves with these major topics. Commercial relations in an era of increasing free trade are also considered, but the Reformers had less to say about colonial trade than about political questions. It is more regrettable that their interest in colonies did not materially extend to social, intellectual, and religious developments, since contemporary English comments on these important aspects of Canadian life would have been interesting and illuminating.

The term "Colonial Reformers" is a vague one and has been variously employed by historians. Some historians have recently argued that this amorphous group lacked a distinctive, consistent outlook, and that the label "Colonial Reformers" should be discarded because it obscures the essential similarity of British opinion about the empire during that period.[39] While this is a valuable caution, the accepted explanations and myths of imperial history will not be dispelled unless detailed examination is given to what individual Englishmen and identifiable groups of individuals actually said about the colonial possessions. It is here suggested that there was something distinctive about the opinions of the particular individuals canvassed in this volume which entitles us to consider them together as a group, whether or not for the sake of convenience we call them by the convential titles of "Colonial Reformers" or "Wakefieldians." Buller, Durham, Molesworth, Roebuck, and Wakefield are generally considered to form the core of the group, and material has accordingly been drawn from their various writings and parliamentary speeches. On the fringes, however, there are a number of individuals who were members of the National Colonization Society or involved in the South Australia or New Zealand schemes, and who might therefore legitimately be described as Colonial Reformers. Since most of these minor figures were neither writers nor members of parliament, they have not left their views on record, but extracts have been included from the speeches of Grote, Hutt, Warburton, and Ward, and from the writings of Charles Tennant. On the other hand, the movement initiated by the foundation of the Colonial Reform Society in 1850 under C. B. Adderley and his associates is considered to lie outside the chronological scope of this volume.

Material has also been taken from editorials and articles which appeared in the *Spectator* and the *Colonial Gazette*. The

---

[39] See John S. Galbraith, "Myths of the 'Little England' Era," *American Historical Review*, LXVII, Oct. 1961, 34-48.

Spectator, begun in 1828 and still being published, was edited throughout the period under consideration by Robert Stephen Rintoul, a Scottish journalist, who was one of Wakefield's earliest sympathizers. Particularly from 1834 onwards, the weekly journal from time to time included articles on colonial affairs which broadly reflected the views of the Colonial Reformers. Since the *Spectator* was primarily concerned with domestic politics and social commentary, however, the Reformers decided in 1838 to found a new journal devoted predominantly to colonial questions. At first the *Colonial Gazette* was conducted independently by the Colonial Secretary of London, obviously another Wakefieldian body, but in August 1839 it was taken firmly under the wing of the *Spectator*, and presumably edited by Rintoul, with Wakefield's undoubted assistance, until it ceased publication in 1847. By this time the weekly may have been encountering financial difficulties or a decline in public interest, though the continuing effects of a paralytic stroke that Wakefield suffered in 1846 may have been a more immediate and crucial cause of the journal's demise.

Although articles and editorials are unsigned, there is reason to believe that Wakefield, Buller, and possibly Molesworth, were contributors to the journals, and the phraseology or content of particular articles strongly points to Wakefield as their author. A series of important letters on Canadian affairs from an anonymous correspondent in Montreal published in the *Colonial Gazette* in 1842, for example, was undoubtedly written by Wakefield during his stay in Canada. Except on rare occasions, it is impossible to assess the influence which the Colonial Reformers exerted over editorial policy. In 1838, for example, Wakefield and Buller were responsible for converting the *Spectator's* initial criticism of Lord Durham's resignation and return to England into vigorous support. There can be no doubt, however, that these journals, and particularly the *Colonial Gazette*, were deliberately employed by the Reformers to express and publicize their views. Since the journals cover the widest range of topics and provide a continuous, colourful, and incisive commentary on passing events, a considerable proportion of the extracts in this volume has been taken from this source. Moreover, this material has been unfortunately neglected and is relatively inaccessible.

In view of its importance as the Reformers' textbook on colonial government, and as the basis of much contemporary comment, extracts from Lord Durham's *Report* have been included, even though this material is well known and easily accessible. Some excerpts have been taken from the Durham Papers located in the Public Archives of Canada, for which permission has kindly been granted.

It has been no easy task to compile from a vast wealth of documentary material a selection which most effectively reveals the views of the Colonial Reformers. For those readers who may wish to pursue any specific topic further, references for all the selections have been cited. Nevertheless, many extracts are deliberately substantial in length, in the belief that some books of documentary material suffer from a predilection for short excerpts which may offer an inspired insight or send up a literary firework, but which arouse rather than satisfy the curiosity of the reader. Except for the chapters on the Canadian crisis and responsible government, the organization of the material in this compilation is necessarily topical rather than chronological. Connecting and explanatory comments have been included where necessary between documents in the hope that each chapter may develop a line of argument and not represent simply an assortment of material. The symbol ~ has been used throughout the text to indicate material interpolated by the editor. The original spelling, capitalization, and punctuation of the documents have been retained even where these may be inconsistent with modern usage.

I would like to express my gratitude to Professor Helen Taft Manning for the advice and encouragement she has so generously given me in the preparation of this volume. I am also grateful to my colleague, Dr. John Flint, who has kindly commented on the text.

PETER BURROUGHS
Dalhousie University
December, 1968

The Carleton Library *The Colonial Reformers and Canada, 1830-1849* is compiled from the following sources:

Lord Durham's Report on the Affairs of British North America, and Charles Buller's *Report on Public Lands and Emigration*, Appendix B to Lord Durham's *Report*, edited by C. P. Lucas (Oxford, 3 vols., 1912).

DURHAM PAPERS, Public Archives of Canada, Ottawa.

Hansard, 3rd Series, vols. I-CVI, 1830-49. Speeches of Charles Buller, George Grote, William Hutt, Sir William Molesworth, J. A. Roebuck, Henry Warburton, and H. G. Ward.

Spectator, 1830-49.

Colonial Gazette, 1838-47.

C. BULLER, *Responsible Government for Colonies* (London, 1840).

J. A. ROEBUCK, *The Colonies of England* (London, 1849).

C. TENNANT, *A Statement of the Principles and Objects of a Proposed National Society, for the Cure and Prevention of Pauperism, by Means of Systematic Colonization* (London, 1830).

E. G. WAKEFIELD, *England and America* (London, 2 vols., 1833); *A View of Sir Charles Metcalfe's Government of Canada* (London, 1844); *A View of the Art of Colonization* (London, 1849).

PART ONE:
ENGLISH ATTITUDES TO COLONIAL AFFAIRS

1 / THE STATE OF PUBLIC AND PARLIAMENTARY OPINION
~ The Colonial Reformers were profoundly concerned about
the degree of ignorance and indifference which they felt characterized English attitudes to colonies and colonial questions
during the second quarter of the nineteenth century. At times
the Reformers tended to exaggerate the extent of public apathy
in order to give added weight and a sharper emphasis to their
own views and activities. Nevertheless, there was much truth
in their charge that British ignorance was the most prolific
source of colonial misgovernment. Evils in imperial administration were allowed to flourish, because colonial matters were
seldom discussed in an enlightened and constructive manner.
This was a conclusive argument for letting the colonies manage
their own local affairs, and to prepare for such an eventuality,
if not hasten its arrival, the Reformers deliberately set out to
educate public opinion at home and overseas, particularly
through the columns of the *Spectator* and the *Colonial Gazette*.
They firmly believed that a favourable reception for their ideas,
a generous settlement of existing colonial grievances, and the
future of the empire itself depended to a considerable degree
on the growth of a more interested and knowledgeable body
of opinion within the British parliament and in the country
at large. As Charles Buller's comments suggest, however, the
Reformers were the first to admit that this was certain to be
a long and arduous task, since apathy towards colonial affairs
was deep-rooted, and the natural result of a lack of both
information and an understanding of colonial questions.~

. . . It is not, indeed, in the nature of men to feel any very
lively interest in the affairs of those of whom they know so
little as the people of this country do of their fellow-subjects
in the Colonies: and the bitter experience of colonists has taught
them how little their condition, and the circumstances which
influence it, are appreciated by the people of this country. The
social state, and the form of government in the Colonies, are
both utterly foreign to the notions of Englishmen. We comprehend neither: we know little of the events that have passed in
them: and the consequence is, that we understand very nearly
as little of what passes in the present day. The newspaper of
the morning announces in some out-of-the-way corner, that

some ship, which left some unknown spot, in some distant corner of the world, some weeks or months before, has brought perhaps a couple of months' files of colonial papers. We are told that the Governor had issued some order, upon a matter of which the nature is utterly incomprehensible to us; or that the Assembly is "still" occupied with some dispute with him, of the commencement of which we had never heard. If perchance there be any thing in this news which interests us enough to make us read through the column of the paper, hunt up the geographical and other points which at first puzzle us, and look with impatience for the sequel of the news, the odds are that we get nothing more on the subject for the next month; and the first time our paper finds room for another set of extracts from the colonial papers, the matter about which we were interested has slipped out of our memory, or some event of importance in Home politics absorbs all our attention. This is the normal state of our ignorance on the subject, varied in the case of the most active-minded by the half-information thus picked up, and the prejudices consequently formed. When some event of great importance suddenly rivets public attention on colonial affairs, we come to the consideration of them with this general ignorance and these misconceptions. Nothing but the news of invasion or revolt gives the people at large a real interest in the colonial news of the day. The events that prepare such calamities have been either unheeded or fostered by the rash decisions which we have given in our inattentive mood. . . .

(C. Buller, *Responsible Government for Colonies* [London, 1840], pp. 66-68)

~ In these circumstances the Reformers were not surprised to find that members of parliament were no more enlightened than the general public in their views on colonial questions. Moreover, as the *Colonial Gazette* explained, the attention of the House of Commons was understandably focused on the many crucial issues of domestic politics.~

. . . The average state of the mind of Parliament with respect to Colonial interests may be fairly described as one of ignorance and indifference. Nor, as we have had occasion to observe before, is this at all to be wondered at. The thoughts of Parliament are necessarily preoccupied with domestic affairs; and no active Member of the House of Commons can spare time from the business which his constituents or his party position demand of him, to bestow zealous attention on the affairs

of a distant province. It would, therefore, be unreasonable to expect that the British House of Commons should occupy itself with Colonial affairs except as matters of inferior moment deemed tributary to the advantage of the Mother-country. More than this, it would be worse than idle, because delusive to hope for. And here, while the most conclusive reasons appear for letting colonies manage their own local affairs in their own way, one learns this useful lesson – that it is a waste of trouble to call upon Parliament to bestow the same attention on the Colonies as if those distant parts of the empire were represented in the House of Commons. The most that can be expected or rationally desired is, that Parliament should see how advantageous it is to the Mother-country to have contented and prosperous colonies; how much the prosperity of England – her safety, perhaps, under the new circumstances of an almost savage competition of capital with capital and of labour with labour – depends on the progressive extension and prosperity of her Colonial empire. This being understood by Parliament, Colonial affairs would obtain as much attention from the House of Commons as it is in the nature of things that they should receive. . . .
(*Colonial Gazette*, 15 January 1840)

~ Parliamentary ignorance was variously displayed, but it always produced serious and unfortunate consequences. Not the least of these concomitant evils, in Charles Buller's view, were the party spirit which animated debates on colonial questions and the irresponsible authority which parliamentary indifference allowed ministers and permanent officials at the Colonial Office to exercise in their unsupervised conduct of colonial affairs.~

. . . As the people judge, so do their representatives act in Parliament. A railway or a turnpike bill ordinarily interests more Members than any measure affecting the most vital interests of our most important colonies. Some of them, it is true, attract the notice of two or three Members, who think that local knowledge gives them the right to assume airs of great wisdom respecting them. Some ignorant and presumptuous Captain in the Navy, some still more ignorant and presumptuous Colonel in the Army, who have passed a year or two in some harbour or garrison of the colony – some retired Judge, whose knowledge of a community has been formed on his experience of the criminals and suitors in his court – some ex-official, mixed up with colonial jobs and cliques – some

merchant, who urges in the House whatever his partners in
the colony tell him is the right thing to promote the interests or
importance of the firm – these, with occasionally some gentleman, whose more than usually extended tour has carried him
to some of our remote possessions, are the only persons, not
compelled by the duties of office or opposition, that take what
is called an interest in a colony. By some one or other of these,
four or five times in a session, questions are addressed to the
Ministers, or returns required, or motions made. But hardly
any one else ever shares in this interest: and such a notice of
motion generally insures the House being counted out whenever it comes on! On some rare occasions the party questions
of the day are mixed up in some colonial matter: the Opposition
come down to fight the battle of the Church, or Education, or
whatever else it may be, on colonial ground; and the mover
is favoured with the unaccustomed honour of an audience and
a division. Sometimes the opportunity of wounding a Ministry
through the sides of one of its measures, or of a Governor of
its own party, occasions similar manifestations of factious force
and zeal. . . . The attention thus given to a colony in these
occasional gusts of party feeling, is productive of so much ill,
that it is far better for them that Parliament should preserve
its usual apathy, and adopt, as it usually does, whatever
legislation the Government of the day may recommend.

There are two modes in which the legislative measures, to
which the Government wishes to get the sanction of Parliament, are framed. Sometimes, though rarely, Parliament passes
an act after the usual fashion of acts of Parliament, settling
by positive enactments every detail of the course on which it
determines. Except, however, in the case of acts settling the
form of government in a colony, this is a labour which is rarely
imposed on Parliament: and experience shows us how unwise
it is to trust the details of such measures to the chances of
Parliamentary attention. . . .

. . . Parliament in general disposes of the details of Colonial
questions in a much more summary way. For some time past,
the impossibility of determining the details of a Colonial
measure in the British Parliament has been so much impressed
upon the Government, that the custom has been to propose
that the Colonial Acts of Parliament be simple *delegations of
legislative powers* to some Ministerial authority in this country;
and they have in consequence simply enabled the Crown to
legislate for the Colonies by Order in Council. . . . Nor has

Parliament taken, in Colonial cases, the precautions for retaining a vigilant supervision of the use made of this power, which it has always retained to itself whenever it has delegated similar authority with respect to the Mother Country . . . and the powers thus given to Orders in Council are exercised without any publicity in this country.

Thus, from the general indifference of Parliament on Colonial questions, it exercises in fact hardly the slightest efficient control over the administration or the making of laws for the Colonies. In nine cases out of ten, it merely registers the edicts of the Colonial Office in Downing Street. It is there, then, that nearly the whole public opinion which influences the conduct of affairs in the Colonies really exists. . . .

(Buller, *Responsible Government for Colonies*, pp. 68-73)

2 / THE INFLUENCE OF PARTY POLITICS

~ Parliamentary debates of the period suggest that colonial questions were generally discussed in the light of domestic political interests and considerations of party. Very seldom were colonial matters handled on their own intrinsic merits. During the 1830's the relative standings of the parties in parliament certainly contributed to this approach. As the decade proceeded, the Whigs' popularity in the country and their majority in the House of Commons gradually declined and an uncertain political equilibrium was created. Furthermore, as the Whigs lost their initial reforming enthusiasm, they came under persistent attack on both the domestic and the colonial front from the radical wing, with whom relations were strained and at times acrimonious. To remain in office was the main concern of Lord Melbourne's ministry. Meanwhile the Tories were equally prone to play politics with colonial issues, though it is clear that in the late thirties they were not anxious to defeat the Whigs and assume office themselves. Although their handling of the Canadian question was irresponsible rather than constructive, the Tories were therefore prepared in the last resort to protect the ministry against any extreme political repercussions that might result from the hostile criticisms and votes of the radicals.

The Colonial Reformers found this situation far from satisfactory, though there was some difference of opinion amongst them concerning the wisdom of voting against the government and letting in the reluctant Tories who would probably adopt even more coercive and retrograde colonial policies. While the voting strength of the Reformers was not significant enough to make this choice a crucial matter, there was much truth in their accusation that both parties considered colonial questions from the standpoint of their effect upon temporary and personal interests, rather than from their bearing on the future and permanent well-being of the empire.

The connection between colonial matters and party considerations was aptly illustrated by the apprehensive excitement aroused amongst the press and politicians alike in March, 1838, by the notice of Sir William Molesworth's unprecedented motion which attacked, not merely Whig colonial policy, but the incompetence of Lord Glenelg as colonial secretary. As the *Spectator* anticipated, the censure failed, but the following year Glenelg was forced to resign.~

. . . The promised motion is altogether of a Colonial nature – appears to affect none but the misused portions of the empire to which it relates – would, in the common course of things, have been little regarded by any one here – and would therefore have been despised by the Colonial Office, against whom it is exclusively directed, if many accidents had not conspired to give it an interest extrinsic from the matter which it embraces. The plain object of the motion . . . "to relieve the Colonies from an imbecile and worthless administration of their affairs." But about this alone, who would have cared? The effect of the motion may be a change of Ministry. . . . Therefore, and therefore only, does everybody talk about Sir William Molesworth's motion.

There can be no doubt, we suppose, of the truth of the honourable baronet's proposition. It would therefore be a vast point gained for the Colonies if the motion should be carried. Though the object of many who voted for it were to turn out the Ministry, yet the turning out of a Ministry for the maladministration of the Colonial Minister, would be an event of inestimable advantage to the Colonies. The succeeding Government would not place any but a superior man at the head of the Colonial Office; public attention would be directed to Colonial affairs; and something like a reform of *the system* might be expected. This would probably happen if Peel or Wellington should succeed Lord Melbourne; it would certainly the case if Lord Durham should be "sent for" upon the solution of the present Government. The possible incidental lt of the motion, therefore, cannot defeat its intrinsic and sible object. This reflection should encourage Sir William

Molesworth to persevere, if his real object in the motion is that which appears upon its face.

We are not amongst those, however, who think it probable that the motion will be carried. Still, the mere debate cannot fail to be of service to the Colonies, whose affairs, for the first time in our day, will become a subject of great interest in Parliament. So that, at all events, the motion should be brought forward, – and also pressed to a division, in order, as its author has said, to "exhibit to the country how many Members, whether Tory, Whig, or Radical, will venture, for mere party purposes, to deny, or abstain from affirming, a proposition which in their conscience they know to be true."

Every doubt as to the success of the motion must be founded on a belief, that, with a majority of the House, "mere party purposes" will outweigh all regard to truth, and all regard for the unfortunate Colonies. A fig for the truth, perish the Colonies, so that *our party* retain office – this is the sentiment with which the Melbourne Whigs and their adherents will go to the division. . . . And lastly, there is Sir Robert Peel, the real leader of the House – what may be expected from him? With his great wealth, what position could be more grateful to him than that which he holds in Opposition – now protecting his political foes – now dictating to them – now exposing them to degradation and shame – and always successfully opposing any principles of theirs with which he disagrees, while he asserts and maintains, and, through them, gives practical effect to his own? Why should he court the cares of office, when he enjoys such high power and honour in Opposition? For him individually, things cannot be in a better state than at present. He will probably, therefore, help Ministers out of their worst scrape, let truth and the Colonies suffer as they may. Upon the whole, we incline to think that one of the most important and truest propositions ever submitted to the House of Commons, will be negatived by a large majority. In that case, the only advantage of the motion, besides an exposure of Colonial abuses, will be a most curious illustration of Parliamentary morality furnished by the division-list.

(*Spectator*, 24 February 1838)

~ The use of colonial questions as legitimate matter for playing party politics was particularly evident and most unfortunate in the case of Canada, where the need for an enlightened policy and a thoroughgoing reform of imperial administration was urgent. As Charles Buller pointed out in July 1839, this was no occasion for inaction and indecision, and no time for the continued postponement of a lasting settlement of the Canadian crisis.~

. . . he really could conceive no mischief to arise from any man's and every man's coming forward to say what he thought respecting the past and future treatment of the Canadas; and he apprehended danger from no other cause than from the absence of discussion – from its not being known what they thought and what they meant to do, and from the consequent prolongation of that system of mystery and vacillation which he looked upon as the main source of the present ills of these colonies. He anticipated evil from the general indisposition of the House to look the present state of the colonies and the whole policy of the colonial government fairly in the face, to determine on what principles that policy was henceforth to be conducted, and to make those extensive changes in our colonial system which must be suggested by calm deliberation on the working of the present order of things. He dreaded the continued ignorance of the real state of affairs which this aversion to discussion was calculated to produce among ourselves; and from all he saw and heard, he apprehended that when all their shifts had been exhausted, and when they could no longer stave off the moment of decision, they would come to that decision with no more settled views, no more complete information than they possessed at present. He dreaded also the effect of their inaction on those colonies. When their inhabitants . . . find that the Session from which they expected the final settlement of their disorders had passed over without a single step being made towards it – that nothing had been done, that only vague indications had been given of what Ministers, none of what Parliament, intended to do, what did they think would be the result on their feelings? Without speculating on the irritation, which he could not but consider the natural fruit of this apparent indifference to their fate, was it not obvious that these people must infer that we had really come to the conclusion either that no remedy was required, or that it was hopeless for us to attempt to devise one – that we left them to their fate to shift for themselves. . . . He supposed, that this one of the apprehended dangers of discussion; that it was said, that the Canadians might discover, that the real cause obstinate inattention to their unhappy condition, was weakness of the Government, and in the unscrupulous and opposition of their opponents. He wished to treat this subject apart from the petty objects and views of the parties of the day; but he must say, that he thought both were equally blameable for it, or that, indeed, the opposition were even more blameable than the ministers. It was the common shame of both, that they made the interests of our countrymen in the colonies the sport of their party manoeuvres. While the Gentlemen opposite, acting on principles which he must be excused for saying appeared to him the most immoral ever avowed by an Opposition pledging themselves to no system; suggesting no more advisable course, thought their functions were discharged by the exercise of a perverse ingenuity in discrediting and thwarting any and every plan proposed by the Government – while the Government, instead of meeting this factious hostility with the vigour which would quell it in a moment, instead of gravely maturing, and boldly proposing large and sound measures, and trusting to the good sense and good feeling of the country to insure their success, and scatter to the winds any party that should dare to thwart them in such a case, attempted to evade the criticism of its measures, by offering no measures to be criticized. While such was the petty and discreditable game of parties, the great colonial empire of Britain was crumbling to pieces on every side of us, and they were involving in certain ruin the dearest interests of thousands and millions of their countrymen. . . .

(*Hansard*, [3rd Series], XLIX, 11 July 1839, 180-2)

3 / PARLIAMENT AND THE CANADIAN CRISIS

~ Parliament's handling of the Canadian problem in the late 1830's aptly illustrates the contention of the Reformers that colonial matters received attention only when they assumed the proportions of a crisis and thus began to have political repercussions in England. Only on such rare occasions was an inquiry into the whole system of colonial government likely to be conducted and the evils of imperial administration exposed. Conversely, when colonies were quiet, their affairs were ignored by parliament and abuses went unheeded.

For this reason the Reformers were optimistic that the Canadian rebellions in 1837 would bring colonial grievances fully into the focus of public attention and secure some measure of redress, provided the discussion of these matters could be dissociated from party interests.~

. . . In consequence of the fighting in Canada, the subject of Canadian grievances will come at last to be understood in this country. So long as the colonists did no more than complain and remonstrate, it was a vain attempt to rouse public attention in England to the causes of Colonial discontent. But the causes of a civil war will soon be inquired into. And it must soon be known that the "practical grievances" of the Canadians, which the officials have altogether denied, are far more serious than those which drove our old self-governed colonies of America into rebellion. Thus, the system on which our Colonial Office governs from a distance will be brought to light. And this more than probable result of the Canadian rebellion is certainly not to be regretted. . . .

(*Spectator*, 6 January 1838)

~ It was equally true, however, that when colonies were peaceful, their welfare was neglected by parliament and the English public. Once the Canadian rebellions had been put down and Lord Durham's *Report* presented early in 1839, the ministry was inclined to procrastinate and postpone a final settlement, or indeed any positive action, since the domestic political situation seemed to demand the minimum of potentially controversial activity. Both the *Spectator* and the *Colonial Gazette* denounced the government's unjustifiable procrastination in 1839.~

We share the dissatisfaction, but not the extreme surprise expressed by most people at the intentions of the Government with respect to Canada. . . . Little else could have been expected from this Ministry. They have been quite incapable for a long while of carrying any important measure; and least of all a good Colonial measure, because in the present state of parties it is impossible that any Colonial subject, however interesting and momentous to this or that distant community, should not be used by the Opposition as a means of harassing the Government. The Colonies – who in England cares much for any of them, except the few who have some direct personal interest in them? The people of England without distinction of class, as of every other mother-country, are necessarily ignorant and indifferent with respect to the state and the fate of far-off provinces. Their national pride indeed takes fire at the idea of losing a dependency; but beyond this they seldom bestow a serious thought on any distant part of the empire. This truism is perfectly illustrated by the case of Canada. For twenty years past, as appears by Lord Durham's searching inquiry, this colony has been governed as if the object of its rulers had been to produce "a state of constituted anarchy." When did the

Parliament or People of England interfere to correct this system of misrule? Never by any accident. The operation and calamitous results of the system have been thoroughly exposed by Lord Durham; but his Report has been on the table of both Houses of Parliament for four months, without exciting a single remark from any Member of either House. . . . Rebellion, civil war, garrison government, foreign aggression, impoverishment, and depopulation − such is the catalogue of the sufferings of her Majesty's subjects in Canada; but her Majesty's subjects here have something else to occupy them than Canadian affairs. With such utter indifference on the part of the British public towards Colonial matters, it would be strange if a powerful Opposition did not seize on Colonial questions as the safest means of annoying the Government; and stranger still if a weak and timid Government, tenacious of place, did not sacrifice Colonial interests to the exigencies of their party. Last year, Canada was made the sport of factions at home: this year, Lord Melbourne would if possible decline the game; and therefore, after four months' reflection on Lord Durham's Report, he proposes to do − nothing. . . .

(*Spectator*, 8 June 1839)

The Colonists of British North America will look in vain to the press of this country for any information as to the causes of the neglect of their affairs by the Imperial Legislature during the present session. Many questions they will ask, but will find no answers. Why has no measure been adopted for the settlement of Canadian affairs? Why was the single debate in each House, if either conversation may be termed a debate, remarkable for the exclusion of nearly every topic of deep interest to the Colonists? Why has the Canada question been *avoided* this year by British statesmen? Ask the London newspapers of the day after the recent mention of Canada in the House of Lords. They answer by a few cold remarks, from which nothing can be gathered but that they care as little about the subject as the Parliament and the public.

This indifference of the British public to the most important Colonial questions, should occasion no surprise. It is remarkable in the present instance, only when contrasted with the state of public feeling in this country on the subject of Canada at the beginning of the year. The puzzle with the Colonists will be how to reconcile that strong and general excitement with the actual indifference. Let us endeavour to explain the apparent contradiction.

The Canadian rebellion of 1837 threatened to destroy the party then in power here, and therefore excited the most lively hopes and fears in this country. The danger – not to the empire, but to the Whig party – was no sooner gone by, than, as the Colonists will well remember, their affairs were forgotten by every one in England. They were forgotten until Lord Durham's Ordinances [of June 1838 concerning the Canadian rebels and the detention of political prisoners in Bermuda] furnished matter for some party proceedings at home. And lastly, Canada once more became a subject of great interest here, when Lord Durham returned without leave [in November 1838], and very important consequences to all the parties at home seemed likely to result from his handling of the Canada question. On each of these three occasions, the true and only cause of a temporary excitement at home about Canadian affairs, was the temporary influence of Canadian affairs on home politics. Thrice in two years the influence and the excitement have appeared together as cause and effect. At all other times during the two years, as little have the people and Government of England cared for Canada, as the inhabitants of Canada usually care about the party politics of this country. . . .

. . . The party exploit of last year in respect to Canada, has left all parties in England with very disagreeable recollections of the subject. They have all been afraid of it. One might say, indeed, that the subject was concluded for this year by Lord Durham's Despatches and Report. Since the publication of those documents, English parties have not ventured even to reproach each other for the past, or to defend themselves from Lord Durham's reproaches. . . . The subject has been dropped through fear and disgust. The very urgency of the question for Canada has led to its postponement in England. . . .

(*Colonial Gazette*, 7 August 1839)

~ In view of English apathy and indifference, the *Colonial Gazette* suggested in August, 1839, that the only effective way of inducing the ministry to act was for the colonists to begin wholesome agitation. If they could create sufficient unrest in Canada, then the government would again be compelled to show some positive concern.~

We have said that if the people of British origin in the two Canadas rely on aught but their own exertions, they may whistle for a permanent settlement of their distracted affairs. Strong pressure from Canada itself, is the only means by which the

Imperial Government can be moved in this matter. Whether the two Provinces shall be united by an act of the British Parliament early next session, or shall remain for years a prey to evils no otherwise curable than by Union, depends not at all upon any circumstances than can originate here, though the question must be here decided. It is a question here, of which course will be the most convenient, the least troublesome to the Whig, Tory, and Radical parties of this country, and especially to the Government of the day, of whatever party that may be composed. During the present session, the balance of convenience and comfort for the parties at home has been on the side of delay: it will be so next year; it must ever be so, as long as the only formidable portion of the inhabitants of Canada – the people of British origin in both Provinces – abstain from pressing their claim to the attention of the Imperial Government. As long as *they* remain quiet, or only waste agitation on disputes amongst themselves, the easiest course for the Government at home will be to do nothing. No first cause can arise here to turn the balance of Party or Ministerial convenience on the side of action for Canada. Hitherto, only the self-interested opponents of Union and free government have brought any Canadian influence to bear on the Ministry and the Opposition at home; and *that* has been in favour of delay, with a view to preserving the two distinct Executives of Canada, and preventing the formation of a colony so strong as to take the management of its own local affairs out of the hands of the Colonial Office in Downing Street. . . .

It would be presumptuous in us, at this great distance, to suggest any specific mode of agitation to the people of Canada. All that we pretend to know, is – and this conviction is founded on a knowledge of home matters in relation to Canada – that nothing but agitation in Canada, nothing but an aspect of things *there* which shall frighten the Government and the parties here, will induce the Imperial Parliament to pass a law next year for the permanent government of Canada. . . . At the beginning of this session, Lord John Russell pledged his word in the name of the Government, that the Canada question should be finally settled this year. You, the people of Canada, have been cheated with false promises; and, to tell you the truth, it is very much your own fault. You will be cheated again, if you let the parties here think that they may again cheat you with impunity. . . . You should so act as to make it probable, that the party, whether in or out of office, which stood in the way of a settlement of your affairs, would be ruined or deeply injured thereby.

To this end, only one sort of means is at your disposal; and that is vigorous, organized agitation. Your declarations of loyalty are unheeded; your great sacrifices for the Imperial connexion are unknown or disregarded; your supplications are in vain; your affection is not valued; you are not respected, *because you are not feared*. "Who cares for Canada?" This is now said by smirking officials, who used to tremble at your name when the Canada question seemed likely to upset the Government. If you would not continue despised, you must make yourselves feared. . . .

(*Colonial Gazette*, 14 August 1839)

~ Eventually the Whig ministry did act in 1840; but once the union of Upper and Lower Canada had been accomplished, public and parliamentary concern for the affairs of British North America lapsed into its former state of indifference and neglect with the advent of a Tory ministry under Sir Robert Peel in 1841.~

The *Colonial* difficulties of Sir Robert Peel's Government are remarkably illustrated by the present state of what used to be called "the Canada Question."

There is indeed no such question now before the British public. The rebel colony seems to be forgotten at home. Although the maintenance of peace between England and the United States depends in no small measure on the "tranquillity" of Canada – although this great colony is now in the act of trying a new constitution and a new system of government devised expressly for the purpose of securing that same tranquility – although, in fact, the state of Canadian affairs was never of deeper importance to England than at this present time – yet nobody here seems to remember that the troublesome dependency even exists. What can be the reason of this curious indifference? . . . Canada is quiet. There are no complaints from the colony. No events there call for the attention of the people of this country; who are, as usual, too busy with their own affairs to trouble themselves about the state of a distant province which does not force itself on their notice. It is plain that, thus far at least, Canada *has been* tranquillized by the measures of the Whigs consequent on the rebellions and Lord Durham's mission: the fact is proved by the universal silence here with respect to Canada. . . .

(*Colonial Gazette*, 18 August 1841)

4 / THE USES OF A COLONIAL JOURNAL

~ In order to keep colonial questions more persistently in front of the English public and so educate opinion by dispelling ignorance, the Reformers decided to found a journal devoted exclusively to colonial intelligence. Since the early 1830's the *Spectator* had from time to time included material on colonial matters, but with the establishment of the *Colonial Gazette* in 1838 the Reformers were able to provide the public both in England and overseas with news and commentary on the affairs of the British empire. The purposes and attitudes of the journal were fully explained in August, 1839.~

We are not amongst those who have imagined that the principal use of a Colonial journal published in London would be to supply information respecting the Colonies to readers in this country. If the information could be procured, the readers would be wanting. Except as regards new settlements, there is no general curiosity here respecting the affairs of any colony, nor any partial curiosity except occasionally as to particular subjects. The Colonial public, again, of this country is divided into classes, as distinct from each other as the colonies in which they happen to be interested respectively, and even more indifferent than the British public in general about every colony with which they have no special concern. It seems impossible, too, to divine any means for producing a common feeling amongst these different classes. Upon the whole, therefore, we are satisfied that there is no demand in this country for a collection of mere intelligence, or news, relating to the Colonies. To afford the supply without any prospect of a demand, would be sheer waste.

But subjects frequently occur relating to various colonies, upon which correct information is desired by numbers in this country who have no means of procuring it. These subjects are of two kinds, – first, those which possess a general interest, because they are really of importance to the empire; secondly, those which affect particular classes residing here. For instance, a London journal which had furnished accurate intelligence respecting the rebellion in Canada, would have had a great circulation in England. . . . The supply must be according to the demand: the matter taken for publication as news, must be carefully selected from an immense mass of useless materials – must consist only of that which will gratify an existing curiosity, and must appear in the form calculated to convey the desired information with the least trouble to the reader. A mere heap of facts would be as rubbish: the success of the journalist in the department of news will depend on his skill in selection and arrangement. Add to this, what it must take time to acquire, a character for accuracy as well as impartiality, and the Colonial Newspaper will make its way here, even though it should consist of a mere record of facts.

But the recording of facts, with whatever skill in selection and arrangement, is, we think, a small part of the business of a Colonial journal. We shall presently notice its uses *in the Colonies*: the purposes which it may most usefully serve *in this country*, otherwise than by furnishing Colonial news, are those of exciting amongst English readers a more general interest than is felt at present in Colonial questions – of enforcing sound principles in Colonization and Colonial Government – of assisting Colonial communities and individuals in the prosecution of their just demands on the Imperial Government – and, above all, of bringing public opinion here to bear upon the only irresponsible, and assuredly the worst-managed branch of the public service. Notwithstanding the general ignorance and indifference about Colonies, there is one Colonial subject on which all men, it may be said, hold the same opinion, – namely, the defects of our system of Colonial Government. Few indeed can specify those defects; still less trace their origin, point out their causes, and suggest fitting remedies for the acknowledged evil. But the existence of the evil is denied by nobody. The inadequacy of the Colonial Office to the purposes for which it was intended, is perfectly notorious. It will be impossible to discuss many Colonial questions without showing, though it should be but incidentally, that the principal vice of the system consists in the secrecy with which vast powers of Colonial Government are exercised in Downing Street. In China, a newspaper is called an *eye*. If any thing is more wanted, in these days, than an eye upon the Colonial Office, public opinion, as well here as in the Colonies, is very much mistaken. This we promise that the *Colonial Gazette* shall be. To watch and report those proceedings of the Colonial Office which have hitherto been shrouded in mystery, will be a leading function of this journal. . . .

It is within the Colonies, however, that a London journal devoted to Colonial interests may perhaps be of the greatest use. The ignorance of the people of this country respecting their Colonies, is not more remarkable than that of colonists in general respecting circumstances in this country which exert the greatest influence on their fate. In all Colonies the powers of the Crown are far greater than in England; in Crown Colonies they are absolute. Now the manner in which the Colonial powers of the Crown are exercised here, including the power of appointing to powerful offices in the Colonies, depends upon a variety of English circumstances, – such as the personal qualities of the Colonial Minister for the time being, the degree of his influence in the Cabinet, his self-reliance or dependence on others, the personal qualities of those on whom he may rely, the stability or insecurity of his own position in English politics, and a hundred other matters with which colonists have no present means of becoming acquainted. Colonial legislation also in the Imperial Parliament, is greatly influenced by the state of parties at home. It is from hidden sources of various kinds in this country, that good or evil reaches the distant parts of the empire. We allude now, not to the secrecy of the Colonial Office, but to those personal and party influences on Colonial affairs, which grow out of events in this country, which affect the Colonial Office itself, and which are as little understood in colonies as if they came from the moon. . . . This topic of home influences on the destiny of colonies, will occupy a large space in our columns; for it is a subject of never-ceasing importance to the Colonies, and to all colonies equally. . . .

. . . We cannot subscribe to the doctrine that such a journal should avoid all expression of political opinion. The public affairs of colonies are as essentially political as those of the mother country or the empire. It would be difficult to name any political subject that has not two sides. To steer impartially, as it is called, between the two sides of a question, is to have no opinion at all. A political journal without opinions would be like a Member of Parliament who should never vote, or a judge who should never decide. Let us avow, therefore, that we have formed opinions on most of the Colonial questions of the day. These we shall express whenever the occasion seems to require it. And further, we are desirous of stating here, that our opinions have not been hastily taken up, but have resulted from the application of a general principle to particular questions. This principle is an especial, not to say an exclusive regard for the well-being and prosperity of our Colonial fellow-subjects. The people of this country and all its various interests have organs and advocates in abundance: the Colonies have been as little represented in the Press as in the Legislature. Our aim then is, to further Colonial interests without reference to any others. Whatever may seem to us conducive to the advantage of any colony, or of the Colonies generally, *that* we shall earnestly support. Error of judgment as to the means, we may not avoid; but about the end in view there shall never be any mistake. We adhere to the original motto of this journal – "Ships, Colonies, and Commerce!" It follows from this declaration, that the party politics of the Mother Country can have no place here. The *Colonial Gazette* is neither Conservative, nor Whig, nor Radical, but purely Colonial. . . .

(*Colonial Gazette*, 7 August 1839)

PART TWO:
COMMERCIAL VALUE OF COLONIES

1 / COLONIAL TRADE AND INVESTMENT

~ During the years which saw the triumph of free trade, when many Englishmen questioned the value of overseas possessions, the Colonial Reformers remained ardent advocates of the commercial benefits of empire. Despite the assertions of critics to the contrary, the *Colonial Gazette* pointed out that the volume of Britain's trade with the colonies was by no means negligible, and it steadily increased with the continued flow of English emigrants overseas and the progress of colonial settlement.~

. . . it will not be difficult to show that the Colonial trade of this country is, next to the home trade, the most valuable branch of its commerce, – giving employment exclusively to British shipping, and putting into activity a greater amount of British labour, in proportion to its extent, than any other part of our trade. It is an important, and, to us, a gratifying fact, that of 388,308 vessels of all flags – British and Foreign, having an aggregate burden of 62,109,462 tons, that entered and quitted the ports of the United Kingdom in the ten years from 1828 to 1837, the large proportion of 109,273 ships of 20,875,712 tons were employed in the Colonial trade, being 28 per cent of the number of ships, and 33½ per cent of the amount of tonnage: – in other words, one-third of the export and import trade of the United Kingdom is maintained with her Colonies and dependencies. This part of our trade, too, unlike that maintained with foreign countries, is not liable to violent fluctuations, nor to the uncertainties arising from rivalry, or from political differences; but is steadily and constantly increasing from year to year. The numbers in the first and last years of the series were –

1828 . . . . 10,026 Ships.   1,821,005 Tons.
1837 11,758   ”   2,330,413   ”

If we look to the value of British products and manufactures exported in the same period, we find, that while the whole foreign and colonial trade of the kingdom amounted to £408,670,046, the proportion sent to the British Colonies amounted to £111,993,953, or 27½ per cent of the whole. There is this further advantage attending the exports to our

Colonies, that more than nine-tenths of the value is made up of goods which have received the last processes of manufacture; while our trade with the Continent of Europe is chiefly composed of raw products, such as coal, iron, lead, and salt, or of goods, such as cotton and linen yarn, which have been subjected to little beyond the initiating processes to fit them for use by foreign manufacturers, by whom they are converted into goods, which not only supply their home demand, but meet and compete with our manufacturers in their markets. . . .

It will place the value of our Colonial trade in a striking point of view to state, as we do on the authority of documents published by the respective Governments, that the tonnage engaged in that trade is considerably beyond twice the amount of that of all the ships under the French flag, which enter and leave the ports of France during the year, including the Colonial trade of that country; and that it is equal to the entire amount of tonnage under the American flag that entered and left all the ports of the United States, taken on the average of five years, from 1831 to 1835, the latest year for which the accounts have been published in this country.

What country in the world, either ancient or modern, could ever exhibit such a proof of Colonial greatness? Our possessions in North America, the West Indies, Australasia, the Mauritius, and the Cape of Good Hope, collectively contain populations amounting to 2,300,000 souls; and in 1837 they took from us manufactured goods to the value of £7,350,000, or more than £3 per head, – while our next best customers, the citizens of the United States, including their slave population, were customers to the value of only 7s. 6d. each, or less than one-eighth of the amount purchased by each of our Colonial fellow-subjects.

(*Colonial Gazette*, 2 March 1839)

~ In 1846 the *Colonial Gazette* again discussed the progress and advantages of Britain's trade with the colonial dependencies, past and present. As these comments suggest, it was common practice amongst contemporaries to refer to the United States as "colonies" of Britain that had simply severed the political connection.~

Among the accounts relating to trade and navigation . . . published in November, there is an account of the declared value of British and Irish produce and manufactures exported from the United Kingdom in 1845, specifying the countries to which they were exported. The sum total is £60,111,082 . . . more than a third were taken off by countries which are either dependencies of the British empire, or colonies still maintaining their political connexion with it, or colonies which have severed that connexion. The colonies still forming part of the empire took seven millions and a half; the colonies which have organised an independent government took upwards of seven millions; and the dependencies took nearly eight millions. Look at the matter from a slightly altered point of view: – The colonies, united and severed, took upwards of fourteen millions and a half; the dependencies close upon eight millions. . . . One-third of our export trade, therefore, is owing to the colonising and *quasi*-colonising efforts of England. The strenuous prosecution of these enterprises dates from little more than two centuries back, yet within that time they have created markets which provide a vent for the disposal of our surplus produce more steady, and relatively carrying off much larger quantities, than rich and populous nations with whom we have traded for triple the number of centuries. . . .

. . . It is obvious, however, from the returns, that to our own colonies and dependencies we are indebted for the greatest expansion of our commerce. The returns show this, and a very little reflection shows the cause. The unwise exclusive system of trade, from which nations are only beginning to depart, is operative, but only to a limited degree: there is a deeper seated and unalterable cause. Our own colonies are in reality an extension of the home market. . . . The tastes and habits of the British colonists are the same with those of their fellow-countrymen in the old country; their modes of conducting business, their notions of obligations, are the same; the commodities of the old country suit its colonial market, better than those of any other; trade is carried on between them with a more frank confidence and perfect understanding. The bond thus created to unite the colony to the mother-country has been found to survive political severance. The trade with Great Britain is still immeasurably the most important part of the commerce of the United States, although we parted in anger. . . .

. . . The capital and industry of two independent states, or of one independent state, and the colony of another, may, by commercial exchanges, produce the same amount of wealth and amenities to the parties engaged in them as if they were both citizens or subjects of the same state. But, in the case supposed, the wealth is shared between two independent nations; it goes partially to strengthen the hands of two independent governments. In the case of a trade, equally profitable, between a mother-country and her colony, the whole of the wealth created, and, what is of still more importance, the whole of the energies and mental resources developed, are the reserve fund upon which one government can rely in case of a rupture with another. In the last great European war, during part of which England may be said to have stood single-handed against the other civilised powers of Europe, it was not upon the resources of this little island alone that we depended. Our men did much, but our capital did more; and that capital, whether locally situated here or in the colonies and dependencies, or floating on the sea, belonged only in part to the inhabitants of the mother-country. India and the colonies contributed largely to carry us through the arduous struggle. Had a wise and liberal policy perpetuated the political union between this country and the colonies which now constitute the United States, their capital and resources would have been part of our available fund for carrying on the war: as it was, we sometimes found them brought to bear against us instead of in our defence.

(*Colonial Gazette*, 12 December 1846)

~ The growth of colonial trade and overseas markets was therefore heavily indebted to Britain's colonizing activities. As Wakefield carefully explained, one major reason for this commercial expansion could be traced to the complementary economic needs and products of colony and mother country.~

... Provided, then, that care is taken to prevent temporary gluts of either capital or labour in very young colonies, and provided also that colonial government is tolerably good, it may be affirmed with confidence, that neither too much capital nor too many people can be sent to a colony; for the more of both the colony receives, the more readily will fresh importations of capital and people find profitable employment; certainly without any decrease, perhaps with an increase, in the rates of profit and wages.

The normal state of high profits and wages, notwithstanding the utmost importation of capital and people, in colonies where the proper fruits of enterprize and industry are secured by good government, arises partly from the manner in which the produce of colonial industry is distributed; partly from the great productiveness of industry in a country where only the most fertile spots need to be cultivated. In colonies, as compared with old countries, the landlord and the tax-gatherer get but a smaller share of the produce of industry: the producer, there-fore, whether capitalist or labourer, gets a large share: indeed, they get nearly the whole: and this whole, as before observed, is very large in consequence of the great natural fertility of all the cultivated land, or the small cost of production. Both the labourer and the capitalist, therefore, get more than they consume. The labourer saves, and the capitalist saves: capital augments rapidly. But as nearly all the colonists are either capitalists or labourers, who have more than they can consume, the whole colony has more than it can consume. Colonies, therefore, are, may I say, naturally exporting communities: they have a large produce for exportation.

Not only have they a large produce for exportation, but that produce is peculiarly suited for exchange with old countries. In consequence of the cheapness of land in colonies, the great majority of the people are owners or occupiers of land; and their industry is necessarily in a great measure confined to the producing of what comes immediately from the soil; viz., food, and the raw materials of manufacture. In old countries, on the other hand, where the soil is fully occupied and labour abun-dant, it may be said that manufactured goods are their natural production for export. These are what the colonists do not produce. The colony produces what the old country wants; the old country produces what the colony wants. The old country and the colony, therefore, are, naturally, each other's best customers. . . .

(E. G. Wakefield, *A View of the Art of Colonization* [London, 1849], pp. 82-83)

~ At the same time, the Colonial Reformers argued that the progress of colonization, if systematically conducted, would open up new opportunities for British investors at home and overseas. Although the uncertainty created by political distur-bances in the Canadas in the late 1830's had a deleterious effect on the flow of both capital and emigrants to those colonies, the *Colonial Gazette* maintained that the future prospects of pro-fitable investment in British North America were attractive.~

. . . No sooner will the political Canada question be finally settled, than the stream of emigrating capital and people, which has been diverted from British North America, may be expected to resume its former course. Property has been so greatly deteriorated there by the late disturbances, that no colony will present a more profitable field for the investment of capital as soon as peace and order shall be restored. In Canada there is perhaps more room for improvement, for advance in the value of property, than in any other British colony. Capital will flow to the spot where there is opportunity to buy cheap and the prospect of selling dear: and an emigrant population naturally follows an emigrating capital. We happen to know of more than one plan for the investment of capital in the North American Provinces, whose execution awaits only a settlement of the political Canada question. It may be reasonably hoped, moreover, that as soon as that question shall be disposed of, the Provincial Legislatures and the Imperial Government will concur in the adoption of some comprehensive measure of emigration and local improvement. No part of the world would better repay an outlay, or afford a better security for advances which capitalists might be willing to make for such purposes. . . .

(*Colonial Gazette*, 15 January 1840)

2 / COLONIES: PROFIT OR LOSS?

~ At a time when British opinion was coming to accept that the country's commercial interests could be better promoted by free trade than by protective tariffs, it was natural that Englishmen should reassess the commercial value of colonial dependencies and reconsider how Britain's trading relations with them could be most effectively conducted. The central issue in this debate concerned the relationship between commercial interests and political control. It was argued by the critics of empire that the preservation of a political connection with an overseas country was not a necessary prerequisite for the maintenance of favourable trading relations with it. The example of the United States demonstrated to the satisfaction of many Englishmen that Britain could grant independence to its colonial territories and yet continue to dominate their economies by superior commercial power, and this valuable lesson was capable of extended application. Indeed, it was pointed out that the volume of Britain's trade with the former colonies in America had greatly increased after they had become independent, and this experience suggested the wisdom of severing the political connection with the remaining colonies in British North America.

During a period when British commercial supremacy was not threatened by foreign competition, the argument that "informal" commercial empire was more profitable and effective than "formal" political domination held great weight and was particularly applicable to colonies of European settlement like British North America. Moreover, the important corollary was that "informal" empire would enable England to reduce to a minimum its overseas administrative and military commitments and so drastically diminish the heavy and fruitless burden of expenditure which the dependent empire imposed on the British taxpayer. Critics maintained that whatever the current economic value of colonies, this benefit was completely offset by the exorbitant cost of administering and defending them.

While the Colonial Reformers welcomed the coming of free trade, their attitude to the commercial value of maintaining a political connection with the colonies was not entirely consistent. In the years before the Durham *Report* had shown the possibility of drawing a viable distinction between self-government and independence and of reconciling autonomy with unity, the Reformers were at times inclined to support the view that colonial trade would survive political separation. Henry Warburton frankly avowed this point of view in 1838, during a discussion of the Canadian timber monopoly.~

. . . As to the question of trade, it must be of great importance to carry on trade with such extensive countries as the North American colonies. But then it was well known that England lost a great deal by giving them the monopoly of the timber trade, to which he had always been opposed. The whole amount of the export trade from Canada and New Brunswick was £1,500,000 annually, and of that £1,100,000 was in timber alone; yet rather than go to a war of independence with them, he would willingly give them a lease of the timber monopoly for a term of years, and they would be too happy to accept such a bargain. . . . But it was contended, as one argument for the continuance of the connection, that this extensive trade in bad timber was in some degree the cause of our great naval power, inasmuch as it gave rise to the carrying trade. Now he was prepared to show that a falling off in this latter species of trade, and any injury to our naval power, were not contingencies to be apprehended from the separation of the colony from Great Britain, because it was equally in our power to carry on that trade, as well after an amicable separation as before. If this trade in timber was necessary to the sustentation of our naval power, which he was not prepared to admit, he would say that, in order to give that support the greatest effect, they ought to release the Canadas from their control. For a maritime country the best means of providing for the increase of the navy was to promote in every possible way the increase of the revenue. Now it was never contended that the continuance of the monopoly of the Canada timber trade tended to increase the revenue of this country, but the reverse. Then here was another reason for separation, as the carrying trade might, after such separation, be still retained. . . .

(*Hansard*, XL, 25 January 1838, 482)

~ At other times, and especially after 1839, the Colonial Reformers emphasized the advantages to be gained by preserving an empire of self-governing colonies and argued, though not always plausibly, that colonial independence did not necessarily produce greater commercial benefits nor did political subordination restrict the expansion of colonial trade. As part of their case, the Reformers sceptically examined the lesson popularly drawn from the unique American experience, though, as the comments of the *Colonial Gazette* demonstrate, their attempts to expose a fallacy in contemporary reasoning were not always convincingly performed.~

. . . It is, indeed, a fearful indication of the manner in which Colonial interests are likely to be viewed in an Assembly where they are not directly represented, when we find, in a recent number of the *Edinburgh Review*, – a publication which professes to take the most liberal and comprehensive views on public questions, – such a sentence as the following.–

In Colonial possessions there may be *some advantage; much benefit there certainly is from such settlements, at an early stage of the industry, and especially of the trade of any country; and those advantages do not cease with Colonial dependencies, but are often even more valuable after the political connection has been severed. But for the purposes of political power – as an element in our foreign policy – nothing can be more obvious than the indifference of these North American Colonies either way.*

"Nothing can be more obvious," to all men who have paid attention to these subjects, than the presumption and ignorance displayed in the above-quoted passage. . . . It is a common impression, taken up, we conceive, without reflection, or adopted without investigation, by many persons besides the Edinburgh reviewer, that this country has profited more from its intercourse with the United States of America than it ever would have done if they had remained a part of the British empire.

This is one of those unaccountable fallacies on public questions which are so often brought forward that they have almost ceased to challenge inquiry, but the incorrectness of which everybody has it in his power to ascertain, by a reference to recorded and undoubted facts. Let us test this belief by comparing the state of our trade with America before and since separation. In 1771, which may be considered the last year of uninterrupted trading between England and her North American provinces, before the breaking out of the troubles that led to the separation, the value of English produce and manufactures exported to those provinces amounted to £4,202,474 . . . and we find that if the whole of the British manufactures purchased by them had been equally divided, the share of each Colonist would have amounted to £2.16s. Let us now inquire, and contrast with this the proportion in which the independent citizens of the United States are at present our customers. . . . We shall, perhaps, steer clear of all miscalculations . . . if we assume as the means of comparison the average exports during the ten years from 1828 to 1837. That average we find to be £7,340,190 . . . and the value of all the British manufactures imported, if fairly divided between them, would give to each inhabitant only 10s. 10½d.! To place this fact in another light. If these independent citizens had continued to be the same good customers to us that their colonist forefathers were, the average annual amount of our shipments to the United States, during the last ten years, should have been £37,832,471, more than five times the actual amount, and within about three millions of the value of the entire exports from the United Kingdom to the whole world. . . .

We might enlarge upon this topic, but have said enough to show that such opinions as those put forth by the writer in the *Edinburgh Review*, and which (we regret to say it) are shared by many well-meaning persons, are but little entitled to our assent. It will be our endeavour, in following up this subject in future numbers of the *Colonial Gazette*, to set forth some of the advantages, both commercial and political, which attend upon the possession of our present Colonies; and thus, to combat the assertion so thoughtlessly, and we must say, so mischievously, hazarded in the quotation to which we have so frequently referred.

(*Colonial Gazette*, 26 January 1839)

~ The attitude of the Reformers to the commercial value of the empire was also influenced by their desire to secure a substantial reduction in the current level of colonial expenditure. Particularly in the 1830's, they were to a considerable extent in sympathy with the prevailing view of contemporaries that the cost of governing and defending the colonies outweighed the commercial benefits derived from their possession. In the years before a more optimistic view of the future of the empire had emerged, the Reformers occasionally admitted that this serious imbalance might even necessitate the early grant of independence if colonists could not be persuaded to pay their own civil and military expenses. In January 1838 the *Spectator* contained some critical remarks on the commercial value of the Canadas.~

. . . We begin with the trade. Great Britain has a monopoly in the Canadian market, and the Canadians have a monopoly in ours. The total value of the exports from the two Canadas, in 1833, was £965,000, and that of the imports was £1,665,000. If the accounts were correctly kept and the trade of a natural and wholesome character, the two ought of course to be nearly the same; and the enormous discrepancy of £700,000 is only to be accounted for by the fact that it is made up chiefly by Treasury bills for the maintenance of our expensive establishments civil and military. The smaller sum, or less than a million, represents consequently the actual *bona fide* value of the trade of the two Canadas. The greater part of the imports are consumed in the Upper Province. . . . Supposing, then, the whole value of the trade to be a million, the value of that of the Lower Province will be about £330,000. So much for the mere numerical amount of the trade. A mercantile profit of 10 per cent on the whole capital invested, would be just £100,000 a year; and on the share of the Lower Province, £33,000. This is all that we can discover that is gained by Lower Canada; and we agree entirely with Sir Henry Parnell, that "no case can be put to show that we should not have every commercial advantage we are supposed now to have, if it (Canada) were made an independent state" [*On Financial Reform*, London, 1830, p. 257]. . . .
(*Spectator*, 13 January 1838)

~ By the 1840's, however, the new-found optimism of the Reformers was reflected in their attacks on Richard Cobden and other free traders who seemingly advocated the dissolution of the empire. This debate largely took the form of attempts to draw up a balance sheet, with the value of colonial trade set against the cost of administering and defending the empire.

The debit written by Cobden in the imperial ledger drew strong criticisms from the *Colonial Gazette* in 1843.~

. . . Mr. Cobden set out by informing his auditors that our colonial trade did not amount to quite one-third of our whole trade, and from that he most logically inferred that it was not worth keeping. Does Mr. Cobden mean to assert that this country would suffer no injury from having one-third of its trade suddenly lopped off? If the trade in colonial produce were thrown free immediately, it is possible that foreign dealers might drive the colonists out of the market, although they could not supply as much as themselves and the colonists had done before. They could sell at a price which would not be remunerative for the colonists, and the colonists could not continue to produce without a remunerative price. But the produce of the foreigners is limited, and cannot be increased for some time. The colonial producer may therefore be driven out of the market, though there is no one to supply his place. . . .

His remarks on the cost of the colonies to this country are in the same fair and consistent spirit. He sets down to the account of the colonies all the naval and military expenditure of the colonial stations, as if ships and soldiers would not be required to protect our commerce in distant seas even though we had no colonies; as if the possession of colonies did not enable us to keep up at less expense these guards of our distant traders. He sets down to the account of the colonies the expense of Corfu, Gibraltar, Malta, and Heligoland, which are not colonies. He sets down to the account of the colonies the expenses incurred for the suppression of the slave-trade, and the expenses of stipendiary magistrates whom the colonies neither needed nor wished for. He sets down the expenses incurred in South Australia and New Zealand by the blundering or jobbing of Governments, as the legitimate expenses of the colonies. And, having by these disingenuous means run up an exorbitant account, he exclaims, your colonial trade is only worth so much per annum, and your colonies cost you so much per annum. . . . And, even after thus exaggerating the cost of the colonies and undervaluing their returns, he has not dared to give a corresponding statement of the cost of our home traders to the public, as compared with what they bring in. Even from his own exaggerated statements, it would appear that the colonial share of the whole expenditure for army and navy is as one to three, and this is nearly the proportion he states the colonial trade bears to the trade of the whole empire. . . .

(*Colonial Gazette*, 24 June 1843)

. . . The two main objections urged against colonization by the Cobden school of economists proceed palpably from a confusion of ideas. Colonies, they say, are expensive; and colonies are in their eyes obstructions in the way of free trade. That the expenditure of Great Britain and the colonies must be greater than the expenditure of Great Britain alone, is true: but. . . . Beyond this, any increased expenditure entailed on the state by colonies must come from mismanagement; it is no necessary part of a colonial system. To speak of giving up our colonies, (and to this length the Cobden principles must be carried, or the talk about them is idle,) because the Colonial Office is extravagant, is nearly as wise as if a gentleman on being told that he was cheated by his house-keeper or house-steward should propose to mend the matter by pulling down his house. . . .

(*Colonial Gazette*, 19 April 1843)

~ Nevertheless, the Colonial Reformers admitted the need to reduce substantially the existing level of imperial expenditure. With the emergence of a self-governing empire by the end of the 1840's, and commercial relations based on the principle of free trade, expenditure on the preservation of colonial dominion seemed unnecessary. If the principle of free association was fully accepted as the future basis of imperial relations, Sir William Molesworth argued that it would be pointless to spend large sums to avert the possibility of colonies enacting hostile tariffs against British goods. The abandonment of the former system of colonial monopoly, signified by the repeal of the Navigation Laws in 1849, heralded the emergence of a very different type of empire.~

. . . I now come to the colonies, properly so called, which have been planted in North America, the West Indies and Australasia. For what purposes, I ask, were colonies originally planted by England? What benefit does this country derive from her dominion over her colonies? Our ancestors would have answered these questions in the following manner. They would have told us, how a little more than two centuries ago some of the inhabitants of this island, being uneasy at home, had migrated to America; they were prudent and energetic men, of the true Anglo-Saxon breed, which is the best fitted to wage war with the savage and the forest; and being left alone, they flourished; and in the course of a few years, without costing one farthing to this country, they became a numerous and a thriving people. Then the shopkeepers and other traders of England wished to secure their custom, and, according to the notions of the day, they petitioned Parliament that the colonists should be confined to the English shop; first, for buying all the goods they wanted in Europe; secondly, for selling all such parts of their colonial produce as the English traders might find it convenient to buy. Parliament acceded to this request. Thence the old system of colonial monopoly, which was the sole end and aim of the dominion which England assumed over her colonies. To maintain that monopoly and that dominion, vast sums were expended, costly wars were waged, and huge military and naval establishments were kept up; but it was always supposed that the expense thus incurred was repaid by the benefits derived from the monopoly of the colonial trade. I will not attempt to strike the balance of profit or loss. It is evident, however, that with the abandonment of colonial monopoly, the arguments in favour of colonial dominion, which were derived from that monopoly, must likewise be abandoned. Now, to monopoly free trade has succeeded, and the last relic of the colonial system, in the shape of the navigation laws, is about to perish. Our colonies are free to trade with whom they will, and in what manner they will. Therefore, they will only trade with us when they can do so more profitably with us than with other countries. Therefore, as far as trade is concerned, the colonies are become virtually independent States, except that they may not enact laws to restrain their inhabitants from buying from us, or selling to us, if it be for their interest so to do. It is evident, however, that if the colonies were independent States, they never would be so foolish as to prevent their inhabitants from selling to us; but it may be said that they might be so foolish as to prevent their inhabitants from buying from us. If this be all the mischief which, as far as trade is concerned, is to be apprehended from the colonies become independent States; then it follows that all the benefit which, as far as trade is concerned, we derive from the sums which we expend on colonial dominion, consists in the power which we thereby possess of averting the possibility of the colonies enacting hostile tariffs against our produce and manufactures. The amount of this benefit must evidently depend upon the value of our export trade to the colonies. Now, the declared value of the export of British produce and manufactures to the North American, West Indian, and Australasian colonies for the year 1844 (last complete return) was about £6,000,000; the direct expenditure by Great Britain, on account of those colonies, cannot be less than two millions sterling a year. I ask, is it worth our while to spend a couple of millions a year to guard against the possibility of a diminution in an export trade of £6,000,000 a year? I put this question to any mercantile man: would it be worth his while to pay 6s. 8d. in the pound on the value of his goods, to secure that those goods shall freely compete with the goods of other nations in the markets of the North American, West Indian, and Australasian colonies? And if it be not worth his while, is it worth our while to pay it for him? This is undoubtedly a great and marvellous empire, in many respects unparalleled in history, but in no respect more marvellous than with reference to its colonies. Every other nation has attempted, in some shape or form, to draw tribute from its colonies; but England, on the contrary, has paid tribute to her colonies. She has created and maintained, at enormous expense, an extensive colonial empire for the sole purpose of buying customers for her shopkeepers. This (as Adam Smith has justly observed) was the project, not of a nation of shopkeepers, but of a Government influenced by shopkeepers. It may be said that I have omitted to consider the value of the import trade; but no one fears that the colonies would, if they became independent States, refuse to sell to us; they would only be too happy so to do. We do not, therefore, require colonial dominion in order to buy from them; and in fact, we do not really require colonial dominion even to sell to them; for if we buy from them, it would be for their interest to receive payment in our produce and manufactures, if cheaper than those of other countries, and that interest would in the long run prevail. It does appear to me, therefore, to be a manifest absurdity to spend vast sums of money on colonial dominion for the purpose of securing free trade with the colonies. I now ask is this large colonial expenditure by Great Britain necessary in order to maintain the connexion between Great Britain and her colonies, which shall secure trade between them, and the other benefits which I do believe Great Britain may derive from her colonies? . . .

(*Hansard*, c, 25 July 1848, 829-31)

3 / IMPERIAL PROTECTION OR FREE TRADE?

~ During the course of contemporary discussion concerning the merits of free trade, the Reformers argued unanimously against the preservation of protective duties or imperial monopolies. Not only did they check the expansion of trade and prosperity at home and overseas, but commercial privileges and restrictions created ill-feeling in both imperial and foreign relations.~

... all restrictions upon the trade either of the mother-country or the colony with foreign nations – all superior privileges granted to either in the markets of the other, over foreign traders – are disadvantageous to both. The foundation of the reciprocal benefits of mother-country and colonies is that they afford good markets to each other. The richer the market, the more advantageous to the seller; and inasmuch as every restriction upon trade shuts men out from some possible source of increased wealth, every such restriction impoverishes a country and injures those who trade with it. Besides, it is uniformly found that exclusive privileges are favourable to indolence. Both parties have an interest in the extension, not in the restriction of the trade of each. Add to this economical view of the subject, the ill-will that is apt to grow up towards the possessor of an exclusive privilege. The monopoly of the market of the continental colonies of North America was the main source of a grudge against Great Britain, which the triumphant assertion of their independence has not entirely succeeded in effacing from the minds of the citizens of the United States. . . .

(*Colonial Gazette*, 24 February 1841)

~ J. A. Roebuck explained more fully in 1849 the beneficial effects that free trade might be expected to have on future imperial relations.~

... As the new community grows, the wants of the inhabitants increase also, and with them the desire and the power to purchase the commodities which the metropolis can produce more easily and more cheaply than the colony for itself. Thus a new market is created for the produce of the mother country. Trade between people so intimately related is sure to arise, and needs no coercive laws to force it into being. With unfettered trade there will arise a community of interests and of feeling. Instead of hostile and envious rivals, we shall have made willing and friendly customers, into whose ports we can enter without restriction and untaxed; who will not be desirous of placing upon our productions the check of a hostile tariff, or eager to refuse to us the benefits of an untrammelled commerce. If in a spirit of true liberality we regulate our whole conduct towards the new nations which our people from time to time create, they in their turn will deal generously and in a spirit of friendship with us. But if we permit the narrow views

of a protective policy to be the guides of our system, and by
restrictive laws thwart and check the energy and ingenuity of
the growing communities while subject to our sway; if we force
upon them the monopoly implied and really expressed in the
shibboleth of "ships, colonies, and commerce," we prepare our
colonies for a race of rivalry and hostility when they are able
to cast off our dominion. Unfortunately this course we have
hitherto pursued, and we see the fruits in the conduct of the
United States. We taught them, while colonies, to believe
restriction wise policy, and we proved to them that we were
selfish enough to insist upon a cramped and restricted trade,
though it was plainly mischievous to the colonies, and though
it was at every stage of their history strenuously resisted by
them. They naturally believed what we taught, and imitated the
example which we had so pertinaciously set. The doom, however, of this protective policy is sealed. We are bound, if wise
and just, to begin at once, and give the world a proof of our
sincerity, by establishing with all our colonies, in every part of
the globe, a perfectly free trade; by allowing to the whole
world free access to our colonial ports. We thus shall lay the
sure foundations of a lasting intercourse by means of a thriving,
because unrestricted commerce. . . .

(J. A. Roebuck, *The Colonies of England* [London, 1849], pp. 14-15)

~ The Reformers were convinced that free trade was as beneficial to colonial economic interests as to those of the mother
country. If some colonists doubted the wisdom of this commercial principle, however, the *Colonial Gazette* warned them
that they had simply to face the fact that protests against its
adoption as the basis of imperial policy would be unavailing.~

. . . The second thing of which the colonists may rest assured,
is that the restrictions and protections imposed under the
impression that they would benefit the Colonies and the Mother-
country cannot exist much longer. The people of Great Britain
are as apt as their neighbours to do charitable things, but they
will not sacrifice themselves in order to do good things to others;
much less will they persist in self-sacrifice after it becomes
doubtful whether it benefits others any more than themselves.
. . . All classes alike are beginning to feel that our protective
system of duties diminishes the supply and increases the price
of what have become necessaries of life to all, and of what, by
becoming necessaries to all, have increased the physical comforts and moral worth of all. The colonists must see that it is

in vain to struggle against such a growing conviction, and that whether the present protective system of duties be for them the best or the worst, they must make up their minds to relinquish it.

. . . The true interests of the Colonies require, that instead of struggling to retain restrictions in their favour, which must ere long be abrogated, they should use the interval which must elapse before their repeal, to get those restrictions which press upon and impoverish them annulled. But in addition to this, they ought to consider that a man or a community burdened with restrictive duties can never derive advantage from having restrictive duties imposed on others. Colonies are advantageous to a mother-country, and a mother-country is advantageous to her colonies, in proportion as each furnishes a good market to the other. The richer any community is, the better market it is: any thing which tends to impoverish either colony or mother-country hurts both. Now the restrictions upon our Colonial navigation and trade, and the prohibitive duties upon certain necessaries of life, impoverish the Colonies – take money out of their pockets. On the other hand, the restrictions upon the importation of Tropical product, fish, and timber, (our Colonial produce,) from other countries, impoverish the Mother-country. . . . Our system of Colonial trade proceeds upon the assumption, that by keeping each of two parties less wealthy than they need be, you make both of them richer – that two subtractions are equivalent to one addition – that two blacks make a white. This is not mere theory; the United States of America are an experimental demonstration of its truth. The American Union has been a better customer to England since it has been at liberty to trade with any part of the world, than the Plantations were when their custom was tied to our shop by navigation-laws, and the heterogeneous contradictory compound of bounties, prohibitive duties, and drawbacks, called by courtesy a commercial system. The Union is a better customer than the Plantations were, because it is richer: it is richer, because it sends its produce to the market where it is sold dearest, and buys what it cannot produce in the market where it is sold cheapest. By having its trade liberated, the Union has acquired greater power to purchase from England; and the hereditary tastes of the American nation have proved sufficiently strong and enduring to keep English wares more in demand with it than those of any other country, notwithstanding the latitude of selection allowed by its political severance, and the ill-will engendered (for a time) by the hostilities which effected that separation.

America is still a Colonial market to England: its experience ought to teach the true policy of Colonial trade in respect to those Plantations which have remained in political union with the empire. . . .

The present moment is favourable to the establishment of Colonial Free Trade. . . . From Government, therefore, we do not anticipate any serious opposition to the liberation of Colonial trade, if earnestly asked for. . . . It rests therefore with the colonists, and the Colonial interest in this country, to say whether they will have free trade or not. . . .

(*Colonial Gazette*, 9 December 1840)

~ The advantages of free trade and the evils of preferential tariffs were illustrated by the Canadian timber monopoly. The Colonial Reformers considered the discriminating duties in favour of Canadian timber highly disadvantageous to Britain, since they involved a substantial loss to the exchequer for the sake of importing a more expensive and less satisfactory product than timber brought from the Baltic. Moreover, the *Spectator* maintained that lumbering was not the type of industry on which the colonies should be encouraged to depend, and so the removal of this particular monopoly would be equally beneficial to the colonists.~

. . . But now for the master grievance to this country – the timber monopoly. According to the official returns, the total value of all the timber exported from the St. Lawrence, in 1833, was in round numbers, £700,000; and most probably full one half of this price arising out of the monopoly which the timber of Canada enjoys in the markets of England. To give North American timber a monopoly of the British market, there is imposed on almost all other timber, but particularly on the timber of the Baltic, duties which on the average may be reckoned at sevenfold the Canadian. By a return made to the House of Commons in 1830, it appears that if the same duty had been levied on the Canadian, for that year, which was levied on Baltic timber, the revenue accruing on the first would have been above £1,580,000; whereas it was little more than £232,000, – making a loss to the treasury equal to £1,348,000. If, then, for the further difference which must have arisen on the increased consumption of timber for the last eight years, we add even so small a sum as about £150,000, we may estimate the clear annual loss to the exchequer, and hence to the nation, at *a million and a half sterling*. Would Baltic timber, however, be consumed to the extent of yielding to the treasury the revenue which appears to be sacrificed by the present system? Not the least doubt of it. It is now consumed to a considerable extent, in spite of a *discriminating* duty against it of 600 per cent; and except for a limited quantity of a particular kind of pine, which would still be brought from Canada, would wholly supersede the Canadian wood. . . .

The immediate effects to the consumer are, a high price for a bad article, when a good article might be had instead, – dry rot, unsafe ships, and perishable houses, with an unnecessary tax on every branch of national industry. In short, if we had taxed our ingenuity to discover the *worst* market to go for timber, Canada is the very country we should have hit upon. . . .

But would not the Canadians be losers by the change? The whole value of the timber exported from the Canadas, as we have seen, is but £700,000; and the natural value is not probably one half of that amount. If it had been the whole, however, the trade is not one that would benefit the Canadas. On the contrary, it is highly detrimental to their interests. The *lumberers*, as the woodcutters and others concerned are ominously called, are the very pests of society. "They are," says an eye-witness, "made and kept vicious by the very trade by which they live." When the inhabitants of Canada give up lumbering, says another, "agriculture will begin to raise its head". . . . In short, while the British nation is a heavy loser by the timber monopoly, that monopoly is at the same time a heavy tax on the industry and morality of the Canadians. But a section of the clamorous shipowners of England benefit by the general calamity, and their partners and correspondents in Quebec and Montreal are partakers. The first are naturally the loudest, on this side of the Atlantic, for a war against Canadian liberty; and it is the latter who, with a crowd of dependent book-keepers, shop-keepers, lumberers, functionaries, and sinecurists, modestly assume to themselves the designation of the "British party," although they constitute but a moderate portion even of the English population. Is, then, such a monopoly as we have described "a noble object," as was said of the American Colonies in 1775, "to fight for"? Is such a "British party" as we have described one for which our blood, our treasure, or our character ought to be wasted? . . .

(*Spectator*, 13 January 1838)

~ The timber monopoly was broken in 1842, but similar arguments against colonial duties were adduced in favour of abolishing the tariff on Canadian corn imported into Britain. Provided sufficient protection could be secured against unfair competition from the neighbouring United States, and against the flooding of the British market with cheap American corn sent *via* Canada, the Reformers believed that free trade in corn would liberate Canada's agricultural potentialities and contribute to the alleviation of British domestic problems. In 1842 the British government agreed to reduce significantly the duty on Canadian wheat once the colonists had imposed a duty of 3*s.* a quarter on American wheat imported into Canada. In two issues in February 1843 the *Colonial Gazette* elaborated the substantial commercial advantages that were expected to flow from these changes.~

. . . Lord Durham in his *Report on British North America,* says – "The whole of the great peninsula between Lakes Erie and Huron, comprising nearly half the available land of the province, consists of gently-undulating alluvial soil, and, with a smaller proportion of inferior land than probably any other tract of similar extent in North America, is generally considered the *best grain-country on that continent.*" The soil and climate of this region are indeed pre-eminently adapted to the growth of wheat. The quantity yielded is immense in proportion to the cost of production; the quality is uniformly the very best; and the harvest never fails. Better and cheaper wheat is here raised than perhaps anywhere else in the world excepting an equally fertile portion of the neighbouring States. This "garden of Canada" is as yet but partially colonized; but it is of sufficient extent to supply the entire demand of the British corn-market; and there can be no sort of doubt, that if its more rapid colonization were encouraged by means of an increased demand for its surplus produce, it might speedily raise enough wheat to supply any conceivable demand from the United Kingdom. Two circumstances, however, stand in the way of a vast trade in wheat or flour between the United Kingdom and this portion of Canada. The first is, certain impediments in the navigation of the St. Lawrence, (the outlet from the Lakes to the Ocean,) which are in course of being removed by means of constructing canals at places where the river is obstructed by rapids. The second is, the duty levied in the United Kingdom on wheat and flour imported from Canada. The canals will be finished in the summer of 1844. Lake vessels will then meet sea-going vessels at Montreal and Quebec; as respects wheat there will be no occasion for breaking bulk more than once between the Lakes and the British port . . . and thus the cost of carriage, whether for wheat or flour, from Canada to this country, will be so much diminished as to admit of a highly profitable trade if it were not for the duty. Supposing the duty taken off, this profitable trade would be extended in proportion to the progress of colonization in the region described by Lord Durham. The certainty of a demand for its surplus produce would lead to the rapid settlement of that fertile country; the wheat and flour imported into the United Kingdom would be paid for with British manufactures; the very capital employed in raising the wheat would be provided, through the trade, by this country, where capital is as superabundant as labour; the labour employed in raising the wheat would be furnished by emigration from Britain; and the new employment for British capital and labour on the fertile soil of Canada, would create employment for more capital and labour at home in producing manufactured goods for the producers of the wheat and flour. Supposing the duty taken off, such would in 1844 be the extension of the field of employment for British capital and labour, by means of free trade and colonization helping each other. . . .

(*Colonial Gazette*, 8 February 1843)

. . . The change cannot but work wonders for Canada. The producing-powers of the colony have never yet been fairly tried. The duty, together with the fluctuating prices of the British market, has hitherto prevented the colonists from using the great natural advantages at their disposal. When the tax shall be abolished, and still more when (no improbable supposition, as well appear presently) steadiness of price shall be imparted to the British market by the facility of importation from America, the colonists will have every motive for not only extending the cultivation of wheat, but for systematically establishing the manufacture of wheat into flour by means of the unlimited water-power furnished by the St. Lawrence and its tributaries. By that time, probably, no wheat will be imported into England from America, but flour alone will be sent across the Atlantic. When the manufacture of flour in Canada shall have received the great improvements of which it is susceptible, and flour shall have entirely superseded wheat as an article of export from the colony, the cost of produce at the market-place will be so much reduced, without any diminution of profit, as to admit of a continually increasing demand at the lower price in proportion to the increase of population in this country. These anticipations are familiar to the minds of the deeply-interested inhabitants of Canada. We may expect, therefore, as an immediate result of Sir Robert Peel's intended legislation, that the colonists will vigorously set about the extension of the growth of wheat and the improvement of the milling processes. The utmost improvement of their internal navigation, or means of carriage from the interior to the ocean, is already in progress. Within two or three years, perhaps, a great agriculture, manufacture, and carrying-trade, will have grown up in Canada, far more than sufficient to compensate the colonists for the loss of their lumber business. The capital for these new pursuits will inevitably be supplied from this country, by means of advances on produce to come; and the additional labour required will give occasion to extend emigration. Free trade and colonization, as we remarked last week, will help each other in bestowing in Canada a degree of prosperity which the colony has never yet enjoyed.

But as respects the internal carrying-trade and the manufacture of flour, the good for Canada will not stop here. Much inquiry and reflection on the subject induce us to believe, that a duty of three shillings per quarter on American wheat will not prevent the importation of such wheat into Canada for the purpose of being manufactured into flour for the British market. If this very moderate *fixed* duty should not raise the price too high for the British market, its only effect will be to establish a sort of bounty in favour of Canada produce. In that case, the profit of the producer in Canada will be at the rate of three shillings per quarter higher than the profit of the American producer; and the colonists will gain, moreover, a further employment for capital and labour in carrying and manufacturing the American wheat. . . . The British market, not being dependent upon Canada alone, but being open to supply at a very moderate fixed duty from the fertile regions bordering on Canada, would be spared those fluctuations of price which are the greatest discouragement of production. The Canadians should not merely be satisfied with the sort of bounty in their favour as agriculturists, carriers, and millers, but ought to rejoice at a provision which promises to give steadiness to their market. . . .

(*Colonial Gazette*, 15 February 1843)

~ The discussion over the Canadian corn duty raised a wider issue. Here was an instance where justice demanded that the colonial agriculturalist should be placed on an equal footing with farmers living in the home counties of Kent or Sussex. In agriculture, as in other matters, the *Colonial Gazette* maintained that colonists should be treated, not as foreigners, but as Englishmen living overseas.~

. . . The Toronto Board of Trade very properly suggest, that the emigrant from the Mother-country deserves encouragement and the prospect of being able to make the best use of his produce; whereas our tariff treats him as an alien, and rejects the fruit of his industry. This injury in the Customs appears to arise from a misconception as to the relation between the Parent State and its Colonies. They are called "her Majesty's foreign possessions"; but there is nothing *foreign* about them, except that they are literally beyond the limits of the Three Kingdoms: it would be as well to call an English traveller in France or Italy a foreigner. The colonies of the ancient world were indeed foreign lands; for the people went forth to found distinct states, from whom the parent land claimed no allegiance, to whom she gave no succour, except at the dictate of an affectionate regard. England does not permit that relation to subsist with her Colonies: they are governed by the Central Government in a more arbitrary way than the Mother-country herself; they are denied self-government, even in a multitude of affairs of purely local interest. England does not permit her citizen, in leaving her shores, to throw off his allegiance, to cast behind him his obligations to the state, and become a foreigner: why then throw aside her allegiance to him and treat him as a foreigner? why deny the privileges while imposing the penalties of being a foreigner? We hold it to be sound, both in sense and law, that a British subject, by the mere act of sailing from England and setting himself down on a vacant spot in the lands of the empire, can no more claim to be rid of his allegiance than the builder of a mud hovel on a common: he is, morally, still in England. But let him have the advantage to that inextricable tie. . . . The farmer who migrates from England to Canada ought no more to be treated as a foreigner than he who migrates from Kent to Sussex . . . the colonist is a British citizen: he is identically the same man, subject to the same government, having the same affections, looking to the same protection, liable to the same ties, as when he still ploughed the land of England. The dominant race in every one of our colonies is the same as our own, the Anglo-Saxon; and in every particular the population is less alien from us than that of Ireland, a constituent part of the United Kingdom.

Keeping these principles in view, we perceive, that if it is desirable and just to protect the British agriculturists from

the competition of the foreigner, – a question which is not
mooted here, – it is neither desirable nor just to protect them
against the competition of a part of their own body who endure
considerable hardship in the great enterprise of enlarging the
field of British production. Could any body of men add a Kent
to the area of England, would any legislator dare to propose
laying a duty of discouragement on the produce of that acquisition in order to favour less enterprising agriculturists? The
colonist performs that service to the country; only he goes to
the further quarters of the globe, at his own risk and expense,
to do so. Does he not rather deserve a reward, therefore, than
a penalty – a bounty, rather than a duty on his produce?
especially when it is considered, that in the very act of sending
it to market he has to bear charges from which the home-grower
is free. . . .

(*Colonial Gazette*, 23 February 1842)

PART THREE:
SYSTEMATIC COLONIZATION

1 / WAKEFIELD'S THEORY SUMMARIZED

~ Gibbon Wakefield's theory of systematic colonization was specifically designed to alleviate the unemployment and distress which then prevailed in the British Isles by calling upon the colonies to furnish homes and jobs for emigrant labourers and profitable new fields for the investment of surplus British capital. Wakefield thought that current domestic difficulties could be traced to a superabundance of labour and a glut of capital. Labourers were competing amongst themselves for limited opportunities of employment, and capital was accumulating in the hands of British capitalists faster than it could be profitably invested at home. This strange coincidence of widespread unemployment and dormant wealth Wakefield attributed to the rapid growth of population and capital in England since the end of the Napoleonic Wars and the restricted field which existed for their productive application within the British Isles. His solution was to expand the field of employment for both capital and labour by including within it settlements overseas, as if a strip of territory had been attached to the English coast. Wakefield noted that the needs of the mother country and the colonies were complementary in this respect: Britain possessed an excess of labour and capital, but a shortage of land; the colonies, on the other hand, possessed an abundance of land, but lacked the labour and capital to exploit it. By means of systematic colonization these idle resources could be brought into a fruitful association.

Although Wakefield was fundamentally concerned to provide a remedy for British problems, his whole scheme came to centre on conditions in the colonies. He believed that most colonies suffered from an acute shortage of labour, and that until this deficiency had been remedied, they would not become attractive to English capitalists and emigrants of rank and substance, nor economically capable of alleviating Britain's domestic difficulties. Wakefield attributed this basic deficiency to the facility with which immigrant labourers and other colonial workers had apparently been able to acquire their own land, and so establish themselves as independent proprietors.

As a means of securing a more productive balance between land and labour, Wakefield looked to the British government to exercise an active control over the management of colonial lands and the progress of colonial settlement. In place of the wasteful system of free grants by which crown lands throughout the empire had generally in the past been alienated, he proposed that all land, irrespective of quality or location, should in future be sold at what he termed a "sufficient price" — that is, a price which would be restrictive enough to prevent labourers from immediately becoming landowners and would thus create and preserve a supply of labour for settlers with capital. Although Wakefield refused to state what the "sufficient price" would be in any particular instance or give precise instructions how it might in practice be calculated, he envisaged that the price should be manipulated to maintain the maximum productive balance between the amount of land passing into private ownership and the available supply of colonial labour to develop it: increased to discourage the purchase of land if labour became expensive and scarce; reduced to encourage purchasers if labour was plentiful and cheap. It was for this reason that Wakefield came to prefer the sale of colonial land at a uniform, fixed price rather than by public auction at a minimum upset price, a method of sale which he had at first advocated as a result of his admiration for the efficient practice of the United States government. Public auction would stimulate competition and so increase for the mere sake of revenue a price that was by itself a sufficient restriction on landownership. Nevertheless, the whole system would be most advantageously promoted, and to some extent self-regulating, if the revenue produced by the sale of colonial land was used to pay the passages of selected emigrants from the English labouring classes, with a preference being given to young married couples. On arrival in the colonies such immigrants would enter the labour market to meet the increasing demands of extended settlement and replace workers who had acquired sufficient money and experience to entitle them to become purchasers of land and smallholders in their own right.

As a further means of maximizing the productivity of capital and labour in the colonies, Wakefield stressed the advantages of concentrating settlement. Although he regarded the compact farming communities of rural England as the ideal pattern, he did not intend that settlers should be densely huddled together within certain narrow geographical limits. By concentration, Wakefield meant the establishment of a productive division of labour within any given district, or what he described as a combination of labour and a division of employments. Settlers should be encouraged to assist one another in the task of pion-

eering a wilderness, instead of being allowed to disperse themselves over a wide expanse of territory and struggle alone with
limited resources of labour and capital. At the same time,
colonial communities should comprise a wide range of diverse
occupations, with tradesmen, professional people, and others
not dependent on cultivating the soil for a livelihood.

In addition to its economic benefits, Wakefield's concept of
concentrated settlement possessed distinct social advantages
which he was anxious to emphasize. He discovered in Britain
what he called the uneasiness of the middle classes, a feeling
of discontent and frustration amongst professional and business
people who were struggling to maintain their standard of living
at a time when incomes and profits were low. These were the
individuals whose interests he also wanted to attract: respectable, thrifty, and industrious citizens of small means who
possessed ambition and enterprise but lacked the opportunity
to improve their fortunes and their social status. Wakefield
therefore stressed both the vast opportunities overseas and the
degree of civilization that could be achieved even in colonial
communities. Systematic colonization represented an attempt
to transplant in the colonies a cross-section of English society,
purged of its grosser economic and civil restrictions, but with
its refinements and vital social distinctions carefully preserved.
The unfortunate tendency of a pioneering environment towards
egalitarianism would thereby be successfully checked, and new
countries would be rendered attractive to all classes of Englishmen if colonial communities were in all essential particulars
extensions of English society overseas.~

2 / ADVANTAGES OF COLONIZATION

~ The various facets of Wakefield's theory could be amply
illustrated by extracts from his writings, but it is more important
for the present purpose to suggest the particular relevance to
British North America of his ideas on emigration and crown
lands administration. In general, his views were influential
because he provided a cogent and plausible analysis of the
urgent domestic problems with which British politicians were
then struggling, and because he demonstrated the way in which
colonies might be more effectively employed to alleviate these
acute economic and social difficulties. Colonies would obviously
provide convenient outlets for England's surplus population,
and of the various parts of the empire open to settlers, none
were more attractive than the colonies of British North America.
As Charles Buller commented in 1843,~

. . . I should regard any practical scheme of colonization as most defective and unsatisfactory which proposed to leave British North America entirely out of the field of colonization. These colonies have one obvious and great advantage, as every one must be aware, over all other portions of our empire, in their greater nearness to the mother country. The emigrant, who can avail himself of steam, could, with ease, be at the westernmost point of Canada, in about a fortnight. Even the poorest, though compelled to resort to the slowest means of communication, need not provide for more than a six weeks' sea voyage, and might count on reaching the same distance in two months. The nature of our Canadian trade renders the outward voyage peculiarly cheap in proportion even to its length. And though the unoccupied regions of our American dominions present no such vast field for the future extension of our race as are offered by the wide regions of our Australian and, perhaps, of our African quarters of the globe – though they promise no such vast variety of produce of such value – though they fill our imaginations with no such certain, though distant, prospects of boundless empire – they offer us an immense space more than any other available for the immediate wants of this and many succeeding generations. Millions might live and thrive on a vast extent of rich land, in which climate, soil, and water unite in favouring the easy production of food, whether for the consumption of the people or for exportation to other countries; and to and from which the most capacious harbours, and the most abundant facilities for internal communications afford the amplest means of access and of carriage. . . . In all these portions of our possessions, there is room enough to establish in plenty, at least half the present dense population of the British islands; and it would certainly be a lamentable thought for the advocate of colonization, were he compelled to abandon this noble field, placed so peculiarly within our reach, as one which was never to be rendered available to us by the application of vigorous efforts, and a sound system. . . .

(*Hansard*, LXXI, 15 August, 1843, 766-7)

~ Lord Durham had already eloquently enunciated in his *Report* some of the attributes that made British North America a valuable field of British colonization.~

. . . No portion of the American Continent possesses greater natural resources for the maintenance of large and flourishing communities. An almost boundless range of the richest soil still remains unsettled, and may be rendered available for the purposes of agriculture. The wealth of inexhaustible forests of the best timber in America, and of extensive regions of the most valuable minerals, have as yet been scarcely touched. Along the whole line of sea-coast, around each island, and in every river, are to be found the greatest and richest fisheries in the world. The best fuel and the most abundant water-power are available for the coarser manufactures, for which an easy and certain market will be found. Trade with other continents is favoured by the possession of a large number of safe and spacious harbours; long, deep and numerous rivers, and vast inland seas, supply the means of easy intercourse; and the structure of the country generally affords the utmost facility for every species of communication by land. Unbounded materials of agricultural, commercial and manufacturing industry are there: it depends upon the present decision of the Imperial Legislature to determine for whose benefit they are to be rendered available. The country which has founded and maintained these Colonies at a vast expense of blood and treasure, may justly expect its compensation in turning their unappropriated resources to the account of its own redundant population; they are the rightful patrimony of the English people, the ample appanage which God and Nature have set aside in the New World for those whose lot has assigned them but insufficient portions in the Old. . . .

(C. P. Lucas (ed.), *Lord Durham's Report on the Affairs of British North America* [Oxford, 3 vols., 1912], II, 12-13)

~ Nevertheless, the Colonial Reformers drew an important distinction between mere emigration, which did no more than transfer people to existing colonies, and the broader process of colonization, which led to the formation of new settlements to receive British emigrants. Colonization, as Wakefield envisaged it, therefore offered an admirable means of opening up fresh markets overseas, expanding trade, and creating opportunities for the profitable investment of surplus British capital.~

. . . Can we then sufficiently enlarge the whole field of employment for British capital and labour, by means of sending capital and people to cultivate new land in other parts of the world? If we sent away enough, the effect here would be the same as if the domestic increase of capital and people were sufficiently checked. But another effect of great importance

would take place. The emigrants would be producers of food;
of more food, if the colonization were well managed, than they
could consume: they would be growers of food and raw materials of manufacture for this country: we should buy their
surplus food and raw materials with manufactured goods. Every
piece of our colonization, therefore, would add to the power of
the whole mass of new countries to supply us with employment
for capital and labour at home. Thus, employment for capital
and labour would be increased in two places and two ways at the
same time; abroad, in the colonies, by the removal of capital and
people to fresh fields of production; at home, by the extension
of markets, or the importation of food and raw materials. . . .
The common idea is that emigration of capital and people
diminishes the wealth and population of the mother-country.
It has never done so; it has always increased both population
and wealth at home. And the reason is obvious. In the case
supposed of a great colonization, and of our actual free trade,
viewing Great Britain and all new countries as one country
for the purposes of production and exchange, there would be
in the whole of this great empire an increase of production
exceeding the utmost possible increase of capital and people.
Capital and people, therefore, would increase as fast as possible.
Some of the increase would take place in the new-country or
colony part of the empire; some here: and it might well happen
that our share of the increase would be greater than our present
increase of wealth and population. . . .
(Wakefield, *Art of Colonization*, pp. 91-93)

~ Moreover, Wakefield and his supporters regarded colonization, not only as a subject which had previously been neglected
by writers on political economy, but also as a lost art which they
wanted to revive. If colonization was conducted according to
a systematic plan and waste land properly administered, Molesworth argued that it would be possible to create civilized and
prosperous communities overseas that would attract emigrants
of rank and substance, capitalists as well as labourers. ~

. . . to colonise beneficially, it is necessary that the higher
and richer, as well as the poorer classes; that the employers of
labour as well as the employed; that all classes of society should
migrate together, forming new communities, analogous to that
of the Parent State. . . .
. . . Not dissimilar in principle was the old English mode of
colonising, except that our colonies, instead of commencing

their existence as independent States professed their allegiance to the mother country; but their charters gave them all the essential powers of self-government, and complete control over their internal affairs. They flourished rapidly, were most loyal, and sincerely attached to our empire, till we drove them into just rebellion by our new colonial system. Very different from these successful modes of colonising has been that of the Colonial Office. It has been either a shovelling out of paupers or a transportation of criminals, whereby some of the fairest portions of the British dominions have been converted into pest-houses of pauperism, or sinks of iniquity, polluting the earth with unheard-of diseases and unmentionable crimes. No gentleman, no man of birth or education, who knows anything about the matter, would ever think of emigrating to a colony, to be under the control of the Colonial Office. But if the colonies were properly planted, and self-governed according to the old fashion, then our kinsmen and friends, instead of overstocking the liberal professions, instead of overcrowding the Army and Navy, where no career is open for them, would seek their fortunes in the colonies and prosper. For we are by nature a colonising people. The same destiny that led our forefathers from their homes in the farthest east, still urges us onwards to occupy the uninhabited regions of the west and the south; and America, and Australia, and New Zealand, anxiously expect our arrival to convert their wastes into happy abodes of the Anglo-Saxon race. . . .

(*Hansard*, c, 25 July 1848, 855-6)

~ If colonization were to be advantageously conducted and English society transplanted overseas, Buller pointed out how essential it was to create conditions in the colonies that would attract both capitalists and labourers.~

. . . It is our duty, it seems to me, to render Canada available to our people, and our people available to Canada. And in order to do that we must in Canada, as in our other colonies, endeavour to get over the great impediment to colonization, by securing the simultaneous emigration of capital and labour; we must tempt the capitalist to embark his money in the improvement of Canada by ensuring him labour for the cultivation of his property, and we must invite the labourer thither by holding out to him the certainty of being employed by others, until he shall have accumulated sufficient means for becoming a thriving proprietor. This we can only do by applying to Canada the principles on which our colonization should be conducted elsewhere. There, as elsewhere, the placing a sufficient price on waste lands must furnish the means of colonization, while it would serve the yet more important purpose of concentrating the population, which your former system seemed devised with a view of scattering as widely as possible. . . .

(*Hansard*, LXXI, 15 August 1843, 774-5)

~ If a sufficient price was imposed to restrict the acquisition of land and concentrate colonial settlement, Wakefield was convinced that substantial economic and social benefits would result.~

. . . In any colony where this perfect rule for treating the chief element of colonization should be adopted, colonization would proceed, not as every where hitherto, more or less, by the scattering of people over a wilderness and placing them for ages in a state between civilization and barbarism, but by the extension to new places of all that is good in an old society; by the removal to new places of people, civilized, and experienced in all the arts of production; willing and able to assist each other; excited to the most skilful application of capital and labour by ready markets for disposing of surplus produce; producing, by means of the most skilful industry in the richest field, more than colonial industry has ever produced; obtaining the highest profits of capital and the highest wages of labour; offering the strongest attraction for the immigration of capital and people; increasing rapidly; enjoying the advantages of an old society without its evils; without any call for slavery or restrictions on foreign trade; an old society in every thing save the uneasiness of capitalists and the misery of the bulk of the people. . . .

(E. G. Wakefield, *England and America* [London, 2 vols., 1833], II, 175-6)

3 / THE ROLE OF GOVERNMENT IN EMIGRATION

~ The Colonial Reformers and many other contemporaries argued that, if large-scale emigration was to become an effective method of alleviating distress in Britain, some means had to be found of financing the passages of emigrants without placing additional burdens on the British taxpayer. During the 1820's fear of excessive imperial expenditure had made parliament unwilling to sanction extensive schemes of assisted emigration and subsidize them with public funds. Wilmot Horton's experiments of sending paupers and disbanded soldiers to Upper Canada and the Cape in the 1820's had shown how easy it was to spend considerable sums of public money without securing any tangible return. Indeed, nothing is more instructive of contemporary political philosophy than the fact that practical schemes for assisting emigration during the twenties remained out of favour, despite the acuteness of Britain's domestic difficulties, and despite a general agreement that emigration would provide the most appropriate solution.

In 1831, however, the Colonial Office decided to set on foot a plan for providing limited financial assistance from colonial funds to British emigrants going to Australia. Although the decision cannot be attributed solely to Wakefield's influence, this emigration came to be financed by proceeds from the sale of crown lands. Thereafter assisted emigration to Australia proceeded spasmodically as and when colonial funds were available, but the government refused to contribute money from the British Treasury for free passages. Meanwhile it was decided that the shorter and cheaper journey to North America should not be financed from public funds, and it never became so, principally on the ground that financial intervention by the state might check the existing flow of voluntary emigration and seriously undermine the initiative and self-reliance of individuals. Moreover, many emigrants already found their way to the United States, and no ministry with a passion for economy was anxious to provide free passages for individuals whose sole intention was to reach the United States by way of British North America.

The Colonial Reformers condemned the government's unwillingness to promote emigration as shortsighted in view of the many economic benefits it would produce. The *Colonial Gazette* argued in 1842, as Wilmot Horton had previously done, that it would be more beneficial and more economical to use public funds to send unemployed labourers overseas than to maintain them in idleness at home.~

. . . The British nation, with its twenty-six millions of population, possesses, besides the three little islands in which all its wealth is sown, inhabitable lands of greater extent than all Europe. As the produce of the three islands does not suffice to feed the twenty-six millions, the obvious process is, to send some of those people to the lands now lying fallow. But, exclaims some economist, it will cost something to do so! And what does it cost *not* to do so? Setting aside national ruin, popular destitution, bloodshed, and other costly evils incurred or threatened, there is a direct expense incurred by the country which it is not difficult to point out: could the country produce as much food and exchangeable produce with fewer people? ... Could the United Kingdom spare a million, and yet produce as much wheat, beef, cotton, woollen and iron ware, as at present? Unquestionably. Then the subsistence of a million of people is a direct yearly charge on the nation. The cost of conveying a person to a colony, taking one person with another and one distance with another, does not much exceed the cost of that person's annual subsistence: to remove the million to the Colonies would need an outlay about equal to the maintenance of that million every year, bad years with good. ... The gain to the Mother-country therefore from emigration is this – she is relieved from the cost of subsisting the surplus population; the full amount of riches extracted by the emigrant from the new soil is added to the Imperial wealth; a great portion is sent back to the Mother-country in barter for the goods which the emigrant desires to follow him. But whatever the profit on the transaction, the great needful primary gain is, that the emigrant, instead of being fed at the cost of the nation, (whether directly, in the shape of poor-rates, or indirectly, in the shape of abstracted wages and profits,) earns his own subsistence out of the land. ...

(*Colonial Gazette*, 13 July 1842)

~ Although substantial revenue might be raised from the sale of colonial lands, the Reformers maintained that public money spent on assisting emigration would produce a far greater and more advantageous return than expenditure on keeping up colonial defence and putting down colonial wars and rebellions. As Molesworth cogently argued in 1848, a reduction in these exorbitant expenses would make available considerable funds for the promotion of systematic colonization.~

... To show the utility of colonies as outlets for our population, I may refer to the reports of the Emigration Commissioners, from which it appears that in the course of the last twenty years 1,673,803 persons have emigrated from this country, of whom 825,564 went to the United States; 702,101 to the North American colonies, 127,188 to the Australian colonies, and 19,090 to other places. It would be interesting to know what has been the cost of this emigration, and how it has been defrayed. I cannot put it down at less than £20,000,000 sterling, of which about £1,500,000 were paid out of the proceeds of land sales in the Australian colonies. This emigration has varied considerably in amount from year to year; from the minimum of 26,092 persons in 1828, to the maximum of 258,270 persons last year. . . . Therefore, the habit of emigrating is confirmed, and becoming more powerful every day; and therefore colonies are becoming more useful as outlets for our population. . . .

I do not propose to abandon any portion of that empire. I only complain that it is of so little use to us; that it is a vast tract of fertile desert, which cost[s] us £4,000,000 sterling a year, and yet only contains a million and a half of our race. Would it not be possible to people this desert with active and thriving Englishmen? . . .

To carry such a plan into execution, two things would be requisite. First, funds wherewith to convey the poorer classes to the colonies . . . sufficient funds could be obtained by the sale of waste lands, according to the well-known plan of Mr. Wakefield. . . . I firmly believe that with continuous and systematic emigration, sufficient funds could be so obtained. But I will suppose, for the sake of argument, that they must be obtained, for the present, from some other source. Now, I ask the House to consider, first, that we spend four millions sterling a year in the colonies on Army, Navy, Ordnance, Commissariat, Kafir wars, Canadian rebellions, and the like; secondly, that for half four millions – the sum which I propose to save by a reduction of colonial expenditure – we might send annually to Australia 150,000 persons, and to Canada twice that number. I ask the House, at the expiration of ten or fifteen years, from which of these two modes of expending the public money would the nation derive the greater benefit? Our Army, Navy, and Ordnance cost us at present from six to seven millions sterling a year more than they did in 1835, when their force was ample for the defence of the empire. What have we to show in return for this enormous increase of expenditure? A Canadian insurrection suppressed, a Kafir war terminated, barren trophies in India, the gates of Somnauth, Hong-Kong, Labuan, and the Falkland Islands. What should we have had to show for it had only a portion of it been expended on colonisation? A third part of it – the two millions a year which I affirm can be spared from our colonial expenditure – would have been sufficient in ten years to double or triple the British population of our colonial empire.

For instance, that sum would in ten years . . . have conveyed to North America some three millions. . . . I do grudge the four millions a year which we squander upon our colonies, when I consider what might be done with half that sum for the benefit of this country, and of the colonies, by means of systematic colonisation. . . .

(*Hansard*, c, 25 July 1848, 853-5)

~ Apart from retrenchment, politicians were also confronted with the problem of deciding how far the state should accept active responsibility for regulating an activity that many contemporaries felt ought ideally to be left to private enterprise and individual initiative. Emigration was a field of administration where the government did not initially feel that the state should assume more than minimal responsibility, lest it became extensively involved in a host of expensive administrative arrangements for the selection and superintendence of emigrants. These fears were amply justified by subsequent events. Despite the government's care to avoid paying the cost of passages and other unwelcome commitments, the imperial authorities soon became increasingly involved in the many administrative responsibilities which large-scale emigration necessarily created. In 1837 Thomas Elliot was appointed Agent-General for Emigration and, assisted by a growing corps of emigration officers at the various ports from which thousands left for North America and Australia, he supervised shipping arrangements and did what he could under the terms of the passenger acts to ensure the safety, comfort, and health of emigrants during the voyage. Attempts were made to protect the poorer class of emigrants from the many frauds practised by unscrupulous shipowners, brokers, and others who performed essential services at the ports of embarkation.

By the end of the 1830's, however, it was obvious that the sheer range and volume of business had become too exacting for even a conscientious administrator like Elliot, and that the provisions of various passenger acts from 1803 onwards were inadequate and ineffectually enforced. Emigration had become an administrative responsibility of the state, and it required an organization to match its new importance. It was this basic deficiency which formed the central theme of persistent criticism in and out of parliament by the Colonial Reformers and all those who felt that emigration ought to be placed on a more organized basis. Their perseverance was finally rewarded with the appointment of the Colonial Land and Emigration Commission in 1840 and the overhaul of legislation and the executive corps in 1842.

As part of the background to these measures, the investigations and *Report* of the Durham commission provided an influential commentary on the evils of inadequate superintendence. In his *Report on Public Lands and Emigration*, Buller strikingly demonstrated the shortcomings of existing regulations from the colonial point of view, which until this time had largely been ignored in London.~

. . . Upon this subject very great misconceptions appear to prevail in England. It seems that all those who have made inquiries into the subject of emigration from the United Kingdom, have imagined that no interference was required with respect to that to the North American provinces; and that although some trifling matters of detail might require correction, the general character of that emigration was such as to forbid any intermeddling. This misconception is undoubtedly attributable, in a great degree, to the circumstance, that all the evidence obtained on the subject, was collected in the country from which the emigrants departed, instead of that at which they arrived. Had the position of the inquirers been reversed, they must have arrived at very different conclusions, and have discovered that no emigration so imperatively demanded the regulating interposition of the Legislature as that for which they specially refused to provide. . . .

It is not necessary that I should attempt to prove, that it is the duty of Government to regulate the emigration that it continues to encourage, and to establish an efficient system of control over emigrant vessels; because this is admitted in principle at least, by the appointment of an agent-general for emigrants, and of subordinate agents at some of the ports of embarkation. But the measures adopted have been partial and incomplete; and though in some cases they have prevented, in many they have permitted the continuance of all the evils against which they were intended to guard. If looked at by an individual residing in England, it is probable that they may appear adequate and effectual, because in that country attention is directed exclusively to the evils they prevent. In the colonies their deficiency is apparent, since there, attention is naturally fixed upon those evils which they leave untouched. . . .

The great amount of voluntary emigration to the North American Colonies, which has been assigned as a reason for the non-interference of Government, even if it be admitted as an argument against the offer of a free passage to any class, lest this offer should operate practically to deter many who emigrate upon their own resources, forms at the same time one of the most powerful arguments for the adoption of an effectual system of control over this voluntary emigration. Of the tens of thousands who emigrated every year, it must have been known that the vast majority were ignorant of the existence of any law to which they could appeal for protection against extortion or ill treatment. All of them were proceeding to a place where employment could be furnished to but a very small portion; and to these only for a limited period. The place of ultimate destination of nearly all the emigrants, was several hundred miles from the port of debarkation; and there existed no means of forwarding them to the spot where their labour would be in demand, upon the adequacy or permanency of which it would be safe for the Government to rely. . . . If, however, the Imperial Government refused to take upon itself the entire direction of emigration, in the fear that they might lessen its amount, they were the more bound to take such measures as were obviously within their power to protect or to assist the emigrants.

The measures which Government have adopted are however deplorably defective. They have left untouched some of the chief evils of emigration, and have very incompletely remedied those even against which they were especially directed. Although the safeguards for the emigrant during the passage are increased, and in many places enforced, yet there is still no check of any sort whatever over a large proportion of the emigrant vessels. The provisions for the reception of the emigrants at Quebec, so far as the Government is concerned, are of the most inefficient and unsatisfactory character; and the poorer class would have to find their way as they best might to the Upper Province, or to the United States, were it not for the operation of societies, whose main object is not the advantage of the emigrants, but to free the cities of Quebec and Montreal from the intolerable nuisance of a crowd of unemployed, miserable, and too often diseased persons. The government agent at Quebec has no power; he has not even any rules for his guidance; and no monies are placed at his disposal. At Montreal there has not been any agent for the two last years. The whole extent therefore of the interference of the Government, has been to establish in England agents to superintend the enforcement of the provisions of the Passenger Act in respect of the emigrants from some ports, and to maintain an agent in the Province of Lower Canada, to observe rather than to regulate, the emigration into that province. . . .

(C. Buller, *Report on Public Lands and Emigration,* [Appendix B to Lord Durham's *Report*], in Lucas, *Lord Durham's Report,* III, 117-22)

4 / COLONIAL LAND ADMINISTRATION

~ In their writings and speeches the Reformers emphasized the importance of land administration both to colonial development and to the pursuit of imperial designs. Not only was land the most valuable natural resource of a colony, but since all unalienated or "waste" land belonged to the crown, the government could, through the regulation it adopted, exercise a profound influence over the progress of settlement, the pattern of land utilization, the structure of landownership, and the rate of economic growth. Consequently, there was a very close and fundamental correlation between the way in which the British government discharged its responsibility for the management of crown lands and the extent to which individual colonies could be made to satisfy British commercial demands and act as outlets for surplus population.

In his *Report* Lord Durham showed a keen awareness of the significance of land administration and its complexities.~

. . . I allude to an operation of Government, which has a paramount influence over the happiness of individuals, and the progress of society towards wealth and greatness. I am speaking of the disposal, by the Government, of the lands of the new country. In old countries no such matter ever occupies public attention; in new colonies, planted on a fertile and extensive territory, this is the object of the deepest moment to all, and the first business of the Government. Upon the manner in which this business is conducted, it may almost be said that every thing else depends. If lands are not bestowed on the inhabitants and new comers with a generous hand, the society endures the evils of an old and over-peopled state, with the superadded inconveniences that belong to a wild country. They are pinched for room even in the wilderness, are prevented from choosing the most fertile soils and favourable situations, and are debarred from cultivating that large extent of soil, in proportion to the hands at work, which can alone compensate, in quantity of produce, for the rude nature of husbandry in the wilderness. If, on the other hand, the land is bestowed with careless profusion,

great evils of another kind are produced. Large tracts become
the property of individuals, who leave their lands unsettled and
untouched. Deserts are thus interposed between the industrious
settlers; the natural difficulties of communication are greatly
enhanced; the inhabitants are not merely scattered over a wide
space of country, but are separated from each other by impas-
sible wastes; the cultivator is cut off or far removed from a
market in which to dispose of his surplus produce, and procure
other commodities; and the greatest obstacles exist to co-
operation in labour, to exchange, to the division of employments, to combination for municipal and other public purposes,
to the growth of towns, to public worship, to regular education,
to the spread of news, to the acquisition of common knowledge,
and even to the civilizing influences of mere intercourse for
amusement. Monotonous and stagnant indeed must ever be the
state of a people who are permanently condemned to such
separation from each other. If, moreover, the land of a new
country is so carelessly surveyed that the boundaries of property are incorrectly or inadequately defined, the Government
lays up a store of mischievous litigation for the people. Whatever
delay takes place in perfecting the titles of individuals to lands
alienated by the Government, occasions equal uncertainty and
insecurity of property. If the acquisition of land, in whatever
quantities, is made difficult or troublesome, or is subjected to
any needless uncertainty or delay, applicants are irritated,
settlement is hindered, and immigration to the colony is discouraged, as emigration from it is promoted. If very different
methods of proceeding have effect in the same colony, or in
different parts of the same group of colonies, the operation of
some can scarcely fail to interfere with or counteract the
operation of others; so that the object of the Government
must somewhat, or at some time, be defeated. And frequent
changes of system are sure to be very injurious, not only by
probably displeasing those who either obtain land just before,
or desire to obtain some just after, each change, but also by
giving a character of irregularity, uncertainty, and even mystery, to the most important proceeding of Government. In this
way settlement and emigration are discouraged; inasmuch as
the people, both of the colony and of the mother country, are
deprived of all confidence in the permanency of any system,
and of any familiar acquaintance with any of the temporary
methods. . . . If the disposal of public lands is administered
partially – with favour to particular persons or classes – a sure
result is, the anger of all who do not benefit by such favouritism

(the far greater number, of course), and consequently, the general unpopularity of the Government. . . .
(Lucas, *Lord Durham's Report*, II, 203-5)

~ As part of a reformed system, the advocates of systematic colonization wanted to introduce a greater degree of restriction into imperial land administration. Colonial prosperity and the emergence of civilized communities could be fostered most effectively by a system of land sales which would control and regulate access to landownership and concentrate settlement. Amongst several writers, Charles Buller emphasized the disadvantages of allowing emigrant labourers to become landed proprietors.~

. . . I cannot recommend that any measures should be adopted to settle these emigrants upon land of their own. The previous habits of English labourers are not such as to fit them for the severe and painful labours to which they would thus be exposed, or to give them the forethought and prudence which such a position especially requires. Habituated to provide for the subsistence of the week by the labour of the week, they are too often found to shrink from a toil cheered by no prospect of an immediate return; and having exhausted all the means furnished for their temporary support, to leave the land upon which they were placed, in order to obtain subsistence as labourers for hire. The exceptions to this result are few and unimportant. They rather confirm than invalidate the rule, and have been procured at a cost utterly disproportionate to the object attained. It is rather to be feared, that in spite of any measures that can prudently be adopted, the majority of the labouring emigrants will be tempted, by the desire of becoming independent landholders, to settle themselves upon farms of their own at too early a period for their own comfort and prosperity. It cannot, however, be the duty of Government to precipitate this period, nor in any way to interfere with the natural and profitable order of things – that the possession of capital, and an acquaintance with the modes of husbandry practised in the colonies, should precede settlement. . . .
(Buller, *Report on Public Lands and Emigration*, in Lucas, *Lord Durham's Report*, III, 125-6)

~ A further evil of land administration in Canada, according to Charles Tennant, was the extent to which settlement had been widely and sparsely scattered.~

. . . in Canada infinite pains have been taken to scatter the people, and to reduce them to a condition similar to that of some of the inhabitants of the Pampas. The greater the concentration, the greater must be the division of labour, the quantity of production, and the accumulation of wealth; the greater consequently must be the demand for labour – provided always, that if the people are increasing, they may be gradually concentrated on an increasing territory. One man, isolated on a square mile of land, and obliged, of course, to do every thing for himself, might not produce more than enough food for his own subsistence; ten men in the same situation might produce a great deal more food than they could consume, and would thereby provide employment for other labourers, who, united with them, would produce still more food in proportion to their consumption; and the number of labourers might constantly increase, with benefit to all, until the whole square mile were well cultivated. That degree of concentration, therefore, which is required to enable a new people easily to repay the cost of their creation, would not operate as a check to high wages and the greatest possible increase of people, but would, on the contrary, insure them, by giving the greatest possible produce to the greatest possible number. . . .

(C. Tennant, *A Statement of the Principles and Objects of a Proposed National Society, for the Cure and Prevention of Pauperism, by Means of Systematic Colonization* [London, 1830], pp. 40-41.)

5 / EVILS OF LAND ADMINISTRATION
   IN BRITISH NORTH AMERICA

~ It was the great merit of Wakefield and the Reformers that they exposed the evils of generous free grants as a method of colonization. Wakefield persistently criticized the wastefulness with which colonial lands had invariably in the past been alienated throughout the empire.~

. . . It has been said above, that government may dispose of land with a niggard hand. Do not suppose that any colonizing government has ever done so. All colonizing governments have done just the reverse, by disposing of land with a profuse hand. The greediness of colonists has been equal to the profusion of the governments. The colonists, full of the ideas about land which possess people in old countries – emigrating indeed because at home the cheapest land had got or was getting to be scarce and precious – could never obtain too much land for the satisfaction of their desires: and the governments, universally down to the other day, seemed to have looked upon waste land as a useless property of the state, only fit to be squandered in satisfying the greedy desires of colonists. Throughout what may be termed the colonial world, therefore, allowing however for a few exceptions in which a colony has grown to be as densely peopled as an old country, there has at all times existed a proportion between land and people, which almost prevented competition for the cheapest land, and enabled every colonist to obtain some land either for nothing or for a price little more than nominal. Whatever may have been the price of the dearest land in a colony, the price of the cheapest has never, with the above exceptions, been sufficient to prevent labourers from turning into landowners after a very brief term of hired service.

. . . However profusely land may be granted, some of it acquires in time a value depending on advantages of position: and this consideration explains why people are so greedy to obtain land for nothing, even though at the time of being obtained it has no market value. This consideration also shows that under the plan of granting, however profusely, the government has the opportunity, and the strongest temptation, to favour its friends, to practise favouritism and official jobbing in the disposal of land. There is no instance of a colonizing government that was able to resist this temptation. Official favouritism and jobbing in the disposal of land by grant, constitute one of the most prominent and ugliest features of colonial history: and they have been one of the most effectual impediments to colonization, by producing an immense crop of disappointments, jealousies, envies, and irritations. . . .

(Wakefield, *Art of Colonization*, pp. 333-6)

~ Charles Buller's investigations in Canada led him to condemn the many evil effects of free land grants on colonial development.~

. . . The evidence collected upon this subject, and appended to the present Report, discloses the existence of evils in every colony similar in kind and in degree, having a common cause, and involving similar consequences. The settlers, separated from each other by tracts of appropriated but unoccupied land, whether Crown or clergy reserves, or private property, have been placed in circumstances which rendered it impossible that they should create or preserve the instruments of civilization and wealth. Their numbers are too few, and their position too distant, to allow them to support schools, places of worship, markets, or post-offices. They can neither make nor maintain roads. The produce of their farms, owing to the necessarily imperfect methods of cultivation pursued under such circumstances, is small in quantity, and, owing to the difficulty and expense of conveying it to market, of little value. The money that has been expended in the acquisition and improvement of the land they occupy yields them no adequate return; and though the means of subsistence are within their reach, yet these are rude, and not unfrequently scanty, and have to be purchased by severe and oftentimes unremitting toil. The experience of the past warrants no expectation of any improvement. With very few and irregular exceptions, such a state of things has prevailed in every district of every colony, from its establishment to the present time; any increase of population having led rather to an extension of the limits of settlement than to the occupation of the unsettled lands in the midst of the old occupants. To an individual placed in this position there is, consequently, only one means of escape; the total and immediate abandonment of his farm, either selling it for what it will fetch at the moment, or allowing it to remain unoccupied till he can obtain what he considers a fair price. . . .

. . . The enormous disproportion between the granted and cultivated land in every Province, and the great re-emigration to the United States, admit of no contradiction. Allowing that during the last few years there has been a very considerable augmentation in the number of the inhabitants, and in the agriculture and commerce of the colonies, and that, compared with their previous condition, their present circumstances exhibit hopeful signs of improvement and activity, this does not affect the truth of the representations I have made. It is still incontestably true, that after the lapse of a period varying from 60 to 10 years, less than a 20th part of the land granted by the Crown has been reclaimed from the wilderness, and that a very large proportion, if not the majority, of the emigrants from the United Kingdom, who have arrived in these colonies, have left them for another land, with no greater natural advantages of soil or position, and where they are surrounded by a people whose habits and institutions are unfamiliar to them. . . .

(Buller, *Report on Public Lands and Emigration*, in Lucas, *Lord Durham's Report*, III, 67-70)

~ Despite the evils and deficiencies of land administration exposed in the Durham *Report*, the British government was slow to remedy the situation. In an impressive speech in August 1843 Charles Buller recalled the attention of parliament to the continuing abuses of the past and the need for thoroughgoing reforms.~

. . . I will not now trouble the House with describing the various forms in which the mismanagement of the public lands of Canada affected their disposal. Where ignorance, carelessness, and jobbery ran riot, unchecked through every department, there was not a stage in the process in which some abuse or another did not interfere to mar all public objects, and check all private enterprises. . . . They will see how, from first to last, the entire system proceeded on no principle at all; how one system prevailed in one colony, and exactly the reverse in its neighbour; how the system of to-day was changed on the morrow to one of the most contrary nature; and how, without formal change, it was violated from day to day by the caprice of the governor or his subordinates. They will see with what perverse ingenuity it was contrived, that while the most undue facilities were given for the acquisition of large masses of land by persons who could make no good use of it, every obstacle was placed in the way of the purchaser who was really to be a settler; what trouble, expense, and delay preceded his choice of the spot, and, again, what incalculable trouble, expense, and delay were interposed by the carelessness and extortion of the Government offices before a title could be got to the land selected and purchased. They will also see how worthless that title was rendered by the blunders of the surveys. . . .

. . . I wish to fix your attention on the one great mischief, which is the result of these and other faults, namely, the reckless profusion of grants which has taken the wild lands of Canada out of the hands of the public and placed them in the nominal possession of a few proprietors, who can neither use them themselves, nor render them subservient to the promotion of any great public purpose, or general plan. This is the main difficulty which meets us in the outset of any attempt to colonise Canada. The country is still unsettled, but not unappropriated; the lands are wild, but the Government cannot use them. In its bad days its property was jobbed away. Some was granted to governors, some to executive councillors, some to the dependents of men in power; a large portion was assigned to form a provision of of the most objectionable kind for the clergy and a still larger portion was allotted to other classes of persons who were considered to have claims on the Government, which were satisfied by grants of land instead of pensions. . . . You may fairly say, that the whole of the surveyed land has been alienated;

and is now the property either of large absentee proprietors, who, with the exception of the Canada and other companies, and a very few private individuals, do nothing for the settlement of them, or of very poor persons, who have got almost for nothing, tracts, which they have neither capital nor labour to cultivate. The low price for which land could be got, has tempted every settler to become a proprietor; almost every man is a proprietor of more than he can use, and is either a rich absentee without the disposition, or a needy settler, without the means of hiring labour. These are the inevitable results of giving undue facilities to the acquisition of land. . . . It has scattered the population over a wide extent of country, in little farms separated by vast tracts of unsettled land in the possession of absentee proprietors, and unconnected by roads either with each other or with markets. The settler can raise food for himself, but can with difficulty sell, and, therefore is not much tempted to raise a surplus produce. He has no motive, and no means for employing labour; but tilling with his own hands, and those of his family just enough of his land to support themselves and keeping every body else off the remainder of his property, he goes on just raising from year to year enough for the consumption of the year, without making any progress in comfort or in civilization. And thus you have the greater part of Upper Canada, and the townships, cultivated in scattered patches by small proprietors, who neither accumulate nor improve. . . . The emigrant, who arrived in the colony with means to buy and clear a farm, sometimes settled on it, and, after long years of hardship, arrived at the state of rude and mere competence which I have described. Even of this class a great number were tempted to go on into the States, whither great facilities of acquiring land, a greater choice of situation, and every chance of a more civilized existence, and a more improving lot invited them . . . the greater portion of the mere labouring class landed in Canada merely to go on into the United States, where certain employment at high wages was to be had. . . .

(*Hansard*, LXXI, 15 August 1843, 769-74)

~ The Colonial Reformers were particularly struck by the apparent contrast which existed between the bounding prosperity of the United States and the stagnation of neighbouring British North America. Lord Durham attributed this divergence largely to the respective systems of land administration and the marked superiority of American practice.~

. . . The system of the United States appears to combine all the chief requisites of the greatest efficiency. It is uniform throughout the vast federation; it is unchangeable save by Congress, and has never been materially altered; it renders the acquisition of new land easy, and yet, by means of a price, restricts appropriation to the actual wants of the settler; it is so simple as to be readily understood; it provides for accurate surveys and against needless delays; it gives an instant and secure title; and it admits of no favouritism, but distributes the public property amongst all classes and persons upon precisely equal terms. That system has promoted an amount of immigration and settlement, of which the history of the world affords no other example; and it has produced to the United States a revenue which has averaged about half a million sterling per annum, and has amounted in one twelvemonth to above four millions sterling, or more than the whole expenditure of the Federal Government.

In the North American Colonies there never has been any system. Many different methods have been practised, and this not only in the different colonies, but in every colony at different times, and within the same colony at the same time. The greatest diversity and most frequent alteration would almost seem to have been the objects in view. In only one respect has there been uniformity. Every where the greatest profusion has taken place, so that in all the colonies, and nearly in every part of each colony, more, and very much more land has been alienated by the Government, than the grantees had at the time, or now have the means of reclaiming from a state of wilderness; and yet in all the colonies until lately, and in some of them still, it is either very difficult or next to impossible for a person of no influence to obtain any of the public land. More or less in all the colonies, and in some of them to an extent which would not be credited, if the fact were not established by unquestionable testimony, the surveys have been inaccurate, and the boundaries, or even the situation of estates, are proportionably uncertain. Every where needless delays have harassed and exasperated applicants; and every where, more or less, I am sorry but compelled to add, gross favouritism has prevailed in the disposal of public lands. . . .

. . . I allude to the striking contrast which is presented between the American and the British sides of the frontier line in respect to every sign of productive industry, increasing wealth, and progressive civilization.

By describing one side, and reversing the picture, the other would be also described. On the American side, all is activity and bustle. The forest has been widely cleared; every year numerous settlements are formed, and thousands of farms are created out of the waste; the country is intersected by common roads; canals and railroads are finished, or in the course of formation; the ways of communication and transport are crowded with people, and enlivened by numerous carriages and large steam-boats. The observer is surprised at the number of harbours on the lakes, and the number of vessels they contain; while bridges, artificial landing-places, and commodious wharves are formed in all directions as soon as required. Good houses, warehouses, mills, inns, villages, towns and even great cities, are almost seen to spring up out of the desert. Every village has its school-house and place of public worship. Every town has many of both, with its township buildings, its book stores, and probably one or two banks and newspapers; and the cities, with their fine churches, their great hotels, their exchanges, courthouses and municipal halls, of stone or marble, so new and fresh as to mark the recent existence of the forest where they now stand, would be admired in any part of the Old World. On the British side of the line, with the exception of a few favoured spots, where some approach to American prosperity is apparent, all seems waste and desolate. There is but one railroad in all British America, and that, running between the St. Lawrence and Lake Champlain, is only 15 miles long. The ancient city of Montreal, which is naturally the commercial capital of the Canadas, will not bear the least comparison, in any respect, with Buffalo, which is a creation of yesterday. But it is not in the difference between the larger towns on the two sides that we shall find the best evidence of our own inferiority. That painful but undeniable truth is most manifest in the country districts through which the line of national separation passes for 1,000 miles. There, on the side of both the Canadas, and also of New Brunswick and Nova Scotia, a widely scattered population, poor, and apparently unenterprising, though hardy and industrious, separated from each other by tracts of intervening forest, without towns and markets, almost without roads, living in mean houses, drawing little more than a rude subsistence from ill-cultivated land, and seemingly incapable of improving their condition, present the most instructive contrast to their enterprising and thriving neighbours on the American side. . . .

(Lucas, *Lord Durham's Report*, II, 209-13)

6 / THE RELEVANCE OF SYSTEMATIC COLONIZATION TO CANADA

~ The Wakefieldians believed that the principles of systematic colonization were capable of universal application. Although the scheme would operate more successfully in an entirely virgin field of colonial activity than in a country where settlement had already proceeded under a different method of colonization, the *Colonial Gazette* argued that its benefits would accrue wherever Wakefield's ideas were adopted. The theory therefore had obvious relevance to British North America, since the sale of crown land might be used to promote the influx of labour and capital to the advantage of the colonies and Britain.~

Labour is the first great demand throughout our Colonial possessions, in Canada among the number. But Canada wants something else – capital. Not that capital would be unwelcome in other colonies: in the rich West Indies, for instance, and in flourishing New South Wales, capital is a desideratum; but in Canada it is a positive *sine qua non*. . . .

Settling upon land is unquestionably no holiday task without capital; and that must be particularly the case in a country where a great part of the population have already made some advance beyond the mere rude beginning of colonization. Abundant labour may be placed upon the finest land in the world, and yet make but slow progress towards riches, especially in a land where the process of cultivation is so laborious as in Canada. But the Canadians have ready to their hands the means of procuring the requisite immigration of capital, if they will but know it. The grievous want of labour has been the rod which has beaten one good lesson into them, and has partly reconciled them to that system of which they had so great a dread, the "Wakefield system." All other evils, real and imaginary, were eclipsed by the obvious and pressing want of labour. They want money to transport labour: the Wakefield system offers an immigration-fund; and without too nicely examining that system in its general scope, their ignorant fear of it has been allayed by their avidity to obtain the fund. They have begun, too, after long practical experience of the ill, to recognize the mischief of the lavish free-grants which have alienated such wide tracts of land, and now prevent the immediate realization of the desired immigration-fund. The Wakefield system supplies not only the means of preventing that waste of natural resources, but Lord Durham's Report has shown how it may be applied to remedy the evil which has already accrued.

That is another reason that begins to reconcile the Canadians to the formidable Wakefield system. There is a third incident which may help to complete the reconcilement: the system tends to promote the immigration of capital. The inevitable tendency of the "sufficient price" is, not only to restrict the undue appropriation of land, but to throw it into the hands of capitalists; not necessarily of large capitalists, but of persons possessing some amount of capital. Where an actual and valid price is exacted for land, of course the purchaser must have some money to buy with; his means are tested by the very act of purchase; he is not a penniless pauper. Grant that he afterwards may prove insolvent, yet even then, his land, not depreciated in value by being part of an alienated desert, maintains its price in the market; and as soon as his insolvency is proved by the difficulty of turning his possessions to profitable account, he cedes them to more substantial owners. The "sufficient price" necessarily supposes a proprietary of capitalists: the Canadians have only to make up their mind to exchange their present nominal proprietary for a real proprietary, and capital would flow into the province with the labour which it helped to convey. The fertile lands of Canada are surely as capable of attracting any kind of immigration as the lands of the colonies at the Antipodes.

(*Colonial Gazette*, 16 June 1841)

~ Nevertheless, the Reformers admitted that the theory would require some modification if it was to be successfully introduced into British North America. Charles Tennant pointed out that the proximity of the United States, for example, had to be taken into account when a price was fixed for crown lands in Canada. If English emigrants were not to be attracted over the border, the price of crown land would have to be regulated by the price charged by the American government rather than by what would be most appropriate in British North America alone.~

. . . The measure is not equally applicable to all the three great British colonies, Canada, South Africa, and Australasia. To Canada it could be but partially applied; but a slight notice of the causes and consequences of this difference will place the merits of the scheme in a forcible point of view. In Canada, the British Government cannot regulate at pleasure the degree of concentration which its subjects shall enjoy, because it does not possess an absolute power over waste land. In the immediate neighbourhood of the British settlements there are immense tracts of new land, over which the Government of Canada has no control whatsoever; and to these the colonists would emigrate if the Colonial Government should require a higher price for waste land than that which is required by the Governments of the neighbouring United States. . . . Hence it appears that the Government of Canada must necessarily regulate the price of its waste land by that which should obtain in the United States. That price is now . . . far too low for the most desirable degree of concentration – for causing the greatest possible demand for emigrant labour and the largest means of obtaining it. But, such as it is, it would be productive of very great advantages to Canada. It would produce there the same concentration of people and accumulation of capital that takes place in the States of Massachusetts, New York, and Pennsylvania; it would provide a considerable fund for the conveyance of British paupers to the colony, and, by furnishing them with employment, would prevent them from emigrating once more to the United States, as is now the practice with a large proportion of the labourers conveyed from Britain to Canada. In every one of the accounts of Canada, published during the last twenty years, there occur expressions of wonder and regret at the disposition of poor British emigrants to abandon "a British colony" for "a foreign state". . . . There is no disloyalty in the case. The labourer is a practical political economist. Conveyed either by Government or an individual capitalist from his English workhouse or Irish cabin to a place where he can save a part of his earnings, he has the means to remove to another place where labour is in yet greater demand; and his eagerness to aid in supplying that demand is no more disloyal than the anxiety of the Liverpool merchant to sell Manchester goods at New York. . . .

(Tennant, *A Statement of the Principles and Objects of a Proposed National Society, for the Cure and Prevention of Pauperism, by Means of Systematic Colonization*, pp. 60-62.)

~A further obstacle to the successful introduction of systematic colonization into British North America was the vast amount of land that had already passed into private ownership but was not being effectively exploited. As Buller pointed out in 1843, unless the government could regain possession of these undeveloped lands through enforced resumption or voluntary surrender, it would be impossible to promote a better system of administration based upon land sales.~

. . . The plan by which I propose to promote colonization

to Canada, though proceeding on the same principles as that which should be applied to Australia, New Zealand, and other colonies, would differ from it considerably in detail . . . we have a class of difficulties to contend with there, which, though not unknown, though not otherwise than very formidable in every one, even of our newest colonies, exist there in gigantic dimensions. These are the difficulties created by former mismanagement, by that perversion of the ends, and exhaustion of the means of colonization, which has naturally been the result of long perseverance in the oldest of our extensive colonies in a system of colonization founded on no principle at all, and conducted with languor, caprice, and a total recklessness of public interests. . . .

. . . here in the outset the difficulty meets us that almost the whole waste land of Canada is at the present moment appropriated; but the Government has no power to make it available for any sound system of colonization; and that the greater part of the proprietors not only cannot be induced to adopt the best system, but do not even use their land at all. It would be useless . . . to attempt to try any better system on the comparatively small portion of surveyed, or even on the large extent of unsurveyed waste lands, which still remain in the Crown; because every right step taken with respect to them will be neutralized by the bad system allowed with respect to the land of individuals. It is quite obvious that while a large extent of property is allowed to lie uncultivated in the possession of individuals, the improvement of a colony is hopeless. The experience of every colony has proved this. The public feeling of every colony has determined that no respect for private property must allow it to become a public nuisance; and the legislation of every colony contains some device or another for preventing the mischief. The two most common plans have been a law of escheat, whereby property, of which a certain proportion had not been reclaimed after a certain period, becomes forfeited to the Crown; and a wild land tax, which in one form or another is generally adopted over the United States, and in some of our present colonies. My report to Lord Durham recommended the imposition of a wild land tax, which was to be payable in land, and which would inevitably have had the effect, in course of time, of bringing almost the whole of the wild lands into the possession of the Crown. . . . But I am inclined to think that a much more speedy process for getting the wild lands into the possession of the Government is wanted in the present state of things, than any which could be effected by a wild land tax, unless you mean it to be a measure of summary confiscation. . . .

(*Hansard*, LXXI, 15 August 1843, 768)

~ Furthermore, Wakefield's preference for devoting the whole proceeds of land sales to assisting emigration could be usefully modified in the case of British North America. As Buller again explained, the cost of a passage across the Atlantic was relatively inexpensive compared with the voyage to a distant country like Australia, and so the land fund might more profitably be spent on public works and opening up the Canadian interior with roads and bridges.~

. . . I would do this by reverting to the precise recommendations of my report to Lord Durham. I did not, or rather Mr. Wakefield did not, therein, by any means insist on applying the proceeds of the land-sales to defraying the passage of emigrants. I am rather surprised to find Lord Sydenham, in one of the letters recently published, arguing against the application of Mr. Wakefield's views to the colonization of Canada, on the ground that it is not to be effected by selling land at a high price, in order to get the means of carrying out emigrants. In that report, which contains Mr. Wakefield's own deliberate application of his principles to Canada, it is not proposed to set a high price on land; nor is it proposed to apply the proceeds in the first place to emigration. The means are varied to attain the great end of colonization. In new colonies, especially in those of Australia, the great difficulty of colonization is the carrying out the emigrants to the colony; and this is the expense which it is of most urgent necessity to defray by the proceeds of your land sales. The people will not, cannot get out without; and the getting them to the colony is the first necessity. But with respect to Canada the case is exactly the reverse. There, as we see, the means of getting across the ocean are within the reach of a vast number of the poorest of the population, not only of Great Britain but also of Ireland. Without any aid except that which friends, which parishes, and which liberal landlords have been in the habit of giving, a vast influx of labourers and their families has taken place. I should propose that, in the first place, at least we should leave emigration to be carried on independent of the Government; and I should suggest, as my report does, that the primary object, to which the proceeds of the land-sales should be devoted, should be the opening up the interior of the country by roads, bridges, and other public works, so as to render it accessible; and to the building churches, schools, and other public buildings, which should render it really habitable by a civilized community. . . . The construction of such works would in another way facilitate the emigration of poor labourers, by affording them a certain means of getting employment on their arrival in the colony. Government, if conducting the whole operation on a combined plan, would do right in employing emigrants in preference to other persons on their works; and would direct them thither on their arrival. As the labours of these men opened up the country, capitalists would be induced to purchase and settle, and would employ another portion of the labouring emigrants. These labourers, either in public or in private employment, would be sure, in course of time, to accumulate sufficient savings out of their wages, to enable them to purchase and stock small farms; they would then not only make way for a fresh supply of labouring emigrants, but would create a fresh demand for labour. This is the sure result of a sound system of coloniza- tion; the more labour and capital that are supplied to a colony, the larger is the field laid open for additional capital and labour; and the means of employing both go on continually augmenting in geometrical progression, while there remain any waste lands to be reclaimed. . . .

(*Hansard*, LXXI, 15 August 1843, 779-81)

7 / GOVERNMENT AND COLONIZATION

~ The Colonial Reformers were dependent for their success in British North America on winning the support of officials at the Colonial Office and persuading them to adopt Wakefield's ideas as the basis of imperial land administration. The propa- ganda of the Reformers contributed to the character and content of the Ripon Regulations of 1831, when sale by public auction was adopted as the basis of imperial practice throughout the empire. This important reform was supported by an appeal to arguments taken directly from Wakefield's writings along with his distinctive phraseology and method of explanation. Never- theless, the amount of land already alienated by the government in British North America and the continuing effects of past abuses rendered these sales regulations largely inoperative. Moreover, as the comments of the *Colonial Gazette* suggest, the Reformers were not satisfied that the Colonial Office had gone far enough towards the adoption of their principles of colonization.~

. . . considerable ignorance seems still to prevail of the fact, that land, however new and fertile, is only valuable in so far as it furnishes a productive field for the labour of the colonist. It is from colonization that its value is derived. But, up to a late date, the British government has acted as if it had been insensible that its colonial territories could, from any circumstance, acquire a value at all. It has disposed of them upon no systematic plan; but has granted them away, by large tracts, in all the colonies, either without price, or at nominal quit-rents and conditions, with unexampled profusion, not to say favouritism and jobbing. . . .

The year 1831 was the commencement of a new æra in Colonial administration. Lord Howick, then Under Secretary for the Colonies, established regulations for the disposal of lands upon the principle of sale only. This was an important step towards improvement; but these regulations, even with some subsequent modifications, are to be regarded as mere approximations to a sound system; for not only are the existing Government prices obviously insufficient, but provision is wanting for the proper application of the land-revenue, and for the establishment of other incidental requisites of the true plan. The system of the United States, though they sell at the low price of 5s. 7½d. per acre, is far better than ours, and was recommended as, in many respects, worthy of imitation, by the Select Committee on Colonial Lands, of 1836, whose valuable Report is before the public. . . .

It is scarcely possible to doubt that the application to the Canadas, and the other North-American colonies, of a system by which the whole of their waste lands should be disposed of at a uniform and sufficient price, and a labour-fund created out of the proceeds, would be a powerful stimulus to the advancement of those provinces in wealth and prosperity. The wilderness would be opened to British enterprise and industry, – a new path would be cleared for the progress of civilization in the far West. . . .

(*Colonial Gazette*, 8 December 1838)

~ The failure of the British government to adopt Wakefield's ideas on land administration more readily or to promote an extended and systematic programme of emigration led the Reformers to denounce the Colonial Office as hostile to colonization. It appeared to the *Colonial Gazette* that Mr. Mother-country and the other bureaucrats comfortably ensconced in Downing Street did not want to be troubled by the demands of this urgent national question.~

. . . The members of the Colonial Office have four distinct reasons for disliking any extension of colonization by means of the interference of Parliament. In the first place, there is the interference, which they resent as an invasion of *their* property. Secondly, it is contrary to the nature of things that *they* should colonize successfully; and this, combined with the jealousy of others, and of all innovation, which belongs to the subordinate official character, gives rise to the sentiment which has become proverbial through the story of the dog in the manger. Thirdly, every extension of the Colonial empire adds grievously to the trouble of the permanent officials of Downing Street. Several new colonies have been established of late years, but without any addition to the working force of the Colonial Office. We are far from supposing that the officers of that department work much harder than before; but, the quantity of business being greater, they are compelled, according to the usual practice of attending only to the matter which presses most, to leave a greater number of questions unsettled and even applications unnoticed, and are thus subject to more reproach and annoyance. If "extensive and systematic" colonization were undertaken by the State, either so many new colonies would be founded, or the old ones would be so rapidly extended, that the demands on the labour of the Colonial Office would be grievously enlarged. Stagnation, therefore, or what they call "letting well alone," is the state of colonization which the men of desks and red tape desire to preserve. And lastly, in proportion as colonization extends upon a plan which creates great colonial interests in this country, the members of "the Office" suffer extreme annoyance from the existence of an active and intelligent public, disposed to look into their doings and call them to account for wrong or neglect. . . . Every other department of Government is more or less influenced and controlled by public opinion: the Colonial Office alone has hitherto done or left undone just what it pleased; and the thought of becoming responsible to an intelligent and interested public is hateful to the permanent officials, who have never imagined that such a misfortune awaited them. . . .
(*Colonial Gazette*, 1 March 1843)

8 / LAND ADMINISTRATION AND IMPERIAL RELATIONS

~ One major reason why the Colonial Reformers maintained that Britain should retain the colonies was that they provided a convenient outlet for Britain's surplus population. But if this advantage was to be effectively preserved for the future and an extensive programme of systematic colonization adopted, the imperial government had to retain control over the administration of colonial lands. This power could not be surrendered into colonial hands, because only the imperial authorities could reform the abuses of the past, ensure the necessary uniformity of practice throughout the empire, and safeguard the interests of the empire as a whole against local and selfish demands of any particular colony. Although Lord Durham therefore recommended in his *Report* the reservation of this power to imperial control as part of his scheme of colonial self-government, authority over this vital area of administration could not be denied the colonists. While the Reformers emphasized the crucial importance of land affairs in the economic life of colonies, Buller's comments in 1839 indicate that they failed to realize that the promotion of systematic colonization and colonial self-government would be mutually incompatible.~

. . . The measures which I shall have to propose are of a character to demand the exercise of the powers of the Imperial Legislature; but they are, at the same time, such as that Legislature may perhaps shrink from adopting. It may be deemed that they involve too great an interference with the property of individuals, and with the rights of the provincial legislatures, to render their adoption safe or just; and it may be argued that the subject is one which appertains of right to the colonies, and upon which they alone ought to legislate . . . but, independently of those reasons, the present appears to me to be a case in which it is the plain duty of the Imperial Legislature to interfere. It is not merely that the evils in all the colonies are similar in their nature and their origin, and requiring the same remedy; nor that it is for the interests of each of these colonies that in all an uniform system should be adopted, so that the results of one system in one colony may not be counteracted by the operation of another system in one or more of the neighbouring colonies; nor that the nature of the only adequate remedy is such as to require a central control, and some efficient guarantee for its permanency; and that therefore upon all these grounds the interests of the colonies require that the supreme and central authority of the empire should interpose; – but higher interests than those of the colonies, the interests of the empire of which they form a part, demand that Parliament should establish at once, and permanently, a well-considered and uniform system. The waste lands of the colonies are the property, not merely of the colony, but of the empire, and ought to be administered for imperial, not merely for colonial, purposes. And in whatever measures may be adopted to promote emigration, or facilitate settlement, the interests of the empire are involved, and should be consulted as much as those of the colonies.

It is true that hitherto, while in name the property of the Crown, and under the control of an English minister, these lands have been in effect administered by colonial authorities for purely colonial purposes. It was indeed impossible that it should be otherwise. The execution of the instructions from time to time issued by successive Secretaries of State, or Lords of the Treasury, has of necessity been entrusted to those who, in the colonies, were the peculiar representatives of the English Crown; the Governor acting with the advice of his Executive Council. But the power nominally given to the Governor vested in effect entirely in his Council; and the members of that Council, being residents in the colony, having interests of their own to promote, or friends whom they desired to benefit, or it may be enemies whom they were willing to injure, have uniformly exercised their power for local or personal objects, unchecked by a control, which in this respect could only be nominal. Some recent proceedings of the Home Government would seem also almost to have assumed, that the practice thus pursued was right in principle, though it might be wrongly carried out, since the Government has offered to relinquish to the Colonial Legislature the future control of these lands, or at least of the funds arising from their disposal. It still, however, appears that the principle, no less than the working of the former method, was erroneous. There can surely be nothing in the fact, that the Crown has granted to one person, or to any number of persons, a certain portion of land in any colony which can give to those persons any right to dispose of the land which has not been granted to them: but rather the first grantees, having had their share of the land, are less entitled to any voice in the disposal of the remainder than the other citizens of the empire. The only rights which they can possess are of precisely the same character and extent as those possessed by any other subject of the Crown; a right to demand that these lands shall be administered in such a manner as to promote the prosperity of the colony, and to advance the interests of the empire. These objects, properly regarded, are identical, though experience has amply shown that the one may be pursued at the expense of the other. It is for the Imperial Parliament to reconcile these different interests, and by providing for the greatest development of the resources of the colonies, to enable them to offer a market for the manufactures, and a home for the surplus population of the United Kingdom. . . .

And the same reasons exist for vesting in the Imperial Parliament the application of remedies for past mismanagement in the disposal of these lands. I should be far from recommending any needless interference with merely local matters, which in almost every case are most effectually provided for by those who are immediately conversant with them. This, however, is not merely a local matter. If regarded solely as it affects the present inhabitants of the colonies it is a matter of comparative unimportance. The present position of these countries, in reference to their unoccupied land, derives its significance and import from the fact, that it not merely retards the prosperity of the thousands by whom they are now peopled, but that it prevents the millions, to whom they might eventually afford an asylum, from enjoying the advantages to which they are entitled. And without desiring to undervalue the importance of these possessions, I may perhaps venture to say, that if Parliament will not interpose its authority for the accomplishment of these objects, if it will not devise means of cure for the evils which the Imperial Government has caused or permitted, and at the same time provide effectual securities against similar evils for the future, the North American Provinces must be nearly valueless to the empire . . .

. . . while in all the measures I shall have to recommend, I have proceeded upon the assumption that the Imperial Legislature will exercise its undoubted rights, I am also bound to recommend, that in the event of such a course not being deemed expedient, the whole control of the property should be vested in the most ample and unconditional manner in the Colonial Legislature . . . if the local assembly should not legislate for the greatest advantage of the mother country as well as of the colony, it would take care that the mismanagement of the public lands was not, as has hitherto been the case under imperial management, a source of great evil to the colony. . . .

(Buller, *Report on Public Lands and Emigration*, in Lucas, *Lord Durham's Report*, III, 37-40)

~ Even by 1847, the *Spectator*'s comments on the advantages of colonies as outlets for British emigration predicted continued imperial control over the crown lands of the empire.~

It seems as if circumstances would force upon our statesmen

some great measure of colonization. Free Trade has struck at the foundation of the antiquated "Colonial system," and made it necessary to devise other modes than commercial restriction for keeping up the connexion between mother-country and colonies. . . .

. . . If statesmen know the interest of the country and their own duty, a time is approaching which will shame even the superficial economists who talk of "abandoning the Colonies" as "useless incumbrances." It is true that this country has parted with large tracts of waste lands to the local legislatures, or locked them up by recognizing absurd litigious claims; but the interest of the parent state in the waste lands of her colonies does not cease with their alienation – does not cease until those waste lands are covered with people. Until that be done, the parent state has a claim on those lands; they do not belong exclusively or chiefly to the colonists. This is a truth which is too often overlooked – its opposite, indeed, being taken for granted; but it lies at the bottom of a right understanding as to the mutual relation between parent state and colony. . . .

Let us go back to the time when the lands are unsettled. A highly-civilized and densely-populated state possesses extensive waste lands in the colonies. Those lands derive their value in part from their natural qualities and geographical features, but still more from the acquired resources of the parent country. . . . In a state possessing those waste lands, all citizens have equal rights – all have a share in the collective right to those waste lands; and if a few hundreds or even thousands by settlement acquire a further right of occupancy in certain parts of those lands, that right cannot extend to deprive the whole community at home of its interest in the whole. On the contrary, even when the lands are overspread with settlers and nominally alienated to private holders, the parent state retains its interest in the colony, as a colony, so long as it remains capable of absorbing any part of the redundant population from home. . . .

Nor does the advantage of the colonists in the colonizing process cease with the nominal alienation of the lands. It is for the advantage of the actual settlers, in common with the whole of the state from which they spring, that the parent country should retain and recognize her interest in the waste lands. The wants of a colonial community are correlative with those of the parent state: she wants space of land; they, labour and capital; and the same process which appropriates to the use of the parent state the waste lands of the colony, conveys to them the labour and capital which they lack. The more those elements abound in an old country, the more valuable is that country to any colony as its parent state. The true connexion between a colony and a parent state consists in this efflux, until the distribution of people and capital upon land has in an approximate degree been equalized. When that has been done, the relation of parent state and colony ceases *ipso facto*: separation is then but a more convenient distribution of government; trade is but the usual commerce between nations. If, through political blundering, separation take place before that process has been completed, it is premature, and both countries lose many chances of advantage. And if, through a misconception of the colonial relation, the process of active colonization be suffered to fall into abeyance, the Ministers have suffered the true connexion of parent state and colony to be broken off prematurely by a gross neglect of administrative duty.

It is a dim instinctive perception of this truth which has made statesmen cling to colonies although sage economists denounced them as useless and costly appendages – which has made colonies cling to the connexion even when they were despised and ill-treated. But a more intelligent insight into the truth has now been created by the Free-trade movement . . . the withdrawal of commercial protection has made the Colonies somewhat angrily ask, "What are the advantages of the colonial relation?" but having thus been stimulated to inquire, they are beginning to perceive what the real advantages are. It would be most unwise to allow the colonists to learn simultaneously those advantages and the determination of the parent state to refuse them. . . .

(*Spectator*, 18 September 1847)

PART FOUR:
FACETS OF IMPERIAL ADMINISTRATION

1 / COLONIAL OFFICE RULE

~ The Reformers were chiefly preoccupied with the question of colonial government: its abuses and reform. In writings and speeches they exposed the many deficiencies they detected in the existing system of imperial administration and denounced the evils which these shortcomings produced. In their view, Britain's government of the empire was characterized by irresponsible authority, exercised in London by anonymous but permanent officials at the Colonial Office and in the colonies by councils and cliques which remained for the most part at odds with local assemblies. The Reformers argued that the effective solution to these evils lay in a greater decentralization of authority and the establishment of responsible colonial ministries.

At home the attacks of the Reformers were focused on the Colonial Office and the deficiencies of its bureaucratic administration. It was a point of persistent criticism that public and parliamentary indifference towards colonial affairs shielded the actions of officials at the Colonial Office from publicity and wholesome scrutiny, while the short terms of office served by politicians as colonial secretary further reinforced the effective power of the permanent civil servants. In 1838 Molesworth blamed these men for having instigated the Canadian rebellions.~

. . . He had enumerated a series of grievous wrongs inflicted on the Canadian people by the tools of the Colonial Office, and for which the Ministers who had presided over that department of the State ought to be held strictly responsible. But it should be remarked that of all the high functionaries the Colonial Secretary was the one least exposed to effective responsibility, because the people of a mother country are necessarily uninterested and unacquainted with the affairs of their remote dependencies. Therefore it was only on extraordinary occasions that the public attention could be directed from matters of nearer interest to colonial concerns: it was rarely that the Colonial Office could be made to feel the weight of public opinion, and to fear censure and exposure. Where, however, responsibility was wanting, the experience of all ages had proved, that abuses would exist, and continue to exist, unredressed, until at last they reached that amount which induced them [the colonists] no longer to trust to prayer and humble petition, but raise the cry of war, and have recourse to arms. Such had been the case of Canada. In that province for the last thirty years acknowledged abuses had existed; acknowledged by Committees, and by Members of every party in the House of Commons. Great changes had taken place in the Government of this country, yet no changes had taken place in the administration of colonial affairs. The same odious system of colonial misgovernment which was pursued by the Tories had been acted upon by the Whigs. The causes for the continuance of the same colonial system under Ministers of the most adverse principles were easily to be explained. The Colonial Secretary seldom remained long enough in his office to become acquainted with the concerns of the numerous colonies which he governed. In the last ten years there had been no less than eight different Colonial Secretaries. They had seldom, therefore, the time, and still more seldom the inclination, to make themselves acquainted with the complicated details of their office; their ignorance rendered them mere tools in the hands of the permanent Under-Secretaries and other clerks. It was in the dark recesses of the Colonial Office – in those dens of peculation and plunder – it was there that the real and irresponsible rulers of the millions of inhabitants of our colonies were to be found. Men utterly unknown to fame, but for whom, he trusted, some time or other, a day of reckoning would come, when they would be dragged before the public, and punished for their evil deeds. These were the men who, shielded by irresponsibility, and hidden from the public gaze, continued the same system of misgovernment under every party which alternately presided over the destinies of the empire. By that misgovernment they drove the colonies to desperation – they connived at every description of abuse, because they profited by abuse – they defended every species of corruption, because they gained by corruption. These men he now denounced as the originators and perpetrators of those grievances in Canada, the evil effects of which this country had already begun to experience. He trusted the experience thus gained would convince the people of the necessity of a sweeping reform in the Colonial Office....

(*Hansard*, XL, 23 January 1838, 384-6)

~ These criticisms were elaborated by Buller in 1840 in his well known book, *Responsible Government for Colonies*, in which he introduced the English public to Mr. Mothercountry, the anonymous but allegedly all-powerful administrator who governed the British empire from the recesses of Downing Street.~

. . . Thus, from the general indifference of Parliament on Colonial questions, it exercises in fact hardly the slightest efficient control over the administration or the making of laws for the Colonies. In nine cases out of ten, it merely registers the edicts of the Colonial Office in Downing Street. It is there, then, that nearly the whole public opinion which influences the conduct of affairs in the Colonies really exists. . . .

But even this does not sufficiently concentrate the Mother Country. It may indeed at first sight be supposed that the power of "the Office" must be wielded by its head; that in him at any rate we generally have one of the most eminent of our public men, whose views on the various matters which come under his cognizance are shared by the Cabinet of which he is a member. We may fancy, therefore, that here at last, concentrated in a somewhat despotic, but at any rate in a very responsible and dignified form, we have the real governing power of the Colonies, under the system which boasts of making their governments responsible to the Mother Country. But this is a very erroneous supposition. This great officer holds the most constantly shifting position on the shifting scene of official life. Since April 1827, ten different Secretaries of State have held the seals of the Colonial Department. Each was brought into that office from business of a perfectly different nature, and probably with hardly any previous experience in Colonial affairs. The new Minister is at once called on to enter on the consideration of questions of the greatest magnitude, and at the same time of some hundreds of questions of mere detail, of no public interest, of unintelligible technicality, involving local considerations with which he is wholly unacquainted, but at the same time requiring decision, and decision at which it is not possible to arrive without considerable labour. Perplexed with the vast variety of subjects thus presented to him — alike appalled by the important and unimportant matters forced on his attention — every Secretary of State is obliged at the outset to rely on the aid of some better informed member of his office. His Parliamentary Under-Secretary is generally as new to the business as himself. . . . Thus we find both these marked and responsible functionaries dependent on the advice and guidance of another; and that other person must of course be one of the permanent members of the office. We do not pretend to say which of these persons it is that in fact directs the Colonial policy of Britain . . . for here we get beyond the region of real responsibility, and are involved in the clouds of official mystery. That Mother Country which has been narrowed from the British Isles into the Parliament, from the Parliament into the Executive Government, from the Executive Government into the Colonial Office, is not to be sought in the apartments of the Secretary of State, or his Parliamentary Under-Secretary. Where you are to look for it, it is impossible to say. In some back-room – whether in the attic or in what storey we know not – you will find all the Mother Country which really exercises supremacy, and really maintains connexion with the vast and widely-scattered Colonies of Britain. We know not the name, the history, or the functions of the individual, into the narrow limits of whose person we find the Mother Country shrunk. Indeed, we may call him by the name, of which we have thus shewn him to be the rightful bearer; and when we speak of Mr. MOTHERCOUNTRY, the colonist will form a much more accurate notion than heretofore of the authority by which he is in reality ruled.

. . . Mr. MOTHERCOUNTRY's whole heart is in the business of his office. Not insensible to the knowledge or the charms of the power which he possesses, habit and a sense of duty are perhaps often the real motives of the unremitting exertions, by which alone he retains it. For this is the real secret of his influence. Long experience has made him thoroughly conversant with every detail of his business; and long habit has made his business the main, perhaps with the exception of his family, the sole source of his interest and enjoyment. By day and by night, at office or at home, his labour is constant. No pile of despatches, with their multifarious enclosures, no red-taped heap of Colonial grievances or squabbles, can scare his practised eye. He handles with unfaultering hand the papers at which his superiors quail: and ere they have waded through one half of them, he suggests the course, which the previous measures dictated by himself compel the Government to adopt. He alone knows on what principles the predecessors of the noble or right honourable Secretary acted before: he alone, therefore, can point out the step which in pursuance of the previous policy it is incumbent to take: and the very advice, which it is thus rendered incumbent on the present Secretary of State to take, produces results that will give him as sure a hold on the next Secretary of State.

. . . The power of Mr. MOTHERCOUNTRY goes on increasing from Secretary to Secretary, and from month to month of each

Secretary's tenure of office; and the more difficult the government of the Colonies becomes, the more entirely it falls into the hands of the only men in the public service who really know anything about Colonial affairs.

This is perhaps the best result of such a system . . . Mr. MOTHERCOUNTRY'S management is better than that of the gentlemen whom he generally gets put over his head. But the system of intrusting absolute power (for such it is) to one wholly irresponsible, is obviously most faulty. Thus, however, are our Colonies ruled: and such is the authority to which is committed that last appeal from the Colonies themselves, which is dignified with all these vague phrases about the power, the honour, the supremacy, and the wisdom of the Mother Country.

(Buller, *Responsible Government for Colonies*, pp. 73-81)

. . . It must not be inferred from this that we think it a really good system. It has all the faults of an essentially arbitrary government, in the hands of persons who have little personal interest in the welfare of those over whom they rule – who reside at a distance from them – who never have ocular experience of their condition – who are obliged to trust to second-hand and one-sided information – and who are exposed to the operation of all those sinister influences, which prevail wherever publicity and freedom are not established. In intelligence, activity, and regard for the public interests, the permanent functionaries of "the Office" may be superior to the temporary head that the vicissitudes of party politics give them; but they must necessarily be inferior to those persons in the colony in whose hands the adoption of the true practice of Responsible Government would vest the management of local affairs.

A thorough knowledge of the internal economy of this vast number of different communities, situated at the most distant points of the globe, having the most diverse climates, races, productions, forms of government, and degrees of wealth and civilization, is necessarily one which the best-employed experience of the longest life can never be supposed to give. From his entrance into his office, the necessary labours of the day have occupied almost the whole of Mr. MOTHERCOUNTRY'S time and thoughts; and though we will give him credit for having picked up such information as elementary books can give, it cannot very well be imagined that he has learnt from books, newspapers, and oral information, all that mass of particulars respecting manners, things, and persons, that is requisite for forming in the mind a complete picture of the social and political, the physical as well as the moral condition of those numerous countries. It is in the very nature of duties so laborious as his, that Mr. MOTHERCOUNTRY should be able to attend to little except to the questions presented for his decision by the parties contending in the Colonies, and should form his notion of their condition from these rather than from more extended reading and observation. Compelled to examine the complaints and answers of the various parties, he gradually imbibes the idea that the whole state of affairs is set forth in these statements and counter-statements. He fixes his eye on the grievances and squabbles that occupy the addresses of Assemblies, the despatches of Governors, and the disputes of officials; and gets to fancy, naturally enough, that these are the matters on which the mind of the colony is intent, and on which its welfare depends. . . . Thus, while the question of contending races was gradually breaking up the whole social system of Lower Canada, Mr. MOTHERCOUNTRY, unconscious of the mischief, thought that he was restoring order and satisfaction by well-reasoned despatches on points of prerogative and precedent. Experience may give Mr. MOTHERCOUNTRY more information respecting the whole mass of our Colonies than any other individual probably possesses. But it is after all a very incomplete information, and one which does not prevent his continually committing those gross blunders of which our Colonial history is the record.

This is the necessary consequence of the variety and distance of Mr. MOTHERCOUNTRY's dominions. He has, in addition, the faults of that permanent and irresponsible power, combined with subordinate position, which we always perceive in a government of bureaus or offices. It is a position which engenders not a little conceit; and in whatever form Mr. MOTHERCOUNTRY appears – even in that of the humblest clerk – you always find out that he thinks that he and his associates in "the Office" are the only people in the world who understand any thing about the Colonies. He knows his power too, and is excessively jealous of any encroachment on or resistance to it. It is a power, he well knows, which has its origin in the indolence and ignorance of others: he fancies therefore that it is assailed by any one who understands any thing of the Colonies, or takes any interest in them; and to all such people therefore he has a mortal dislike.

And though Mr. MOTHERCOUNTRY has none of a fine gentleman's aversion to work, but on the contrary devotes his whole energies to his business, he likes to get over his work with as little trouble as possible. It is his tendency therefore to reduce his work as much as he can to a mere routine; to act on general rules, and to avoid every possible deviation from them; and thus to render the details of his daily task as much a matter of habit as he well can. A hatred of innovation is a distinguishing feature of his as of the general official character. . . .

But the worst of all Mr. MOTHERCOUNTRY's faults is his necessary subjection to sinister interests and cabals. Wherever the public cease to take an interest in what is going on, the reigns of cliques and cabals is sure to extend: and whenever the actions of the Government are not guided by public opinion, they inevitably fall under the influence of some sinister interest. Every one of our colonies has its own jobs, its own monopolies, and its own little knots of bustling and intriguing jobbers. These spare no pains to get the ear of Mr. MOTHERCOUNTRY. Backed by some strong mercantile, or official, or Parliamentary connexion, they press their views on him; relying partly on their better knowledge of the peculiar subject on which they have so deep an interest, partly on the fear they can inspire by the threat of an appeal to Parliament or the press. . . . While these narrow and partial interests have these active organs, the Colonial public and the interests of the colony have rarely any, never equally efficient representatives. A long experience has taught Mr. MOTHERCOUNTRY, that without conciliating these various juntas he never can hope to govern quietly, but that if he manage to get their concurrence, he runs little risk of effectual opposition from either the British or Colonial public. His whole aim, therefore, necessarily is to conciliate all of these bodies, or when their interests happen to run counter, either to give each its turn, or to conciliate the most powerful. . . .

It is, however, not only of the cliques and interests at home that Mr. MOTHERCOUNTRY is thus placed under the influence. The same causes that render the action of small knots of men operative on him in England, place him under the same necessity of courting the good opinion and disarming the hostility of every well-organized interest in the Colonies. Now the strongest and most active interest in a colony is always that of the little knot that governs it – the Family Compact, which Lord Durham has described as being the necessary result of the irresponsible government of our Colonies. Creatures of the Colonial Office, as these Compacts are, they nevertheless manage to acquire a strength which renders them very formidable to Mr. MOTHERCOUNTRY. Even when he gets on bad terms with them, he never abandons the hope of reconciliation with them, or the demeanour necessary to insure it. But you will rarely find him quarrelling with them. A despotic and irresponsible authority is always obliged to govern by a small knot of men; and these Colonial compacts are the natural agents of the Compacts at home. Thus the mischiefs produced by irresponsibility in the colony are augmented and perpetuated by the responsibility to Mr. MOTHERCOUNTRY.

The working of the appeal to Mr. MOTHERCOUNTRY in fact only adds to the amount of Colonial misgovernment; and instead of obviating the mischiefs of the system pursued in the Colonies themselves, it only adds another element of delay, obstruction, and inconsistency. Bad as is the government of Turkish Pachas, the Porte never interferes except to make matters worse; and ill as the Colonial Compacts manage, the appeal from them to Mr. MOTHERCOUNTRY only adds fresh fuel to Colonial irritation and individual grievance. His ignorance of the real state of affairs in the colony, his habits of routine, his dependence on the secret cliques and interests at home, produce an invariable tendency on his part to stave off the decision of every question proposed to him. Every matter referred to him is sure to be referred back to the colony; and every successive answer to every fresh reference only serves him to raise some new pretext for postponing his decision. He is engaged in a perpetual struggle with the Colonial Compacts, in which he and they have no object but that of throwing on each other the responsibility of deciding. With this view, he has perfected a complete art of irrelevant and apparently purposeless correspondence, by which he manages to spin out an affair until it either evaporates into something absolutely insignificant, or until at any rate the patience and interest of all parties concerned is completely worn out. . . .

(Buller, *Responsible Government for Colonies*, pp. 82-92)

~ It was only occasionally that a crisis in imperial relations aroused public interest in colonial matters and a secretary of state was made to feel the weight of public criticism. The Reformers claimed that Molesworth's attack on Lord Glenelg in 1838 and the debate over the Canadian crisis had been responsible for the resignation of the colonial secretary in 1839. The *Spectator* pointed out, however, that this instance was exceptional and did nothing to check the power of James Stephen and the other permanent officials or change the existing system of imperial administration.~

For the first time in its history, "This Office," as King Stephen calls his dominion in Downing Street, has been made to feel some degree of responsibility. Sir William Molesworth's motion of 1838 takes complete effect in 1839. Lord Glenelg and Sir George Grey are dismissed for admitted incompetency. . . .

No similar event ever happened before, because never before did a Colonial question excite sufficient interest here to direct all eyes upon "This Office." The distant sufferers by that course of legislation and administration which takes place in the Colonial Office, never did, and never can exert any steady influence on their rulers. The system forbids it. It is only because the public mind of England happens to be moved for once by an exposure of Colonial misrule, that some punishment is inflicted on the supposed authors of the mischief. The storm will soon blow over. All the vices of the system remain untouched. . . .

The very worst feature of our system of Colonial Government is, that, whatever may happen to the ostensible directors of the Colonial Office, its real directors are never made responsible in any degree. Lord Glenelg's successor will be the ninth Chief Secretary in ten years; and the *Parliamentary* Under Secretaries have been almost as numerous in that brief period. As the removable Secretaries go, others take their place, who are totally ignorant of Colonial affairs, and necessarily dependent, therefore, on that Secretary who never goes. Into his hands they of necessity fall, – hands experienced in the art of moulding pliant ignorance into that state of dependence which renders them ministers of his will; and thus no change in the *personnel* of the Office occasions any material change in its policy or mode or administration. . . .

. . . The present agitation of a Colonial question is, no doubt, very inconvenient and even harassing to the permanent Bumbureaucracy of Downing Street; but as the public mind of this country will soon return to its usual state of indifference towards all Colonial subjects, their distress will soon be over. They must indeed submit to let the Canadas be well governed. Lord Durham's Report has settled that point, whether or not united Canada remain a colony of England. But what of that? Are there not plenty of colonies still too weak to claim good government with any hope of success? . . .

(*Spectator*, 16 February 1839)

~ In view of imperial practice and the evils of bureaucracy, the Reformers persistently denounced the Colonial Office as hostile to overseas possessions and indifferent to their welfare. Both in 1845 and 1848 the *Spectator* found ample evidence to substantiate this charge in the continuing abuses of colonial government, the oppressive policies adopted in all parts of the empire, official resistance to innovation or improvement, and inveterate opposition to systematic colonization.~

The Colonial Office has been called *Anti*-Colonial; and there is more than verbal paradox in the epithet – it seems to be a sad reality. In every colony the great oppressor and obstructer is the Colonial Office. . . . All round the Colonial empire, if the object were to repress the settlers, to mortify them, empoverish them, to check the spread of colonization, and keep waste lands desert, the policy pursued by the Office would be the very thing needed. Adam Smith exposed the abuses of our "Colonial system" of trade; others, confounding that system with the Colonies themselves, have denounced all colonies, declaring that England would be better without any. Judging of men by their acts, one would suppose that the Downing Street officials have adopted that notion. They dare not avow it; first, because England *will have* colonies, and they deem it safer to temporize and cheat than contradict the national will; next, because the existence of colonies occasions patronage, which it is sweet to exercise. But being set to manage the Colonies, they do it so as to keep down as much as possible the use of settlements, their influence, wealth, extent, and population – sometimes, in favourable cases, their very existence. . . . If we are wrong in supposing that the Colonies are or may be made a great benefit to the Mother-country – in thinking that the existence of Canada, the West Indies, and Australia, ought to enlarge the wealth, power, and comforts of the English nation – let the matter be discussed openly and fairly; let the adverse position be proved; let the Colonies be thrown off, and let the Colonial Office be shut up. If it is well to found colonies only as independent states, Government should suffer emigrants to go forth and colonize, instead of stopping them with needless impositions of a local government – as the New Zealand settlers were stopped: let every colony be a New England, independent *ab ovo*; and still let the Colonial Office be shut up. Or if such are not the opinions of the Department, let some one come forth and explain why *the acts* are precisely those which would be performed by officials thinking it right to check the advance of colonization, to thwart the colonists, as such, in all parts, and to foster every influence that can impede and repress the energy, growth, extension, and wellbeing of all settlements. Dares any official – will the man "who writes what is written" – venture an explanation? We doubt it; for it is scarcely possible that the conduct of the Colonial Office can be reconciled to any opinion but that which cannot be avowed – the ingeniously-absurd Anti-Colonial opinion that colonies are an absolute evil and must be kept down.

(*Spectator*, 11 January 1845)

From being burdens our Colonies might be converted into supports for the Mother-country; but the great obstacle to such a truly "blessed change" is the Colonial Office: we have undertaken to show how the Colonial Office effects this obstruction.

Every process which would aid the beneficent conversion presents to the Colonial Office, as it is at present constituted, a substantial reason for hostility . . . the Office may plead that it inherited the Anti-Colonial spirit from previous Governments; but in the special Department the animus has become inveterate, and is now maintained by vested interests. Were the Office now to permit the Colonies to be self-supporting, it must admit all its past conduct to be wrong, and the views of its most able antagonists in all parts of the globe to be right.

The Office will not permit the Colonies to govern themselves, because that would supersede the Department; which makes a world of business for itself by trying to carry on, in Downing Street, the detailed management of the Colonies in both hemispheres. To leave the Colonies themselves the power of self-government, would take from the Department in Downing Street nine-tenths of its work, and by superseding its functions would break up the establishment. . . .

Both Colonies and Mother-country pay dearly for the maintenance of the Downing Street Office. Among the most obvious and notorious consequences are such things as long Caffre wars; Canadian rebellions; aboriginal wars in New Zealand . . . immense expenditure for troops to keep down the Colonies lest they rebel, and to keep up the Colonies against foreign aggression, – to resist which, no one would trust the loyalty or spirit of the Colonies as they are now governed, thwarted, and stunted. All these consequences, and many more, have to be endured in order that the Colonial Office may be kept up; and it is a feeling of self-defence that makes the Office resist any innovation, such as would result in converting our Colonial encumbrances to be stays and supports.

(*Spectator*, 13 May 1848)

2 / PATRONAGE

~ One of the major evils of the bureaucratic and irresponsible authority exercised by the Colonial Office was the profusion of imperial patronage. At a time when economical reform and parliamentary criticism had significantly reduced the supply of sinecures and pensions available in Britain to the ministry of the day for party purposes, the colonial empire provided a substantial and well-guarded source of patronage.~

. . . The worst instance of the operation of these secret influences on Mr. MOTHERCOUNTRY is to be found in the Colonial appointments. If he were left to himself, and could appoint as he chose, he might doubtless job a little, but on the whole, he would probably pay some regard to competence in some of his appointments. But the patronage of the Colonial Office is the prey of every hungry department of our Government. On it the Horse Guards quarters its worn-out General Officers as Governors; the Admiralty cribs its share; and jobs which even Parliamentary rapacity would blush to ask from the Treasury, are perpetrated with impunity in the silent realm of Mr. MOTHERCOUNTRY. . . .

(Buller, *Responsible Government for Colonies*, pp. 89-90)

~ Amongst its many baneful consequences, patronage materially increased the volume of colonial expenditure. Both the *Spectator* and the *Colonial Gazette* argued that patronage reduced the value of the empire in British North America by rendering the colonies a financial burden to the British tax-payer, and it increased the level of salaries which the colonists were forced to pay their public officials.~

. . . our connexion with countries like these, and rapidly rising as they are in wealth and population, is kept up at an annual loss to Great Britain of upwards of two millions. Not for any purpose of commercial advantage; for a very liberal estimate is made for our trading gains, and *deducted*; – not for any warlike object; for they are of no earthly utility as military positions; and in case of a war, they would be a source of weakness, of distraction, and perhaps of disgrace; – not for the benefit of the Colonists themselves; for they are smarting under fiscal exactions from which they would gladly be relieved by the sacrifice of any monopolies they possess, even were they much more valuable; and they are besides weary of tasking the labours of law-makers and Ministers legislating for them at a distance of four thousand miles, and in happy ignorance of their wants, their wishes, and their condition. For whose benefit, then, is this expenditure maintained? We answer, for that of the Aristocrácy; which has found its richest though not its most extensive sources of patronage in the Colonies. At home, the power of public opinion, and the control or rather the check of Parliament, set some bounds to its rapacity: in the Colonies, these were removed, and oligarchic profusion has run riot. . . .

(*Spectator*, 5 January 1833)

. . . There is another practical grievance of which the Canadians have complained, arising out of the system of patronage, as formerly, at any rate, exercised in Downing Street. Appointments to all the higher offices have usually been made in England, and we are free to confess that causes which are still in operation have, to a considerable degree, made this course unavoidable. But this necessity has occasioned the scale of salaries attached to such offices to be fixed far higher than would be necessary if natives were appointed to fill them. A gentleman who is sent from England to perform official duties in a colony, must be paid a salary that will enable him not only to live in a style equal to that of other persons of the same rank with himself, but also to set aside a provision for support when the period of his service shall expire, and when he will retire, not to the cheap and unostentatious mode of living usual in the colony, but to the expensive habits that prevail at home. . . .

(*Colonial Gazette*, 15 June 1839)

3 / COLONIAL GOVERNORS:
  THEIR APPOINTMENT AND FUNCTIONS

~ The prevalence of patronage in colonial appointments meant that governors appointed by the British authorities were often unfitted for their important task. Both Molesworth and Wakefield maintained that weaknesses in the existing system of imperial government were compounded by the choice of personnel to operate it.~

. . . Though the colonies have ample reason to complain of the manner in which their affairs are administered by the Colonial Office in this country, they have still greater reason to complain of the governors and other functionaries who are sent by the Colonial Office to the colonies; for, generally speaking, they are chosen, not on account of any special aptitude for, or knowledge of, the business they will have to perform, but for reasons foreign to the interest of the colonies. For instance, poor relations, or needy dependants of men having political influence; officers in the Army or Navy who have been unsuccessful in their professions; briefless barristers; electioneering agents; importunate applicants for public employment, whose employment in this country public opinion would forbid; and at times, even discreditable partisans whom it is expedient to get rid of in the colonies; these are the materials out of which the Colonial Office has too frequently manufactured its governors and other functionaries. Therefore, in most cases they are signally unfit for the duties which they have to perform, and being wholly ignorant of the affairs of the colony to which they are appointed, they become the tools of one or other of the colonial factions; whence perpetual jealousies and never-ending feuds. . . .

(*Hansard*, c, 25 July 1848, 850, [Molesworth])

. . . With the real disposers of colonial patronage, fitness is the last consideration; and, what is still worse, inasmuch as there is no public at home taking an interest in colonial affairs, colonial patronage becomes the refuge for men, whose unfitness for any office whatever forbids their employment by departments which public opinion controls as well as sustains. Those other departments make a convenience of the Colonial Office: the patronage of the colonies is the receptacle into which they cast their own importunate but very incompetent applicants for public employment. The great bulk, accordingly, of those whom we send out to the colonies to administer government, even those appointed to the highest offices, are signally unfit for the duties imposed on them. . . .

But there are exceptions, more especially as to governors, sometimes by design, oftener by accident. Since the rebellions in Canada, the governors of that province have been men of experience and high reputation in public life. . . .

(Wakefield, *Art of Colonization*, p. 239)

~ It was frequently the practice of the Colonial Office to appoint military men as governors, but the *Spectator* argued that such persons were not well qualified by training or experience to serve as civil administrators of overseas possessions inhabited by free Englishmen.~

The other day, Mr. Charles Buller remarked that the quarter-deck is not the best school for Governors; on which Sir Robert

Peel rejoined, that naval or military service is at least not a disqualification. That was no answer. . . .

In fact, if military pursuits are no disqualification, they are assuredly no qualification for the duties of governorship. They teach what is but a small part of those duties, command over a subordination of rank to rank. The object of that subordination, in military affairs, is destruction: the object of colonization is the very reverse, construction. The subordinates of a military commander have no rule but implicit obedience, their own welfare being a secondary matter: colonists have too much at stake to yield any blind obedience, and they know their own welfare to be a primary matter. The Governor, therefore, must not only command, but he must cooperate, consult, and even serve; that is, he must consider the details of his administration subservient to the well-understood wishes of the people. The responsibility of the Executive to Colonial communities has been officially recognized: the military officer is responsible only to his superior. It is apparent that a service which teaches habits of command so strictly defined and absolute must to a certain extent unfit men for a totally different service, where the requisites are a discretion of much latitude, a cheerful co-operation with all classes, and a reliance upon public opinion – upon anything rather than mere authority and subordination. . . .

Thus much respecting the habits of mind. But a Colonial Governor ought not merely to be a man of a certain kind of training; he ought to have a fund of general knowledge and official experience – information touching the great work of colonization, the resources of the particular colony and its wants. No military career necessarily implies these qualifications. Even the scientific pursuits of the more intelligent class of officers may omit, and almost invariably do omit, political theories and civil experience. A man may cruise round New Zealand to the end of his days, and take soundings on every foot of its coast, without once discerning its political position or fathoming its capacities. . . .

(*Spectator*, 29 March 1845)

~ Nevertheless, while the method of appointing colonial governors was highly unsatisfactory, the form of government that existed in most colonies with representative institutions placed the governor in a difficult and unenviable position. The limitations on his authority in the colony, where he was expected to act as effective head of the executive government, and his responsibility to the authorities in London for every administrative action meant that he could not act effectively either as local administrator or as imperial agent. Such were the difficulties of the office that governors tended to settle for a quiet life by throwing the responsibility for taking decisions on the authorities in London and by allying themselves with a local oligarchic faction that dominated the council and tried to hold the assembly at bay. Lord Durham's comments on the weaknesses of this administrative system in Lower Canada could equally well have been applied at this time to other British colonies in North America.~

. . . The defective system of administration in Lower Canada, commences at the very source of power; and the efficiency of the public service is impaired throughout, by the entire want in the Colony of any vigorous administration of the prerogative of the Crown. The fact is, that, according to the present system, there is no real representative of the Crown in the Province; there is in it, literally, no power which originates and conducts the executive government. The Governor, it is true, is said to represent the Sovereign, and the authority of the Crown is, to a certain extent, delegated to him; but he is, in fact, a mere subordinate officer, receiving his orders from the Secretary of State, responsible to him for his conduct, and guided by his instructions. Instead of selecting a Governor, with an entire confidence in his ability to use his local knowledge of the real state of affairs in the Colony in the manner which local observation and practical experience best prescribe to him, it has been the policy of the Colonial Department, not only at the outset, to instruct a Governor as to the general policy which he was to carry into effect, but to direct him, from time to time, by instructions, sometimes very precise, as to the course which he was to pursue, in every important particular of his administration. Theoretically irresponsible to the Colonial Legislature, the Governor was, in effect, the only officer in the Colony who was at all responsible; inasmuch as the Assembly, by centring their attacks on him, and making him appear the sole cause of the difficulties of the Government, could occasion him so much vexation, and represent him in so unfavourable a light at home, that it frequently succeeded in imposing on him the necessity of resigning, or on the Colonial Minister, that of recalling him. In order to shelter himself from this responsibility, it has inevitably, and I must say very justifiably, been the policy of Governors to take care that the double responsibility shall be as light as possible; to endeavour to throw it, as much as possible, on the home Government, and to do as little as possible without previously consulting the Colonial Minister at home, and receiving his instructions. It has, therefore, been the tendency of the local government to settle every thing by reference to the Colonial Department in Downing Street. Almost every question on which it was possible to avoid, even with great inconvenience, an immediate decision, has been habitually the subject of reference; and this applies not merely to those questions on which the local executive and legislative bodies happened to differ, wherein the reference might be taken as a kind of appeal, but to questions of a strictly local nature, on which it was next to impossible for the Colonial Office to have any sufficient information. . . . The Governor has been enabled by this system to shift responsibility on the Colonial Office. . . . But the real vigour of the executive has been essentially impaired; distance and delay have weakened the force of its decisions; and the Colony has, in every crisis of danger, and almost every detail of local management, felt the mischief of having its executive authority exercised on the other side of the Atlantic. . . .

(Lucas, *Lord Durham's Report*, II, 101-3)

~ Perhaps because he was acutely aware of the deficiencies of Colonial Office administration, Wakefield was very sympathetic towards the predicament in which colonial governors found themselves.~

. . . Justice demands that we should rather pity the lot of governors under this system, than blame them for what the system produces. They are frequently punished, and sometimes with the greatest injustice. A governor of more than common ability is the most likely to disregard or disobey instructions drawn up in London, and so to get recalled. The best of governors enters upon office very ignorant of things and persons in the colony. If a representative constitution enables him to discover the bent of the colonial mind on matters which call for decision, he has still to determine whether he will side with the minority or the majority. If he sides with the minority, he sets going that conflict between representative institutions and a despotic administration of them, which is the ordinary state of our representative colonies; and, thenceforth, instead of governing, he only lives in hot water. At length, perhaps, the conflict of factions in the colony becomes so violent that the House of Commons interferes; and then the governor is re-called by the Colonial Office, which hitherto, under the influence of some clique, or individual at home, has patted him on the back in his quarrel with the majority. If he sides with the majority, between whom and the bureaucracy at home there is a strong natural aversion, the first good opportunity of recalling him is seldom neglected; or, at all events, his life is made uncomfortable, and his capacity for governing much diminished, by the intrigues and secret influences at home, which the colonial minority brings to bear against him in Downing Street. . . .

(Wakefield, *Art of Colonization*, pp. 254-5)

4 / COLONIAL EXPENDITURE

~ While the Reformers persistently advocated the reduction of imperial expenditure on colonial administration and defence, the possibility of successfully pursuing economy and reconciling it with the preservation of the empire was not always so apparent. Many Englishmen argued in the 1830's that substantial retrenchment would be impossible unless Britain rid itself of the colonies, and to some extent the Colonial Reformers shared this view. By the forties, however, they had become more optimistic of cutting colonial expenditure without disrupting the empire. Self-governing colonies would pay their own administrative expenses and provide for their own defence. In this way a major criticism levelled at overseas possessions would be effectively removed.

Colonial expenditure remained an unfathomable item hidden in annual British budgets, and neither members of parliament nor the Treasury itself could disentangle its ramifications. Nevertheless, expenditure fell into the broad categories of imperial contributions to civil administrations in the colonies, military expenditure, including army, navy, ordnance, and commissariat expenses, and a general category called "army extraordinaries." Sir William Molesworth provided a comprehensive survey of colonial expenditure in the course of a parliamentary speech in 1848.~

. . . The whole colonial expenditure of the British empire is about £ 8,000,000 sterling a year; one half of which is defrayed by the colonies, and one half by Great Britain. That portion of the colonial expenditure which is defrayed by Great Britain, consists of military, naval, civil, and extraordinary expenditure.

First, the net military expenditure by Great Britain, on account of the colonies (including ordnance and commissariat expenditure) was returned to Parliament, for the year 1832, at £1,761,505; for the year 1835-36, at £2,030,059; and for the year 1843-44 (the last return) at £2,556,919, an increase between 1832 and 1843 of £795,414. The present military expenditure is probably about the same as it was in 1843-44; for the military force in the colonies amounts at present to about 42,000 men (exclusive of artillery and engineers), or to about three-eighths of the whole military force of the British empire (exclusive of the army in India). . . . To form a fair estimate of the whole military expenditure by Great Britain, on account of the colonies, for one year, it would be necessary to add to this sum of £2,500,000 a very considerable sum, on account of reliefs [troops to relieve overseas garrisons], military establishments at home, and other matters, which are in part required in order to keep up so large a military force in the colonies. It is evident, therefore, that I shall under-estimate the military expenditure by Great Britain, on account of the colonies, when I set it down at only £2,500,000 a year.

Secondly, with regard to the naval expenditure by Great Britain on account of the colonies. At present we have about 235 ships in commission, with a complement not much short of 40,000 men. Of these ships, about 132, with a complement of about 25,000 men, are on foreign stations: some in the Mediterranean, some on the North American and West Indian station, some off the west coast of Africa and the Cape of Good Hope, others in the Chinese and Indian seas, or protecting our interests in New Zealand. . . . I may, therefore, without exaggeration, assume that at least one-third of the ships on foreign stations – that is, one-fifth of the ships in commission – or forty-five ships, with a complement of about 8,000 men, are maintained on account of the colonies. Now I infer from the estimates, and from the returns presented to the House, that these ships will cost the country annually, for wages and victuals of crews, wear and tear of vessels and stores, more than £700,000. In addition to this sum, we shall have to vote this year, in the Navy Estimates, £65,000 for naval establishments in the colonies, another £65,000 for naval works and repairs in the colonies, and £181,000 for freight and other matters connected with the conveyance of troops to the colonies. These sums, added together, will give a total of above £1,000,000 sterling as the direct naval expenditure by Great Britain, on account of the colonies for one year. . . .

Thirdly, the civil expenditure by Great Britain on account of the colonies is chiefly defrayed by sums annually voted in the Miscellaneous Estimates, under the head of colonial services; some portion of it, however, is paid for under Acts of Parliament. It may be estimated this year at £300,000. It consists of numerous items. . . . I will now only mention that we pay £27,000 a year for the Colonial Office, £20,000 a year for ecclesiastical establishments in the West Indies, between £11,000 and £12,000 a year for the clergy of North America. . . .

Lastly, under the head of extraordinary expenditure by Great Britain on account of the colonies, I put down such items as the insurrection in Canada, for which in the interval between 1838 and 1843, there were special grants to the amount of £2,096,000. . . . On the average of the last ten years, £200,000 a year would have been wholly inadequate to cover the extraordinary expenditure by Great Britain on account of the colonies. I will put it down, however, at £200,000 a year. . . .

If the four sums which I have just mentioned be added together, namely, £2,500,000 for the Army, including ordnance and commissariat, £1,000,000 for the Navy, £300,000 for civil services, and £200,000 for extraordinary expenses, the total direct expenditure by Great Britain on account of the colonies, would amount to at least four millions a year; and I am inclined to think that this is very much less than the actual annual cost of the colonies to Great Britain. Now, I beg the House to observe, that the declared value of British produce and manufactures exported to the colonies in the year 1844 was nine millions sterling. . . . Therefore the expenditure of Great Britain on account of the colonies amounts to nine shillings in every pound's worth of its exports; or, in other words, for every pound's worth of goods that our merchants send to the colonies, the nation pays nine shillings; in fact, a large portion of our colonial trade consists of goods which are sent to defray the expenses of our establishments in the colonies. What are the advantages which we derive from our colonial possessions in return for this expenditure? . . .

(*Hansard*, c, 25 July 1848, 817-20)

~ The Colonial Reformers and radicals generally argued that the high rate of imperial expenditure on civil establishments in the colonies was largely the result of superfluous offices and exorbitant salaries. In 1833 the *Spectator* estimated the cost of this category of expenditure in the empire as a whole and in North America in particular, and suggested that this was one principal reason for questioning the value of colonies.~

. . . The Colonial possessions are a very great source of the national expenditure, and a very considerable cause of our commercial derangements. In no other department of Government are abuses so rife; in no other branch of expenditure is there so much room, or perhaps such urgent necessity, for a keen and searching retrenchment. . . . Enormous incomes are enjoyed by officials who never set foot in the settlement; pluralities are as numerous in the Colonies as in the Church, and efficiency as little regarded. Half-pay officers, or subservient and unsuccessful traders, dispense justice; veterans, whose notions of civil government have been formed from the absolute authority of the camp, or aristocratic youths, whose experience has extended no further than the clubs, the turf, or even less reputable associations, are appointed to the delicate and difficult task of governing an unsettled community with discretionary power; and if the statements of the Colonists are to be credited, individuals are appointed to the office of judge who are even ignorant of the language in which the pleadings are made. Out of an expenditure of rather more than two millions, no less than £372,000 is divided amongst 166 persons; being on an average upwards of £2,200 to each individual. Colonies, however closely connected by situation, language, and community of interests and feelings, must be burdened with a *separate* Governor and suite, with their long list of allowances, &c., *separate* Crown Law Officers, and *separate* Courts and Judges. Here, then, is ample field for an economical Government to work upon; and, by a rigid economy in applying the Colonial revenue, as well as by a consolidation of their laws and governments, to enable the Colonies either entirely to discharge their own expenses, or to require no assistance from Great Britain excepting for naval protection. Whatever possessions are unable to accomplish this, should be considered as a dead weight upon the national prosperity. Justice and good faith towards individual interests may compel us to retain them for the present: motives of policy may perhaps render their retention proper for an indefinite period: but let them be set down as what they really are – a cause of expense, and not a source of profit. . . .

(*Spectator*, 5 January 1833)

~ When the *Spectator* came to re-examine the question of colonial expenditure in 1843, it argued that it was colonial government, and not colonies as such, that imposed a heavy financial burden on the British taxpayer.~

. . . the Colonies would not require any great expense for the due performance of the government-functions necessary to them, as we see in the case of very great colonies that have the management of their own affairs. But the English Government chooses to keep up in the Colonies a government which resembles itself in costliness, partly for the credit of the thing, partly because certain acts performed by Colonial Governments are done in behalf, not of the Colonies, but of the Mother-country. . . . This head of expense, however, is the one usually meant when people talk about the cost of colonies: they mean, not the cost of *colonies*, but of colonial *government*. It is the one, too, most beyond the control of colonists; in fact, it is almost entirely under the control of the Colonial Office, who arrange the civil lists, appoint the governors, and shield them from the consequences of their errors. . . . Not the Colonies, but the Colonial Office, it is that cost us so many millions. . . .

(*Spectator*, 15 April 1843)

~ British expenditure on civil establishments in the colonies of settlement was gradually reduced in the thirties and forties as the colonists assumed a greater control over the administration of their own internal affairs. At the heart of the progress of the North American colonies towards self-government lay protracted negotiations between the imperial authorities and the colonial assemblies over the civil list. Discussions centred round the terms under which the casual and territorial revenues, drawn by the crown from colonial lands, fees of office, and other sources not subject to local control or appropriation, would be surrendered to the assemblies in return for the grant of a civil list, by which the legislature undertook to pay the salaries of the leading officers of the colonial government. Progress towards agreement over this contentious issue was slow, but Molesworth produced calculations during a parliamentary speech in 1848 to support his contention that the volume of imperial expenditure was directly related to the degree of self-government enjoyed by the colonists. Such reasoning seemed a powerful plea for decentralization and local control throughout the empire.~

. . . I shall now proceed to the consideration of that portion of the colonial expenditure of the British empire which is defrayed by the colonies themselves . . . it appears that the total expenditure by all the colonies . . . was about £3,350,000 for the year 1845. The population of these colonies was about

3,400,000; therefore, the annual expenditure was at the rate of 19s. 8d. per head of the population. The rate of expenditure, however, varies considerably in different colonies, according as the colonists have less or more control over their own expenses. This is a most important fact, to which I wish to call the especial attention of the House. . . . The colonies, with representative assemblies, have a population of about 2,580,000, and their expenditure, in 1846, was £1,930,000, or at the rate of 14s. 11d. per head of their population. On the other hand, the population of the colonies, without representative assemblies, was about 820,000, and their expenditure, in 1845, was £1,420,000, or at the rate of £1.14s. a head of their population, or 18s. 7d. a head more than in the colonies with representative assemblies. I am convinced that this great increase of the rate of expenditure in the Crown colonies is mainly to be attributed to the want of self-government; for it is most apparent when the rate of expenditure, in each class of colonies, is examined and considered separately.

The rate of expenditure is the lowest in the North American colonies, where there is the greatest amount of self-government; in fact, since the last insurrection in Canada, and the establishment of the doctrine of responsible government, Canada has become, in most respects, an independent State, except as far as the civil list is concerned, and except that it is now and then subjected to some mischievous and foolish interference on the part of the Colonial Office. Now, the expenditure of the North American colonies in 1845, was £1,134,000, their population was 1,700,000; therefore the rate of expenditure was 13s. 4d. per head of the population, or 1s. 7d. less than the average rate of the colonies with representative assemblies. But it should be remarked, that of the £1,134,000 expenditure in 1845 by the North American colonies, £500,000 was an extraordinary expenditure by Canada, on account of new works and buildings, a large portion of which was defrayed by a loan. If a portion of this loan be omitted, as it ought to be, from the annual expenditure, then the rate of expenditure by the North American colonies for the year 1845 would have been nearly the same as it was for the year 1842, when it amounted to about 9s. a head of the population. Though this rate of expenditure is low as compared to our other colonies, yet it is about 30 per cent higher than that of the United States for similar purposes. The difference mainly arises from the high scale of salaries paid to the higher functionaries in the North American colonies. Generally speaking, those functionaries receive from three to four times the amount of the salaries of similar functionaries in the United States. For instance, in the Canadas, with a population of 1,200,000, the Governor is paid £7,000 a year; in the United States, the President has only £5,000 a year, and no governor has more than £1,200 a year; in the State of New York, with a population of 2,600,000, the Governor only receives £800 a year. Again, the Chief Justices of Upper and Lower Canada are paid £1,500 a year each, while the Chancellor and Chief Justices of the State of New York receive only £800 a year each. The puisne Judges of Canada receive £1,000 a year each; those of New York only £200 a year each. The Governor of Nova Scotia is paid £3,500 a year; the Governors of New Brunswick and Newfoundland are paid £3,000 a year each. In Massachusetts, with a population much larger than that of the three last colonies added together, the salary of the Governor is only £500 a year. In fact, the four North American colonies which I have just mentioned, pay £2,500 a year more for the salaries of their four Governors, than the thirty States of the Union do for their thirty Governors. Now in the colonies the salaries are fixed by the various civil lists. These civil lists, being removed for a series of years from the control of the representative assemblies, are perpetual causes of quarrelling and discontent; and there is always a dispute going on between the Colonial Office and some colony or other on this subject, which frequently leads to the most unpleasant results. For instance, the dispute about the civil list of Canada was one of the causes which ultimately led to the insurrection in that colony. . . . In all these quarrels, the object of the Office is to keep up the pay of its functionaries; and the object of the colonists is a reduction of expenditure. There can be no doubt that the salaries of the higher functionaries in the colonies are excessive as compared to the standard of the United States, which is the usual standard of comparison in the colonies. . . . I do not think this rate of pay is too high for noble Lords and other gentlemen of rank and connexion, when they undertake the duties of governors of the colonies; but if we are determined to employ such persons in the colonies, we ought to pay for them ourselves. On the other hand, if we insist upon the colonies paying their governors, it appears to me that, with the exception of the military stations, we should permit the colonies to elect their own governors and other functionaries, and to pay them what salaries they think fit. . . .

(*Hansard*, c, 25 July 1848, 837-40)

~ Military establishments overseas were a very different matter. The cost of defending the colonies entailed a heavy expenditure on garrisons, barracks, fortifications, ordnance, and many other items. The Colonial Reformers considered that these unnecessary military expenses rendered the colonies in British North America expensive liabilities. Not only was this a financial burden, but the Reformers interpreted military expenditure as conclusive evidence of colonial misgovernment; there could be no justification for British rule if it depended on military force rather than the willing loyalty of the inhabitants. Here again, the *Spectator* maintained that local self-government would be the cheapest and most effective means of providing for colonial defence, since the colonists would then possess a freedom which they would be prepared to defend at their own expense.~

. . . Does the possession of the Canadas add to our military strength? The possession of the Old Colonies, now constituting the United States, unquestionably *did*, in so far as we were aggressors on our neighbours; for it was by their means we conquered Canada, Louisiana, and Florida. Moreover, they constituted, before their quarrel with us, probably not less than a tenth part of the population of the empire. It was neither pleasant nor profitable to have our population as it were *decimated* – a population, too, that took off four millions of our produce and manufactures, at that time *one-fourth* part of the total exports of the kingdom. Since the establishment of the invincible republic in their neighbourhood, the Canadas, instead of contributing to our national strength, have always added to our weakness. They have at once produced a dispersion of our force, wasted our treasure, and diminished our trade. *Now* that they are disaffected, these evils are aggravated; but, if ever so loyal, in what possible way could a million or half a million of people – one fiftieth or one twenty-fifth part of our whole population – in a corner of the world three or four thousand miles off, contribute to the military strength of the British Islands? If to maintain costly garrisons as our own sole expense in remote regions, among a people whether affected or disaffected to us, can perform such a miracle, then may the Canadas contribute to our national strength – but not otherwise.

The matter of finance is easily settled. . . . No British colony in America has ever paid its own military charges, or contributed a farthing to the Imperial treasury. The Canadas are by far the most expensive colonies we ever possessed. Profit, then, being out of the question, let us estimate the *loss* for which we are going to fight. According to the very incomplete statements laid before Parliament in 1835, the total annual expenditure on the North American Colonies, by the people of this country, was £425,562. In this statement, the sums voted for the improvement of the water communications of the Canadas, almost purely for purposes of military defence, and the sums laid out in the ridiculous attempt to fortify against American aggression an open frontier thousands of miles in extent, are taken no notice of. From fifty to sixty millions . . . were already laid out on the Canadas down to 1830. . . . The public money expended on the Rideau Canal, the fortifications, and other follies, has been absolutely sunk or destroyed. We shall reckon the annual charge upon it, however, only at the Colonial interest of 6 per cent. The items recapitulated will then be –

Annual national loss through the timber monopoly	£1,500,000
Rideau Canal; capital expended down to 1833, namely, £858,000	51,480
The sixty millions previously expended, including £3,000,000 for fortifications	3,600,000
Annual Civil, Military, and Naval Expenditure of Great Britain	600,000
	£5,751,480

We have an enormous sum, nearly *six millions* a year, spent on our six North American Colonies. Now the total value of our exports to these Colonies, whether in British and Irish produce and manufactures, or in Foreign and Colonial merchandise, – and it includes civil and military stores, with the consumption of civil and military establishments, – is £3,000,000 a year, enhanced even to that value by monopoly price. The owners of this capital may count themselves lucky if on the average of years they clear a profit of 10 per cent. This will make a gain of £300,000. So then, to enable a few merchants to gain £300,000 a year, which they would equally gain in any other trade, or in the same trade without a farthing's loss to the nation, the people must disburse nearly six millions a year; that is, the whole nation must sustain an annual loss of nearly twentyfold the profit which the merchants gain! . . .

(*Spectator*, 13 January 1838)

~ Wakefield also argued that colonies which enjoyed internal self-government could be expected to meet the cost of defending themselves.~

. . . an objection to new colonies, which rests on the necessity of protecting them from foreign violence, remains untouched. That necessity would certainly exist in every case where the colony was unable to defend itself. But colonies, which govern themselves, have commonly been able to defend themselves. The colonies of Greece were able, not only to defend themselves, but to assist their parent states in resisting foreign violence. The chartered colonies of North America were able to defend themselves against their mother-country, when she had the folly to attack their local independence. Dependence teaches colonies to lean upon their mother-country: independence from the beginning teaches them to provide for self-defence; not to mention that a colony, which manages its own affairs, has more, infinitely more, to defend than a colony whose affairs are shamefully managed from a distance . . . when did a colony, that flourished at all, and was independent from the beginning, yield up the main cause of its prosperity, its precious independence? Judging from past facts, we may conclude, that if the art of colonization were skilfully pursued, if colonies were independent, and were founded or extended so as to be, not new societies, but old societies in new places, the defence of them from foreign violence would not require any outlay by the mother-country. . . .

(Wakefield, *England and America*, II, 256-8)

PART FIVE:
THE CANADIAN CRISIS

~ The constitution established in Upper and Lower Canada by the act of 1791 represented an attempt to reproduce in the colonies the structure of the British constitution as far as circumstances would permit. Imperial statesmen attributed the loss of the American colonies in part at least to an excess of popular control in the colonial constitutions, and so it was decided that the growth of democracy and republican sentiment could be most effectively held in check in British North America by strengthening the power of the executive and by stressing the principles of authority in government and of hierarchy in society. The constitution of 1791 thus provided in each of the Canadas for a governor, executive council, legislative council, and assembly, which would be the colonial counterparts of the British institutions of sovereign, cabinet, Lords, and Commons.

The major weakness that eventually emerged in this system of representative government concerned the relations between the two coordinate centres of political authority – the councils and the assembly. The nominated members of the councils formed a small oligarchy of officials and government supporters united by patronage, who were not responsible to the assembly for their actions and therefore could not be removed from office by criticism or censure in the popular branch of the legislatures. At the same time, the elected members of the assembly expressed their dissent from government policy by mounting bitter, though usually ineffectual, personal attacks on officials, without the possibility of being called upon themselves to take over the conduct of affairs. Conflict between executive and legislative authority was resolved in England during the early nineteenth century by the acceptance of the principle of ministerial responsibility to a majority in the House of Commons, though the practice was not fully recognized until the 1830's. In British North America, however, responsible government was not adopted until the late forties, and until that time struggles between the executive and the legislature were reminiscent of the politics of the earlier American colonies, with the assembly using its control over colonial finance to extract reluctant concessions from the executive. This process was not successfully completed in the Canadas in the years down to the rebellions of 1837, because the executives and their family compacts offered determined and resourceful opposition, and because the authorities in London were unwilling to concede the more extreme demands of the assemblies.

This central constitutional struggle was compounded in both the Canadas by a variety of associated grievances and sources of friction. In Lower Canada it was considerably complicated and embittered by a racial contest between an English minority firmly entrenched in the councils and a hostile French majority in the assembly. The problems of Upper and Lower Canada were distinctly different in character, and British attitudes towards the provinces varied accordingly. Since the disputes involving Lower Canada were the more serious and intractable, these preoccupied the attention of British ministers, officials, and Colonial Reformers alike. While the British government leaned over backwards to reassure the Upper Canadians, whose loyalty could not be in doubt, ministers were determined to check the pretensions of the French Canadians in the lower province in a despairing attempt to come to terms with a nationalist movement which Englishmen were unable to understand.

The Canadian question came to the fore and had political repercussions in England as a result of the authoritarian administration in Lower Canada of the Earl of Dalhousie and the report of the select committee appointed by the House of Commons in 1828 to inquire into the civil government of Canada. Thereafter all important decisions concerning the administration of British North America were taken at the Colonial Office, and while closer supervision from London did not produce more successful or enlightened measures, it did give a new consistency to imperial policy. The attitudes and policies of the Whig ministries towards Canada in the 1830's have often been criticized for reflecting a prevailing English indifference towards colonies, but the Whigs were fully aware of the value of British North America as an outlet for English emigration and deeply concerned about the ambitions of the United States. Moreover, British policy towards the Canadas was not unsympathetic or reactionary, as has often been alleged. On the contrary, the Whigs were genuinely prepared to reform the Canadian constitution by changes in the composition of the legislative council and the settlement of disputes over the civil list. Until 1837 British policy was persistently based on conciliation and reflected an awareness that colonial self-government would eventually be conceded.

One major difficulty, however, was to translate generous

sympathies into practical reforms that would be generally acceptable. So long as the Canadians could not agree amongst themselves precisely what kind of constitutional reforms they desired, and so long as conflicting demands were being received in London from governors, councils, and assemblies, the Whigs preferred to postpone positive action. Meanwhile, they deliberately avoided novel constitutional experiment, and they refused to impose a settlement by the intervention of parliament. Furthermore, in the case of Lower Canada, British ministers felt that there was a limit to which they should go towards conciliating French opinion. They hoped to retain the support of the moderate French Canadians, but they were not prepared to concede the demands of extremists like Louis Papineau for such radical reforms as an elective legislative council. For these various reasons, conciliation did not resolve the problems of the Canadas, and it was not until the rebellions in 1837 gave the British government a free hand that ministers could impose a settlement of their own choosing.~

1 / LORD JOHN RUSSELL'S RESOLUTIONS

~ Until 1837 imperial appeasement and procrastination were met by colonial intransigence. To reinforce its demands, the assembly of Lower Canada refused to vote supplies after 1832 until its grievances had been redressed. It persisted in this conduct until 1837, and with inadequate revenue to meet local expenses and mounting arrears of official salaries/the British government was finally forced to act. In a series of Resolutions presented to parliament in March 1837, Lord John Russell set out the government's views on the Canadian question and the measures by which the ministry intended to resolve the present impasse in Lower Canada. In conformity with the report of Lord Gosford's commission of inquiry in 1835, the imperial authorities refused to concede demands for an elective legislative council or a responsible executive. Although severe criticisms of the House of Lords were being voiced at this time by many Englishmen, Lord John Russell included, various proposals to create an elective upper house in the Canadas, or in Nova Scotia or New South Wales for that matter, secured little support amongst imperial officials or politicians. Both elected councils and responsible executives were considered incompatible with British constitutional traditions, a colony's dependent status, and the preservation of the imperial connection. The Resolutions also stated that casual and territorial revenues of the crown would be surrendered to the assembly only in return for the grant of a permanent civil list, and that the governor should meanwhile be empowered to appropriate money in the provincial treasury without local legislative sanction. Although the mood of parliament was broadly sympathetic to the Resolutions, they were condemned by the Colonial Reformers as an unwarranted infringement of the colony's constitution and as evidence that a coercive policy had now been firmly adopted. The following comments of the *Spectator* typically reflect this point of view.~

. . . The week opened with the threatened attack on the constitution of Lower Canada – a constitution willingly conferred and solemnly guaranteed by the British Parliament. The assault was led on by the Reforming Whig, Lord John Russell, in a series of resolutions, which he asked the Reformed House of Commons of Great Britain and Ireland to pass. These resolutions not only negatived all the demands of the Colonial suitors for justice, but authorized robbery. They declared, in effect, that the Legislative Council of Lower Canada should *not* be made elective . . . that the Executive Council should still be irresponsible; and that, in order to make the Provincial Government independent of the Provincial Legislature, the money in the treasury should be seized and applied by the Governor, without the consent of the Assembly. There was a vague intimation that improper persons should not in future be made Legislative Councillors. Behold the Canadian policy of the Melbourne-Whig-Tory Administration, as developed in the resolutions and the speech of the Home Secretary.

The defence of this policy was, the necessity of keeping Canada in this sort of subjection to England; and that the Canadian Assembly was unreasonable, abused its power, and had no real grievances to complain of. The last mentioned assertion was made in utter contempt of the truth. It is upon record . . . that in the Legislative Council of Lower Canada are persons of bad character, the abject tools of the Executive; it is not denied that there are judges on the bench who would not be allowed to hold a commission of the peace in this country – intemperate and profligate men; that defaulters high in office have been screened, and thereby great loss thrown upon the public; that jobbing in public lands prevails to an immense extent; that numerous bills of reform, unexceptionable in character . . . have been rejected by the Legislative Council; and that public funds have been applied to make payments which the Assembly, exercising its constitutional and undoubted right, refused to sanction. Look at this list, and then estimate the assurance of those men who deny that the Canadians have any substantial grievances. The Canadians, at least, think differently; and they have refused the supplies to a Government whose acts proclaim it to be the ally of a faction. To punish the Canadians for their contumacy – for presuming to enforce rights guaranteed by Act of Parliament – Lord John Russell moved the resolutions whose substance we have stated. . . .

. . . it behoves every Englishman to make himself acquainted with the actual state of this question – to look down the precipice to the verge of which the Ministers have led us. For the sake of preserving the irresponsible authority of a faction in Canada and a bureaucracy in Downing Street, we run imminent risk of a war, with all its concomitant evils – loss of trade, loss of treasure, heavy taxes, augmented debt, bloodshed, misery and rapine – with our best friends and natural allies, the people of the United States. The Canadians will not immediately, perhaps, but they must eventually, resist the Downing Street tyranny; they will claim the assistance of their Republican neighbours, and they will not claim it in vain. There can be no Government in the United States with *power* to prevent the inroad of thousands of riflemen, who will pick off our officers like sparrows, or the smuggling of stores of all kinds across the Lakes, or the offer of shelter to fugitives in the American territory, or the settlement of Americans on the Canadian lands. . . . If any one deems that we are speaking at random and conjuring up phantoms of evil, let him recollect how the struggle of the American Revolution began, and how it *ended*. The progress of a quarrel of this kind is like that of fire – once kindled, nobody can tell how long it will burn or how far it will reach. . . .

(*Spectator*, 11 March 1837)

~ In the debate on the Resolutions Molesworth defended the actions and privileges of the assembly of Lower Canada and indicated the dire consequences of the present arbitrary policy of the ministry.~

Sir W. Molesworth had listened attentively to the speech of the noble Lord [Russell], the Secretary for the Home Department, and to those who had spoken on the same side of the question, without hearing any argument which could at all support or justify the extraordinary resolutions which had been proposed for the adoption of the House. He would not go at length into the state of affairs in the Canadas.. . . . On the one side, they had the vast majority of the people – on the other "a miserable monopolizing minority," arrogating to itself superiority of place, and treating the rest of the people as aliens in blood. He called on that House to assist the representatives of the Canadian people. The Canadian people complained of certain grievances, and their representatives had adopted the constitutional mode of refusing to grant the supplies till those grievances were redressed. The noble Lord called on the British Legislature to exercise a sovereign power and interfere with the House of Assembly in its control over the revenues of the province. Now, had the noble Lord any right to do so? He denied that the British Legislature was sovereign in Canada with regard to money affairs. The first question was one of sovereignty. According to the constitution of Canada, the rights, privileges, and powers of the House of Assembly in regard to Canada were in every respect similar to the rights, privileges, and powers of this House with regard to the King. They were founded on precisely the same principle – namely, that the Representatives of the people should alone determine the mode and manner in which the money levied from the community ought to be appropriated. . . . He maintained it was the control of the purse which constituted the essence of freedom; and did they think the Canadian people would permit themselves to be rendered slaves by the resolutions of that House? The people of this country had, in a similar case, brought about the revolution – in a similar case, they denounced the monarch who dared to tax them without their consent – in a similar case, their fellow-citizens of the United States bad them defiance and threw off their yoke; and if the Canadians were of that race which produced Washington, Jefferson, and Franklin, they would feel themselves in that position which made every man of English blood a rebel. He trusted, however, that such an unfortunate state of circumstances would not be brought to a crisis. He firmly believed the people of England would not permit such conduct on the part of the noble Lord, nor allow their representatives to adopt the means which he proposed of putting down their Canadian fellow-subjects. Probably enough the resolutions would be carried. The sympathies existing on the other side of the House would, probably enough, lead to an unholy coalition with his Majesty's Ministers upon the present occasion. Hon. Gentlemen opposite wished to have the conquest of Canada a precedent for the re-conquest of Ireland, and he had no doubt they would join most willingly in this vile and unholy crusade against the rights and privileges of freemen. But the Canadians would act as Englishmen, and attempt, he confidently expected, by every means in their power, to shake off the yoke. The people of England, he was sure, would say they had, in that case, done right; they would never suffer their representatives to give the noble Lord the means of putting the Canadian people down. Let the House look at this question, in conjunction with the present state of the Texas, and ask themselves if, having failed in the case of the United States when they stood alone, they were likely to be more successful in a similar struggle against the Canadas, backed by so many who hated the name of monarchy, and abhorred an act of tyranny such as this? He should resist the Resolutions of the noble Lord in every stage, contending first of all that they had no right whatever to pronounce a judgment on the acts of the Canadian legislature, they not being responsible to that House; secondly, that they had no constitutional right to interfere with their control over their own money; and lastly, because the consequence of such an attempt must lead to the violent separation of the two countries or a dreadful civil war.

(*Hansard*, XXXVI, 6 March 1837, 1331-3)

~ It was a commonplace of radical opinion in the late 1830's that the current Whig administration was no longer recognizable as the heir of the enlightened, reforming ministry that only a few years before had passed the Reform Act. The *Spectator* maintained that the government's reactionary Canadian policy clearly showed just how "Toryfied" the ministry had become.~

The conduct of the Whigs with regard to Canada, throws an important light on home politics. The Whigs, from the first existence of their party down to the passing of the Reform Bill, had always one remarkable characteristic – they were always alive to the popular principle of resistance to oppression . . . any merely arbitrary exercise of power, any act of sheer tyranny, whether at home or abroad, used to excite in them feelings of indignation . . . they have ever been ready to side with the weak against the strong – the small state against the large one – the people against mere power – and, above all, to defend what they termed a "popular right," whether consisting of national independence, or of an elective suffrage for national purposes, or of the meanest privilege of the most insignificant corporation. . . . Such was, until lately, the main political principle or feeling of the English Whigs; it is this which, more than any thing else, has for near a century and a half distinguished them from the Tories.

The transition state of home politics seems to have thoroughly *Toryfied* them, except in so far as some of them (the Melbourne Whigs) disagreed with the Tories just sufficiently for keeping the latter out of office. . . . It is all explained by the state of transition from aristocratic to democratic government. The Reform Bill was forced upon the Whigs by a popular movement, which they led only because they felt that it was irresistible. Their work was no sooner done, than they became so alarmed at its probable effect on the power of the great families, that a sort of reaction impelled them into proceedings which, but a few years before, they would have denounced as shameful. . . . They see or feel that power is departing from the aristocracy of birth, and yet hope that it may be preserved for their own children. It follows that, with respect to all further organic change at home, and to questions of authority in the colonies, they agree with the Tories. Some of them have openly joined the enemies of popular rights: the others, for the sake of enjoying present power themselves, still profess and practise so much Liberalism as is indispensable to their present object: but the propensity of the whole Whig mind is towards Toryism. As respects a defenceless colony, this propensity may be indulged without risk. There are no old Whigs now to do battle against the Tories in defence of a colonial constitution. Therefore the new Whigs cordially unite with the Tories in violating the constitution of Canada. . . .

(*Spectator*, 18 March 1837)

2 / CAUSES OF THE REBELLIONS

~ The Canadian question assumed an entirely new gravity and urgency with the outbreak of rebellions in Lower and Upper Canada at the end of 1837. It was natural that Englishmen should search for the causes of the uprisings, and that they should examine this question in the light of the American Revolution and the lessons drawn from this earlier experience. At first, contemporaries were struck by the obvious parallels between the two revolts, and, as George Grote's comments indicate, this similarity suggested that the Canadians were also struggling for liberty and democratic government in the face of British oppression. There was some discussion of the rivalry in Lower Canada between French and English, but this was initially discounted by most British radicals as the major cause of rebellion.~

   . . . It had been asserted by many Gentlemen in the course of the debate, that there was no analogy between the present state of Canada and that of the provinces of the United States in 1774. But he had not heard one single argument to prove to him that there was any disparity whatever between the two cases. He contended not only that the treatment of England towards Canada was analogous to that of the treatment of England towards the United States, but that the grievances of which the Canadians complained were also in every respect exactly analogous to the grievances of which the United States complained. The principal grievance arose in fact, out of the right of the British Government to take the people's money. That was the chief ground of the complaint of the United States in 1774; it was also the chief ground of the complaint of Canada at the present moment. . . .

(*Hansard*, XXXIX, 22 December 1837, 1483-4)

~ The *Spectator* discussed at greater length the distinct similarities between the Canadian rebellions and the American Revolution, and it dismissed the assertions of some Englishmen that the struggle in Canada was a racial dispute and that it was not concerned with civil liberties or constitutional principles.~

   . . . The parallel between Canada and America is . . . not, indeed, identical, because no two human events were or can be identical; but they resemble each other as much as any two human faces or any two green fields resemble each other. The quarrel in both cases is between England and a colony – between England and a North American colony – between an European state essentially aristocratic and a colony essentially democratic: in both cases the insurrection has been produced by a long train of oppression, insult, and provocation, become at length insupportable. . . .
   . . . The struggle is pronounced to be one between the French and English inhabitants; while it is in reality a struggle between the majority contending for right and liberty, and the minority contending for despotism and the wrong of which it is in the profitable enjoyment. The British colonists of Canada speaking the French language are no more French, than the American inhabitants of Louisiana speaking the French language are French. It is very near eighty years since France ceased to rule

over Canada. There are not perhaps ten Canadians living who were born under the Government of France; not one man who was educated under it exists. As long as the Canadians were French in principle and conduct, they were the ready and servile tools of Tory and Whig Cabinets. They refused to join the American Republicans who invaded Canada in 1775; they joined Burgoyne, and surrendered with him at Saratoga. For almost thirty years they were content to live without a constitution, and submitted to the arbitrary rule of the Colonial Office. In a fit of fear, or of liberality, a Tory Minister gave them a constitution, forty-seven years ago; and for twenty years they made no use of it. The American Republicans once more invaded the Canadas; and by the assistance of the Canadians they were once more defeated. Every one knows that it is simply because the Canadians were French in spirit down to 1814, that the Canadas are now British colonies. Had they been English, they would in 1783 have been the fourteenth state of that Union that secured its independence. . . . About seventeen years ago, the Canadian leaders, having acquired the spirit and knowledge of their own rights which characterize freemen, – having, in short, become practically English colonists, – they began to make a practical instrument of that constitution which had been heretofore a dead letter. From that day to this, they have been denounced as a mischievous faction. For sixty years that they were obedient slaves, they were the pets of the English Aristocracy; now that they are Englishmen in political feeling, although not indeed in phrase, Whig and Tory alike proscribe them as "aliens in blood, aliens in language, and aliens in religion." In the Tories this is natural enough; but in the Whigs it exhibits to our minds the most scandalous example of political dishonesty that can be found on the records of history. . . . The alleged English party consists almost exclusively of Tories, – merchants, shipowners, and functionaries; the two first fleecing the people of this country in the shape of the timber-monopoly, and the last the people of Canada in the form of places and sinecures. Precious representatives of the British nation and its interests! . . .

One of the constant assertions made by the Ministerial, backed of course by the Tory party, is, that the Americans had a great and glorious cause to defend, – that they fought for a principle, and that their struggle was crowned with merit and success; whereas the Canadians have no grievances worth naming, but were happy, contented, moderately taxed, and only stirred up to revolt by wicked demagogues. Precisely the same language was held towards America by the Aristocracy of the eighteenth, that is now held regarding Canada by the Aristocracy of the nineteenth century. . . . To tax the Old Colonies to the amount of £ 60,000 was, then, the original source of a contest which, in the shape of suspension of commercial intercourse or of actual hostilities, lasted more than twenty years, and cost this nation the loss of an empire, accompanied by a mulct on posterity equal to a perpetual annual burden of six millions and a half sterling. . . . The Americans, like the Canadians, had many other grievances; but the matters involving principle are those we have named. The Canadians have been driven to open revolt, by a vote of the Imperial Parliament sanctioning the seizure of the money in their exchequer. Where is the difference in principle between this and the immediate cause of the American Revolution? . . .

(*Spectator*, 30 December 1837)

~ In time, however, this explanation of the rebellion in Lower Canada as an essentially constitutional struggle for popular rights was radically modified. Lord Durham came to the conclusion during his short stay in North America that the conflict in the province had its origins in racial animosities, and after the publication of his *Report* this interpretation was universally accepted in Britain. One of the earliest indications of this change of opinion amongst the Colonial Reformers can be seen in a letter written by Wakefield to the editor of the *Spectator* in November 1838 as part of a campaign to create a favourable public reception in England for the return of Lord Durham and the publication of his *Report*. ~

. . . For a long while before the rebellion in Lower Canada, I had deeply sympathized with the majority of the people as represented by the House of Assembly. I imagined, or rather fully believed, along with yourself and many eminent Liberals in this country, that the contest in Lower Canada resembled the dispute between England and her Old Colonies in America; that the great majority of the colonists were struggling for popular principles and good government, against an arbitrary, corrupt, and oppressive faction; that the act of the Imperial Government which violated the Canadian constitution would justify a rebellion; and that if rebellion for such a cause should succeed, every friend of liberty in the world would have as good ground for rejoicing as when Luther vanquished the religious despotism of Rome and Washington established the United

States of America. Such were my impressions before the rebellion. The remarkable facility with which the rebellion was crushed, first led me to suspect that my view of Canadian affairs must have been erroneous; but I could not tell in what respects erroneous; and I therefore entered the colony with a strong feeling of good-will and compassion towards those whose want of energy or neglect of preparation, alone, as it then seemed to me, had prevented them from maintaining sacred rights by an appeal to the sword. . . .

. . . Personal inquiry on the spot, with the best opportunities of getting at the truth, has induced me to abandon those opinions and sympathies. I have been forced to abandon them, in spite of the deep-rooted conviction and earnest feeling with which they were entertained. I believe now, that I was blinded and misled, as many others have been, (yourself not excepted, allow me to say,) by a course of misrepresentation – a regular system of delusion, to which I was once (however unintentionally, as Mr. Roebuck still is,) an active party, and which, while it occasions the most erroneous views here as to the nature of the dispute in Lower Canada, has a still more mischievous effect in deceiving the French Canadians as to the state of feeling in this country with respect to their position and objects.

As to the nature of that dispute, and that state of affairs in the colony, the truth will probably be known here before long; when many will only have to wonder at the depth of their previous ignorance. . . .

(Wakefield to the Editor of the *Spectator*, London, 22 November 1838, *Spectator*, 24 November 1838)

~ What the Reformers and Englishmen generally came to regard as the real cause of conflict in Lower Canada was first elaborated by Lord Durham in his despatches to the colonial secretary in 1838 and in his subsequent *Report*. ~

. . . The first point to which I would draw your attention, being one with which all others are more or less connected, is the existence of a most bitter animosity between the [French] Canadians & the British, not as two parties holding different opinions & seeking different objects in respect to government, but as different races engaged in a national contest.

This hatred of races is not publicly avowed on either side. On the contrary, both sides profess to be moved by any other feelings than such as belong to difference of origin. But the fact is, I think, proved by an accumulation of circumstantial evidence more conclusive than any direct testimony would be,

& far more than sufficient to rebut all mere assertions to the contrary.

If the difference between the two classes were one of party or principles only, we should find on each side a mixture of persons of both races; whereas the truth is that, with exceptions which tend to prove the rule, all the British are on one side, & all the Canadians are on the other. What may be the immediate subject of dispute seems to be of no consequence: so surely as there is a dispute on any subject, the great bulk of the Canadians & the great bulk of the British appear ranged against each other . . . it appears upon a careful review of the political struggle between those who have termed themselves the loyal party & the popular party, that the subject of dissension has been, not the connexion with England, nor the form of the Constitution, nor any of the practical abuses which have affected all classes of the people, but simply such institutions, laws, & customs as are of French origin, which the British have sought to overthrow, & the Canadians have struggled to preserve, each class assuming false designations & fighting under false colours; the British professing exclusive loyalty to the Crown of England, & the Canadians pretending to the character of Reformers. . . .

This general antipathy of the Canadians towards the British & of the British towards the Canadians, appears to have been, as it were, provided for at the conquest of the Province & by subsequent measures of the British Gov[ernmen]t. If Lower Canada had been isolated from other colonies, & so well peopled as to leave little room for emigration from Britain, it might have been right at the conquest to engage for the preservation of French institutions – for the existence of a "Nation Canadienne"; but considering how certain it was that, sooner or later, the British race would predominate in the country, that engagement seems to have been most unwise. It insured such a strife as has actually taken place. For, notwithstanding the division of Canada into two Provinces for the purpose of isolating the French, the British already predominate in French Canada, not numerically of course, but by means of their superior energy & wealth, & of their natural relationship to the powers of government. It was long before the Canadians perceived that their Nationality was in the course of being overridden by a British Nationality. When the Constitutional Act bestowed on them a Representative System, they were so little conversant with its nature, & so blind to the probable results of British emigration, that they described the constitution as a

"Machine Anglaise pour nous taxer," & elected to the H[ouse] of Assembly a majority of Englishmen. But with the progress of British intrusion, they at length discovered, not only the uses of a representative System, but also that their nationality was in danger; & I have no hesitation in asserting that of late years they have used the Representative System for the single purpose of maintaining their nationality against the progressive intrusion of the British race. They have found the British pressing upon them at every turn, – in the possession of land, – in commerce, – in the retail trade, – in all kinds of industrious enterprise, – in religion, – in the whole administration of government; & though they are a stagnant people, easily satisfied & disinclined to exertion, they have naturally resisted an invasion which was so offensive to their national pride. The British, on the other hand, impeded in the pursuit of all their objects, partly by the ancient & barbarous civil law of the Country, & partly by the systematic opposition of the Canadians to the progress of British Enterprize, have naturally sought to remove these impediments, & to conquer without much regard to the means employed, that very mischievous opposition. The actual result should have seemed inevitable. The struggle between the two races, conducted as long as possible according to the forms of the constitution, became too violent to be kept within those bounds. In order to preserve some sort of Gov[ernmen]t the public Revenue was disposed of against the will of the Canadian people represented by their Assembly. The consequent rebellion, although precipitated by the British from an instinctive sense of the danger of allowing the Canadians full time for preparation, could not, perhaps, have been avoided. . . .

(Lord Durham to Lord Glenelg, 9 August 1838, No. 36, Secret & Confidential, DURHAM PAPERS [Ottawa: Public Archives of Canada], vol. 12; or *Report of the Public Archives, 1923* [Ottawa, 1924], pp. 316-18)

. . . The lengthened and various discussions which had for some years been carried on between the contending parties in the Colony, and the representations which had been circulated at home, had produced in mine, as in most minds in England, a very erroneous view of the parties at issue in Lower Canada. The quarrel which I was sent for the purpose of healing, had been a quarrel between the executive government and the popular branch of the legislature. The latter body had, apparently, been contending for popular rights and free government. The executive government had been defending the prerogative of the Crown, and the institutions which, in accordance with the principles of the British Constitution, had been established as checks on the unbridled exercise of popular power. Though, during the dispute, indications had been given of the existence of dissensions yet deeper and more formidable than any which arose from simply political causes, I had still, in common with most of my countrymen, imagined that the original and constant source of the evil was to be found in the defects of the political institutions of the Provinces; that a reform of the constitution, or perhaps merely the introduction of a sounder practice into the administration of the government, would remove all causes of contest and complaint. . . .

. . . for the peculiar and disastrous dissensions of this Province, there existed a far deeper and far more efficient cause, – a cause which penetrated beneath its political institutions into its social state, – a cause which no reform of constitution or laws, that should leave the elements of society unaltered, could remove; but which must be removed, ere any success could be expected in any attempt to remedy the many evils of this unhappy Province. I expected to find a contest between a government and a people: I found two nations warring in the bosom of a single state: I found a struggle, not of principles, but of races; and I perceive that it would be idle to attempt any amelioration of laws or institutions until we could first succeed in terminating the deadly animosity that now separates the inhabitants of Lower Canada into the hostile divisions of French and English. . . .

The grounds of quarrel which are commonly alleged, appear, on investigation, to have little to do with its real cause; and the inquirer, who has imagined that the public demonstrations or professions of the parties have put him in possession of their real motives and designs, is surprised to find, upon nearer observation, how much he has been deceived by the false colours under which they have been in the habit of fighting. . . . The French Canadians have attempted to shroud their hostility to the influence of English emigration, and the introduction of British institutions, under the guise of warfare against the Government and its supporters, whom they represented to be a small knot of corrupt and insolent dependents; being a majority, they have invoked the principles of popular control and democracy, and appealed with no little effect to the sympathy of liberal politicians in every quarter of the world. The English, finding their opponents in collision with the Government, have raised the cry of loyalty and attachment to British connexion, and denounced the republican designs of the French, whom they designate, or rather used to designate, by the appellation of Radicals. Thus the French have been viewed as a democratic party, contending for reform; and the English as a conservative minority, protecting the menaced connexion with the British Crown, and the supreme authority of the Empire. There is truth in this notion in so far as respects the means by which each party sought to carry its own views of Government into effect. The French majority asserted the most democratic doctrines of the rights of a numerical majority. The English minority availed itself of the protection of the prerogative, and allied itself with all those of the colonial institutions which enabled the few to resist the will of the many. But when we look to the objects of each party, the analogy to our own politics seems to be lost, if not actually reversed; the French appear to have used their democratic arms for conservative purposes, rather than those of liberal and enlightened movement; and the sympathies of the friends of reform are naturally enlisted on the side of sound amelioration which the English minority in vain attempted to introduce into the antiquated laws of the Province. . .

(Lucas, *Lord Durham's Report*, II, 14-16, 21-22)

~ An article in the *Spectator* in 1849 looked back to the events of the late thirties and expressed what had long become the accepted explanation of the contrasting causes of rebellion in Upper and Lower Canada.~

. . . Nearly twelve years ago, there were two rebellions in Canada. The colony was at that time divided into two Provinces, under perfectly distinct Governments. The two rebellions were simultaneous, and so far alike that both were directed to the overthrow of the Imperial power of Britain; but in other respects, they were as distinct as the two local Governments against which they were immediately directed. . . . The population of Upper Canada was exclusively English; that is, composed of people speaking the English language, whether they were of English, Scotch, Irish, or American extraction. In Upper Canada, there was no question of nationality or race. In Lower Canada, on the contrary, the great bulk of the people . . . consisted of French Canadians; that is, people of French origin, speaking the French language, and as different in point of race or nationality from the small number of English colonists as are the inhabitants of Calais from those of Dover.

Lord Durham's ample description of the antagonism of races in Lower Canada, and his representation that this was the cause of the rebellion in that Province, have never been contradicted, and may be taken as settled truths. In Lower Canada, the whole French population (the exceptions were so few as to be of no importance) sympathized with the actual rebels; and the actual outbreaks of rebellion were only put down by the Imperial army, with the aid of volunteers drawn from the small English population of the Province, which, with exceptions too insignificant for notice, took part in upholding the Imperial power. The rebellion in Lower Canada was a civil war of races as well as a rebellion against the Government; and in this war those who were rebels in act and at heart composed the great majority of the people, so that only a small minority sided with established authority... In Upper Canada, on the contrary, although the Provincial Government was very generally unpopular, and those who were called Reformers constituted probably a considerable majority of the people, it was only a very small minority that actually rebelled, or that ever contemplated rebellion, against the Imperial power. The actual outbreak of a small portion of this small minority created a general fever of loyalty in Upper Canada: the rebellion was crushed by the colonists themselves without the aid of Imperial troops. . . .

(*Spectator*, 31 March 1849)

3 / PARLIAMENT DEBATES THE CRISIS

~ In addition to the discussion concerning the causes of rebellion, Englishmen debated the relative merits of coercion and conciliation as the proper and most effective basis of the ministry's policy for handling the Canadian crisis, and speculated on the probable consequences of events for the future of the imperial connection in North America. Debates in parliament indicate that the possibility of maintaining British authority in the colonies on some basis other than that of military force was not confidently entertained by many contemporaries. The Colonial Reformers were ardent advocates of conciliation and strong sympathizers of Canadian aspirations. Largely for this reason they were not confident of the wisdom or the practicability of preserving British rule in North America. Indeed, the most striking characteristic of their speeches in the House of Commons was their prediction of separation as the most probable outcome of the struggle. As the following extracts from speeches by Molesworth, Warburton, and Grote clearly demonstrate, the Colonial Reformers in the winter of 1837-8 were spokesmen of separation.~

. . . Now, what course did her Majesty's Ministers intend to pursue? It seemed to him that they could prudently and wisely adopt but two courses. They ought either to attempt to conciliate the Canadians by acquiescing in all the demands of the House of Assembly, which were not inconsistent with the connexion of the two countries; they ought to grant an elective Legislative Council, and by these and similar measures they might prolong for some time the dominion of this country over Canada; the other and perhaps wiser course would be now to propose a separation of the two countries, as the mass of the Canadian people no longer desired the dominion of this country; and when the greatest portion of the population of a colony felt dissatisfied with the authority of the mother country, then it appeared to him that the period was arrived when a friendly separation would be beneficial to the interests of both countries. These were the only alternatives which could be beneficially adopted – the remaining alternative, the one which he feared Ministers intended to pursue was to adhere to their past policy, and to assert the supremacy of this country over Canada without redressing the grievances of the Canadian people. The inevitable result of such a course would be a civil war. . . . That that dominion [over Canada] should now be brought to a conclusion I, for one, most sincerely desire, but I desire it should terminate in peace and friendship, leaving behind it the memory of past kindnesses and mutual benefits, paving the way to new and more intimate connexions, arising from commercial intercourse and the opening of new channels of beneficial trade, leaving, therefore, to this country all the advantages of a vast and increasing market for our manufactures, without the burden, vexation, and expense of governing a remote region. Great would be the advantages of an amicable separation of the two countries, and great would be the honour this country would reap in consenting to such a separation. . . . I can hardly endure to look at the consequences of a forcible separation. The expenditure of blood and treasure, great as they would be, are not the greatest among the evils which such a war will engender; we must calculate the baneful prejudices, the odious antipathies, which it will produce amongst nations, whose mutual interest it is to cultivate kindly feelings towards one another. . . . I sincerely trust, that the people of this country are enlightened enough to forbid such a war, to disregard the prejudices in favour of extended dominion, and count as little the loss of a useless portion of their territories, when those territories can only be maintained by the infliction of such enormous evils. Should, however, a war take place, I must declare that I should more deplore success on the part of this country than defeat . . . if unhappily a war does ensue, may speedy victory crown the efforts of the Canadians, and may the curses and execrations of the indignant people of this empire alight upon the heads of those Ministers, who, by their misgovernment, ignorance, and imprudence, involve us in the calamities of civil discord, and expend our national resources in an unholy struggle against liberty.

(*Hansard*, XXXIX, 22 December 1837, 1464, 1466-7, [Molesworth])

. . . The remedy which he conceived would remove all disaffection in the colonies was to propose an amicable separation between the mother country and the colonies. He acknowledged that the mother country conferred the greatest possible boon on the colonies when in 1791 she gave them the benefit of popular representation. All the governors had counteracted the effects which might naturally be supposed to flow from popular government, and resisted all the attempts made by the colonists to obtain a full recognition of their liberties. . . . The impression that prevailed amongst the Canadians, that they had not obtained the advantages which usually arose out of popular representation, had led to all the unfortunate events which had taken place between the mother country and the colonies. Let them look to the petitions, not from Lower Canada, but from the whole of their North American colonies . . . and they would find that the people required not only popular representation, but what grew naturally out of it, a responsible executive. What he meant by a responsible executive was, that if there was a majority in the House of Assembly against that government, which was put over them by the colonial government at home, or if the course recommended by the administration at home was disapproved of by them, what they asked was power to dismiss the executive, and to place in their stead ministers who would act in conformity with the wishes of a majority of the inhabitants. . . . It was for this, that all the colonies in North America were now petitioning. But what said the Colonial Secretary? Why, that to make an executive responsible was incompatible with colonial government. Let the House attend to what appeared to him to be the measure by which all that affected the colonies according to their present system was regulated. It was not regulated by its utility as it affected the colonies, but by another rule and standard – by whether it was calculated to assert the superiority of the mother country over her colony or not. That was the standard by which every measure was now to be judged. He would say, therefore, that it was not to be wondered at that extensive disaffection and dissatisfaction should prevail in their colonies, and it must continue to be so until they gave them the benefits of responsible government. In his opinion, by a large and liberal concession at the present moment . . . a reconciliation would take place between the colony and the mother country. But if, on the contrary, they determined not only to restore, but permanently to retain their authority in these colonies, then, in his opinion, no measures that could be proposed would be likely to bring about a lasting reconciliation. . . . When he said, "Emancipate your colonies," he did not mean that this course should be adopted in a hasty or partial manner, but that we ought maturely to consider by what steps we might make that emancipation comprehensive, and include not only Lower Canada, but all the American colonies at the same time . . . it was said, "the time is not yet come for such a change; the Canadians do not themselves wish for it; and so far from having any desire to part from the mother country, they are warmly attached to it." Was it their intention, then, to delay emancipation until disaffection proved the real wants of the Canadians? Was it not, on the contrary, most desirable to bring about this change whilst a good feeling towards the mother country still existed? Why not yield to policy and justice what would be forced in the end by extensive disaffection. . . .

(*Hansard*, XL, 25 January 1838, 477-8, 480, [Warburton])

. . . Although he admitted that in the present circumstances the question of union, or separation between the mother country and the colony, was accompanied with difficulties peculiar to the time, yet he maintained that the British Legislature must not fear or even delay to face the evils of which it had itself been the cause. After matters had come to such a pass as that in which they now stood in Canada, how could the British Legislature hope to govern the colony except by superiority of force – how could it ever hope that its occupation of the country should be other than one of continual disturbance, revolting to the feelings of those who had to keep it, and absolutely intolerable to those who had to submit to it. Surely the material advantages, in point of wealth and commerce, must be great indeed if they could be worth purchasing at the cost of eternal coercion and an unceasing struggle to put down the feelings of the great mass of the Canadian people . . . he implored the House to allow the present disturbances of Canada to serve as a warning for the future, and instead of indulging at all times, when the rights and interests of the colony were discussed, in a tone of triumph at the superior power of England, to allow a little space for conciliation and justice, and to deal with the Canadians as they would with men who, though freemen like themselves, were still desirous of remaining, if they could do so with honour, in connexion with England as the mother country.

(*Hansard*, XXXIX, 22 December 1837, 1484-5, [Grote])

~ The only parliamentary criticism of Whig policy on the Canadian crisis came from the Colonial Reformers, and it was generally agreed that even they had not spoken or acted very effectively. The *Spectator* unsparingly criticized their performance over the bill to suspend the Canadian constitution, and argued that the whole way in which the issue had been handled in parliament proved once again the basic ignorance and indifference of members to colonial questions.~

. . . The debate of the Commons was flat and poor. Lord John Russell spoke in a mode that may have been deemed defunct – the "bow-wow" Tory style of the last French war. He delivered commonplaces and claptraps *ore rotundo*, with an air of insolent triumph, like one who expected thundering cheers at the close of every sentence. Great must have been his disappointment; for the reception was cold – the applause scanty and faint. . . . The Whig Leader of the House of Commons again condescended to become the "utensil" of the Colonial Office. Instead of an impartial and comprehensive statement of the whole case, he aimed at proving that Canada had no grievance; that the Government had acted with uniform justice and discretion – the Assembly like a pack of rogues. . . .

Sir Robert Peel dextrously kept clear of the Durham nomination [as High Commissioner in Canada], announced in the House for effect. He contented himself with some easy hits at Mr. Hume, and a prosy proof that Ministers ought to have brought down a message from the Queen, instead of asking Parliament to find a case in a bundle of papers thrown upon the table. . . .

Replete as it was with gross misrepresentations, defective

as an exposition of the Government plan, and reprehensible for its braggart and insolent tone, Lord John Russell's speech received nothing that could be called a *reply* from the Radicals. Mr. Hume, indeed, spoke two or three columns about and about the subject. Mr. Grote only touched upon portions of it, though what he did say was impressive and to the point. Mr. Leader asked for delay, like one who felt that he required it for a rally. Mr. Charles Buller disported on *both* sides. Altogether the Radicals were tame. Indeed, as Mr. Grote remarked, the loss of Mr. Roebuck was sensibly felt; for there was nobody in the House capable of dealing with the question as a whole – it was nobody's business to approach the discussion with a complete mastery of the subject. This, be it observed, is the confession of one of the best-instructed Members of the House of Commons, himself evincing both competent knowledge and conscientious zeal. It illustrates forcibly the fitness of the British Parliament to legislate for distant colonies. . . .

In the supplementary debate, on the motion for bringing in the bill, Mr. Warburton delivered, in a very calm tone, a philosophic and statesmanlike argument in favour of the early separation of the province from the mother country. He addressed an assembly deaf to reason, and proud of its ignorance and contempt of enlarged views of policy. . . .

(*Spectator*, 20 January 1838)

4 / RECEPTION OF THE DURHAM REPORT

~ The course of events relating to the despatch and conduct of Lord Durham's short mission to British North America in 1838 and the circumstances of his resignation are too well known to require elaboration here. The subsequent publication of his *Report* in February, 1839, was greeted with public acclamation by Englishmen of liberal sympathies. In no quarter were the merits of its analysis and recommendations more enthusiastically championed than among the Colonial Reformers, as the following comments from the *Spectator* and the *Colonial Gazette* clearly show.~

LORD DURHAM'S REPORT ON THE AFFAIRS OF BRITISH NORTH AMERICA is, without any exception, the most interesting state-paper that we ever saw; and will prove, we venture to predict, scarcely less important in its consequences.

The High Commissioner sets out by describing the contest between the French and English races in Lower Canada, their utter incompatibility of character, and their implacable hatred of each other. All this is told so simply, so forcibly, and with such a perfect air of truth, as to leave hardly a doubt of the Reporter's accuracy. He then gives an account of the long struggle between the House of Assembly and the Executive Government. This part of the Report, inasmuch as it passes over with slight notice the stale points which may be termed symptoms of a deep-seated disease, and probes the rotten system to the marrow, is as interesting as if the subject were wholly new. The complicated distractions of Upper Canada are there fully examined, and their causes for the first time made intelligible. The state of the Eastern Provinces is slightly, but sufficiently noticed. Then comes a relation of "evils still unremedied, grievances unredressed, and abuses unreformed at this hour," in all the Colonies, which excite at once indignation and shame. The concluding portion of the Report is occupied with the consideration and suggestion of remedial measures.

It would be a vain attempt, in such space as we can command, to convey to our readers any just impression of the state of affairs which is revealed by this Report. Lord Durham was perfectly warranted in saying at Exeter, that he should make "disclosures of which the Parliament and people of England had no conception." Such excessive, such constant, persevering, obstinate misrule, was never yet brought home to the government of a free people. The Report is one continued censure of the system and practice of our Colonial Government: and this occurs without any apparent design; growing, as it were, naturally out of the circumstances described, and depending far less on argument than on the force of an accumulation of naked facts.

The inherent vice of the system, and the shameful practices to which it has given occasion in all the North American Colonies, are equally placed before us, and in a light so clear that it may be termed glaring. The English reader will for the first time comprehend the question of "hostile races" in Lower Canada. He will learn also, more thoroughly than it has ever been taught by any advocate of the Canadian majority here, what share the irresponsibility of Government has had in the calamities of that province and in the miseries of Upper Canada. It is not too much to say that this Report will teach the best-informed, and stimulate the most indifferent, and convince all those who are open to conviction.

Lord Durham appears to have placed himself from the outset above all parties, factions, and cabals – to have inquired of everybody, and been under the influence of none. His Report is eminently distinguished by the absence of all petty provincial partialities, and by evidence of a desire and a capacity to learn and tell the whole truth without fear or favour. He flatters nobody, – neither the French Canadians nor their English antagonists, neither the Tories nor the Reformers in Upper Canada, nor the officials nor the populace, – nor even the Americans, of whom, nevertheless, and of their national characteristics and various institutions, he frequently speaks in terms of high admiration, when contrasting their condition with that of the disorganized and beggarly British Colonies.

His frank avowal of having arrived in these colonies not merely ignorant, but with very erroneous notions of their real condition, is of a piece with the manly candour which pervades the Report, and leaves a strong impression in his favour. One feels that he must have been sustained by a consciousness of integrity, and that opinions so expressed must be at least entirely sincere.

There is one feature of this Report which will give great offence in some quarters. People in the Colonial Office, and in all the offices, will complain that it is totally deficient in the proper official tone – of unmeaning vagueness and disguised lying. And that is very true. Lord Durham seems to know nothing of the *red-tape* style; he actually calls all things of which he speaks by their right names. . . . Just in proportion, however, as the Report is wanting in the heavy humbug which delights those whose world is "this office," will it be read, understood, and prized by the public. It is impossible to please everybody; and Lord Durham must try to console himself with the approbation of millions, for having incurred the pity of the underlings in Whitehall and Downing Street.

Speaking of millions, the Report should be as gratifying to the American people, as to the Colonists whom it most concerns. For the first time an eminent English statesman treats colonists with the respect which is due to a free people; concealing nothing from them, not attempting to delude them with vague generalities, but admitting and enforcing their just causes of complaint, proving their grievances, and insisting that *their* interests should be consulted by allowing them to manage their own local affairs in their own way. For the first time an eminent English statesman officially avows his respect for the Anglo-Saxon people of the United States, and honestly attributes their wonderful career of prosperity to the English principle of local self-government, which they inherited from their ancestors and ours. . . .

The remedial suggestions appear to us, so far as we can judge of them on a hasty examination, to be at once bold and moderate – sufficient for the purpose, but not involving more change than is required by the exigencies of the case. It is proposed to unite the two Canadas immediately, and all the other Colonies as soon as they may choose to form part of a general union. The French Canadians will thus, sure enough, be "swamped," but not by a *minority*, as others have proposed: they will be outnumbered by a great English majority. The case for a general union, and the necessity of placing the French Canadians in a minority, are treated with a masterly grasp of both subjects. But a perfect equality of rights for this unhappy people is strongly insisted on. . . .

. . . it may be said that the whole of Lord Durham's suggestions are founded on one principle, which has hitherto been utterly violated in these colonies – that of *government responsible to the governed*. Almost from the beginning to the end of the Report, the principle of responsible government is constantly, earnestly, and often most eloquently asserted. And yet in the proposal of means for attaining this end, it is obvious that Lord Durham has carefully observed the greatest moderation – as if he knew how distasteful it would be to many here to bestow good government on any colony. His plans would be adopted by acclamation, if all parties here really desired the wellbeing of the Colonies. We have but little hope of seeing them carried into effect. Not to mention the utter incapacity of Lord Glenelg for giving effect to such wise and vigorous conceptions – not to dwell on the crotchetiness and obstinacy of Lord Howick, who has long been Colonial Minister *in the Cabinet* – not to forebode ill from the Premier's swaggering indifference to every subject that does not involve the loss of his place at the Queen's side – we are of opinion that the aristocracy of this country, now all-powerful in both Houses of Parliament, will never give their consent to measures which, immediately as respects British North America, and before long by the influence of good example in other colonies, would deprive that class of an immense amount of patronage which they ought never to have enjoyed. . . .

It is an ill wind, however, that blows no good. Lord Durham's Report will be a most valuable text-book for Colonial Reformers in time to come and in various parts of the world. It has laid down in the clearest and most convincing manner the principles of good government for colonies, and has sapped the very foundation of our wretched Colonial system. It has made the

misgovernment of our Colonies in North America impossible
for any length of time. They cannot long endure abuses and
grievances, of which the origin and permanent causes have been
so unmercifully laid bare. If we will not govern them well, they
will surely govern themselves without our assistance. . . .
(*Spectator*, 9 February 1839)

Lord Durham's report on the affairs of British North
America, which has now been presented by her Majesty's
command to both Houses of Parliament, deserves and has met
with a degree of attention, on the part of the public, greater,
perhaps, than has been given to any other state-paper of modern
times. Some part of the interest which it has excited is probably
ascribable to the peculiar circumstances under which it has been
produced: to the position in which his Lordship now stands
relatively to the Government, and to the uncertainty in which
the consequent proceedings of the Legislature, in regard to
Colonial disputes, are shrouded. To whatever cause the public
interest in this most valuable document is to be ascribed, we
hail it with the greatest satisfaction, fully convinced that an
attentive perusal of the report, and the general conviction that
cannot fail to follow from that perusal, of the gross misgovernment to which our North American Colonies, and especially the
Canadas, have long been subjected, must produce a powerful
effect upon Parliament, and lead to a more effectual consideration of the subject of our Colonial policy generally, than it
might otherwise receive, pressed upon as the Legislature is, by
matters of nearer, though assuredly not of more vital interest.
Hitherto all questions of Colonial policy have been discussed
in Parliament, in the absence of the necessary information, and
with a view to their bearing upon party views and objects. It was,
therefore, greatly to be feared, lest under the peculiar circumstances in which the consideration of the Canadian troubles
must be entered upon, in the present Session, no departure
from the usual course would have been visible. The perusal of
Lord Durham's masterly report, and the degree of attention
which it has commanded, have done much to relieve us from
this apprehension. The spirit in which that report is conceived,
and the facts by which its reasonings and suggestions are
supported, are of a nature, when known, to overbear all party
considerations, to call into action the purest feelings of patriot-
ism, and to induce all whose voices can influence the result, to
lend their aid towards rendering justice to our fellow-subjects,
in the Colonies, on the one hand, and towards securing their

permanent connection with the British empire on the other. . . .
(*Colonial Gazette*, 16 February 1839)

5 / UNION OF THE CANADAS
AND THE FRENCH-CANADIAN QUESTION

~ One of the major recommendations of the Durham *Report*
concerned the legislative union of Upper and Lower Canada.
While substantial commercial advantages were expected to
accrue from the union, the *Colonial Gazette* regarded it as the
essential prerequisite for resolving both constitutional and racial
conflicts.~

. . . The proposal for the amalgamation of the provinces is,
after all, the question which will excite the greatest attention,
and which will be either the most warmly supported, or the
most strenuously opposed, according to the views or supposed
interests of individuals. We have always been of opinion that
the separation of the Upper from the Lower Province of Canada
was an impolitic measure. The interests, both material and
political, of the two divisions, are wholly identical. If no other
consideration had presented itself to prevent the severance, the
fact of the sole means of communication with the mother-
country and the rest of the world, which cannot be closed
against the Upper Canadians, being through the lower province,
should alone have been sufficient to that end. The St. Lawrence,
with its chain of lakes, the great commercial high road of the
Canadas, requires improvement in order to the full development
of the powers and resources of the provinces, and this can never
be properly undertaken and accomplished while their public
revenues are disunited. It further appears quite evident from the
experience of the last few years, as well as from the facts newly
brought to light by Lord Durham's Report, that there is little
reason to hope for cordiality between the provincial parliament
of Lower Canada and the Government, so long as a majority
of its members shall be sent to represent the feelings and
peculiar interests of the French section of the people; and
there is no other method so simple and natural, and so little
liable to objection whereby that majority can be neutralised,
as the union of the two legislatures, or rather the election of
members from every district of Upper and Lower Canada, to
the same house of representatives. By such a course, the French
party would still exercise a great, though not an overwhelming
influence, while the surplus revenues of the Lower Province

would come in aid of the deficiency of the other, and would be employed for the prosecution of works essential to the social progress of both. . . .

(*Colonial Gazette*, 23 February 1839)

~ Lord Durham's *Report* and the comments of the Colonial Reformers generally on Canadian affairs are distinguished by an overt hostility to the existence of a French nationality in British North America. Durham not only attributed the political dissensions in Lower Canada to racial animosities, but he was clearly convinced of the inveterate backwardness and marked inferiority of the French in all spheres of economic and cultural endeavour. As a solution of present difficulties, he assumed that it was both possible and desirable to eliminate the racial conflict by assimilating the French Canadians in a larger political entity in which they would be swamped by a vigorous English majority. Such a policy was considered in the best interests of both French and English, but Lord Durham was particularly concerned to protect the rights of Englishmen living in the colonies and effectively preserve British North America as an area open for exploitation by settlers and capital from Britain.~

. . . A plan by which it is proposed to ensure the tranquil government of Lower Canada, must include in itself the means of putting an end to the agitation of national disputes in the legislature, by settling, at once and for ever, the national character of the Province. I entertain no doubts as to the national character which must be given to Lower Canada; it must be that of the British Empire; that of the majority of the population of British America; that of the great race which must, in the lapse of no long period of time, be predominant over the whole North American Continent. Without effecting the change so rapidly or so roughly as to shock the feelings and trample on the welfare of the existing generation, it must henceforth be the first and steady purpose of the British Government to establish an English population, with English laws and language, in this Province, and to trust its government to none but a decidedly English Legislature.

It may be said that this is a hard measure to a conquered people; that the French were originally the whole, and still are the bulk of the population of Lower Canada; that the English are new comers, who have no right to demand the extinction of the nationality of a people, among whom commercial enterprize has drawn them. . . . If the disputes of the two races are irreconcileable, it may be urged that justice demands that the minority should be compelled to acquiesce in the supremacy of the ancient and most numerous occupants of the Province, and not pretend to force their own institutions and customs on the majority.

But before deciding which of the two races is now to be placed in the ascendant, it is but prudent to inquire which of them must ultimately prevail; for it is not wise to establish to-day that which must, after a hard struggle, be reversed to-morrow. The pretensions of the French Canadians to the exclusive possession of Lower Canada, would debar the yet larger English population of Upper Canada and the Townships from access to the great natural channel of that trade which they alone have created, and now carry on. The possession of the mouth of the St. Lawrence concerns not only those who happen to have made their settlements along the narrow line which borders it, but all who now dwell, or will hereafter dwell, in the great basin of that river. For we must not look to the present alone. The question is, by what race is it likely that the wilderness which now covers the rich and ample regions surrounding the comparatively small and contracted districts in which the French Canadians are located, is eventually to be converted into a settled and flourishing country? . . . The whole interior of the British dominions must ere long, be filled with an English population, every year rapidly increasing its numerical superiority over the French. Is it just that the prosperity of this great majority, and of this vast tract of country, should be for ever, or even for a while, impeded by the artificial bar which the backward laws and civilization of a part, and a part only, of Lower Canada, would place between them and the ocean? Is it to be supposed that such an English population will ever submit to such a sacrifice of its interests?

I must not, however, assume it to be possible that the English Government shall adopt the course of placing or allowing any check to the influx of English immigration into Lower Canada, or any impediment to the profitable employment of that English capital which is already vested therein. The English have already in their hands the majority of the larger masses of property in the country; they have the decided superiority of intelligence on their side; they have the certainty that colonization must swell their numbers to a majority; and they belong to the race which wields the Imperial Government, and predominates on the American Continent. If we now leave them in a minority, they will never abandon the assurance of being a majority hereafter, and never cease to continue the present contest with all the fierceness with which it now rages. In such a contest they will rely on the sympathy of their countrymen at home; and if that is denied them, they feel very confident of being able to awaken the sympathy of their neighbours of kindred origin. They feel that if the British Government intends to maintain its hold of the Canadas, it can rely on the English population alone; that if it abandons its colonial possessions, they must become a portion of that great Union which will speedily send forth its swarms of settlers, and, by force of numbers and activity, quickly master every other race. The French Canadians, on the other hand, are but the remains of an ancient colonization, and are and ever must be isolated in the midst of an Anglo-Saxon world. Whatever may happen, whatever government shall be established over them, British or American, they can see no hope for their nationality. They can only sever themselves from the British Empire by waiting till some general cause of dissatisfaction alienates them, together with the surrounding colonies, and leaves them part of an English confederacy; or, if they are able, by effecting a separation singly, and so either merging in the American Union, or keeping up for a few years a wretched semblance of feeble independence, which would expose them more than ever to the intrusion of the surrounding population. I am far from wishing to encourage indiscriminately these pretensions to superiority on the part of any particular race; but while the greater part of every portion of the American Continent is still uncleared and unoccupied, and while the English exhibit such constant and marked activity in colonization, so long will it be idle to imagine that there is any portion of that Continent into which that race will not penetrate, or in which, when it has penetrated, it will not predominate. It is but a question of time and mode. . . .

And is this French Canadian nationality one which, for the good merely of that people, we ought to strive to perpetuate, even if it were possible? I know of no national distinctions marking and continuing a more hopeless inferiority. The language, the laws, the character of the North American Continent are English; and every race but the English (I apply this to all who speak the English language) appears there in a condition of inferiority. It is to elevate them from that inferiority that I desire to give to the Canadians our English character. I desire it for the sake of the educated classes, whom the distinction of language and manners keeps apart from the great Empire to which they belong. . . . A spirit of exclusion has closed the higher professions on the educated classes of the French Canadians, more, perhaps, than was absolutely necessary; but it is impossible for the utmost liberality on the part of the British Government to give an equal position in the general competition of its vast population to those who speak a foreign language. I desire the amalgamation still more for the sake of the humbler classes. Their present state of rude and equal plenty is fast deteriorating under the pressure of population in the narrow limits to which they are confined. If they attempt to better their condition, by extending themselves over the neighbouring country, they will necessarily get more and more mingled with an English population: if they prefer remaining stationary, the greater part of them must be labourers in the employ of English capitalists. In either case it would appear, that the great mass of the French Canadians are doomed, in some measure, to occupy an inferior position, and to be dependent on the English for employment. The evils of poverty and dependence would merely be aggravated in a ten-fold degree, by a spirit of jealous and resentful nationality, which should separate the working class of the community from the possessors of wealth and employers of labour. . . .

(Lucas, *Lord Durham's Report*, II, 288-93)

~ The *Colonial Gazette* was quite prepared to accept the cogency of this reasoning, and advocate union as the one practicable means of resolving the Canadian crisis.~

. . . That it will be unpalatable to the French party in the Lower Province is to be expected; and if there were any possible way of dealing with the subject, so as to leave that party independent of every other, and without committing injustice to the settlers of the Anglo-Saxon race within the province, we might feel inclined to adopt that alternative. But this is a course no longer open. It is impossible to insulate the *seigneurs* and *habitans*, or to withdraw English settlers from the country; and to restore the suspended constitution, under present circumstances, would be to give up the minority – the English party – to a repetition of the injustice formerly heaped upon them through the jealousy and ill-feeling of the majority, who are of French extraction. . . .

This insulation being impracticable, the next best course appears to us to be that which is proposed . . . the amalgamation of the French party with the English settlers in the Lower and

Upper Provinces, under such a scheme of representation as will preserve all parties from partiality and injustice, is, perhaps, the wisest plan that could now be devised for retaining the whole permanently in connection with the British Throne. . . .

(*Colonial Gazette*, 8 June 1839)

~ When the Colonial Reformers considered the possible effects of Canadian union on future imperial relations, they found little evidence to suggest that the measure would lead to the disruption of the empire by encouraging separation. On the contrary, the *Colonial Gazette* believed that the union and responsible government would together tend to strengthen imperial ties.~

. . . The opponents of the Union assure us that that measure will presently lead to a separation between Canada and the Mother-country. They see that Canada has now the power to separate if she pleases: but why take for granted that she will use that power for that purpose? They do so because they assume that the United Province will be governed as each of the two has been, upon the mixed system of representation without executive responsibility, and that the verging-on-revolution state thus produced will render the colony discontented. We entirely agree with them, as they indeed agree with Lord Durham, but only on their own assumption, that from United Canada, no longer torn to pieces by a contest of races, executive responsibility to the local Parliament will be withheld. Lord Durham not merely said, but elaborately argued, that if the executive government of United Canada were not carried on in a manner and by persons agreeable to the representative body, the colony would be always in a revolutionary state and apt for separation. There can be no doubt of it. The condition upon which alone the Union can work well for the Imperial connexion, is as plain as the certainty that if that condition be withheld the Union will be a step to separation. . . . Verily there is now no choice but between separation and Responsible Government. This at least is an obvious consequence of the Canada Union; and hence the vast importance of that measure to Colonies in general. . . .

(*Colonial Gazette*, 12 August 1840)

PART SIX:
RESPONSIBLE GOVERNMENT IN THEORY AND PRACTICE

1 / THE DEFECTS OF REPRESENTATIVE GOVERNMENT

~ The Colonial Reformers are renowned for their advocacy of responsible government for colonies. If local executives were made responsible for their actions and policies to the popular voice in the assemblies, the Reformers argued that this would eliminate the major defects in the existing form of colonial government and resolve the constitutional controversies that wracked all the colonies of British North America. The operation in the Canadas since 1791 of representative institutions unaccompanied by responsible ministries might be regarded as a necessary intermediate stage in the gradual evolution of popular liberties and constitutional government overseas, but experience in the 1830's conclusively demonstrated that a further advance in accordance with British precedents was long overdue. The thoroughly unsatisfactory operation of representative government in the Canadas was most incisively exposed by Lord Durham in his *Report.* ~

. . . It is impossible to observe the great similarity of the constitutions established in all our North American Provinces, and the striking tendency of all to terminate in pretty nearly the same result, without entertaining a belief that some defect in the form of government, and some erroneous principle of administration, have been common to all; the hostility of the races being palpably insufficient to account for all the evils which have affected Lower Canada, inasmuch as nearly the same results have been exhibited among the homogeneous population of the other provinces. . . . It may fairly be said, that the natural state of government in all these Colonies is that of collision between the executive and the representative body. In all of them the administration of public affairs is habitually confided to those who do not co-operate harmoniously with the popular branch of the legislature; and the Government is constantly proposing measures which the majority of the Assembly reject, and refusing its assent to bills which that body has passed.

A state of things, so different from the working of any successful experiment of representative government, appears to indicate a deviation from sound constitutional principles or practice . . . when we examine into the system of government in these colonies, it would almost seem as if the object of those by whom it was established had been the combining of apparently popular institutions with an utter absence of all efficient control of the people over their rulers. . . .

It was not until some years after the commencement of the present century that the population of Lower Canada began to understand the representative system which had been extended to them, and that the Assembly evinced any inclination to make use of its powers. Immediately, however, upon its so doing, it found how limited those powers were, and entered upon a struggle to obtain the authority which analogy pointed out as inherent in a representative assembly . . . the Government was induced, by its necessities, to accept the Assembly's offer to raise an additional revenue by fresh taxes; and the Assembly thus acquired a certain control over the levying and appropriation of a portion of the public revenue. From that time, until the final abandonment in 1832 [1831] of every portion of the reserved revenue, excepting the casual and territorial funds, an unceasing contest was carried on, in which the Assembly, making use of every power which it gained, for the purpose of gaining more, acquired, step by step, an entire control over the whole revenue of the country.

. . . A substantial cause of contest yet remained. The Assembly, after it had obtained entire control over the public revenues, still found itself deprived of all voice in the choice or even designation of the persons in whose administration of affairs it could feel confidence. All the administrative power of Government remained entirely free from its influence; and . . . I must attribute the refusal of a civil list to the determination of the Assembly not to give up its only means of subjecting the functionaries of Government to any responsibility.

The powers for which the Assembly contended, appear in both instances to be such as it was perfectly justified in demanding. It is difficult to conceive what could have been their theory of government who imagined that in any colony of England a body invested with the name and character of a representative Assembly, could be deprived of any of those powers which, in the opinion of Englishmen, are inherent in a popular legislature. It was a vain delusion to imagine that by mere limitations in the Constitutional Act, or an exclusive system of government, a body, strong in the consciousness of wielding the public opinion of the majority, could regard certain portions of the provincial revenues as sacred from its control, could confine itself to the mere business of making laws, and look on as a passive or indifferent spectator, while those laws were carried into effect or evaded, and the whole business of the country was conducted by men, in whose intentions or capacity it had not the slightest confidence. Yet such was the limitation placed on the authority of the Assembly of Lower Canada; it might refuse or pass laws, vote or withhold supplies, but it could exercise no influence on the nomination of a single servant of the Crown. The Executive Council, the law officers, and whatever heads of departments are known to the administrative system of the Province, were placed in power, without any regard to the wishes of the people or their representatives; nor indeed are there wanting instances in which a mere hostility to the majority of the Assembly elevated the most incompetent persons to posts of honour and trust. However decidedly the Assembly might condemn the policy of the Government, the persons who had advised that policy, retained their offices and their power of giving bad advice. . . . The wisdom of adopting the true principle of representative government and facilitating the management of public affairs, by entrusting it to the persons who have the confidence of the representative body, has never been recognized in the government of the North American Colonies. . . .

A body of holders of office thus constituted, without reference to the people or their representatives, must in fact, from the very nature of colonial government, acquire the entire direction of the affairs of the Province. A Governor, arriving in a colony in which he almost invariably has had no previous acquaintance with the state of parties, or the character of individuals, is compelled to throw himself almost entirely upon those whom he finds placed in the position of his official advisers. His first acts must necessarily be performed, and his first appointments made, at their suggestion. And as these first acts and appointments give a character to his policy, he is generally brought thereby into immediate collision with the other parties in the country, and thrown into more complete dependence upon the official party and its friends. Thus, a Governor of Lower Canada has almost always been brought into collision with the Assembly, which his advisers regard as their enemy. In the course of the contest in which he was thus involved, the provocations which he received from the Assembly, and the light in which their conduct was represented by those who alone had any access to him, naturally imbued him with many of their antipathies; his position compelled him to seek the support of some party against the Assembly; and his feelings and his necessities thus combined to induce him to bestow his patronage and to shape his measures to promote the interests of the party on which he was obliged to lean. Thus, every successive year consolidated and enlarged the strength of the ruling party. Fortified by family connexion, and the common interest felt by all who held, and all who desired, subordinate offices, that party was thus erected into a solid and permanent power, controlled by no responsibility, subject to no serious change, exercising over the whole government of the Province an authority utterly independent of the people and its representatives, and possessing the only means of influencing either the Government at home, or the colonial representative of the Crown.

This entire separation of the legislative and executive powers of a State, is the natural error of governments desirous of being free from the check of representative institutions. Since the Revolution of 1688, the stability of the English constitution has been secured by that wise principle of our Government which has vested the direction of the national policy, and the distribution of patronage, in the leaders of the Parliamentary majority. However partial the Monarch might be to particular ministers, or however he might have personally committed himself to their policy, he has invariably been constrained to abandon both, as soon as the opinion of the people has been irrevocably pronounced against them through the medium of the House of Commons. . . . It is difficult to understand how any English statesman could have imagined that representative and irresponsible government could be successfully combined. There seems, indeed, to be an idea, that the character of representative institutions ought to be thus modified in colonies; that it is an incident of colonial dependence that the officers of government should be nominated by the Crown, without any reference to the wishes of the community, whose interests are entrusted to their keeping. It has never been very clearly explained what are the imperial interests, which require this complete nullification of representative government. But if there be such a necessity, it is quite clear that a representative government in a colony must be a mockery, and a source of confusion. For those who support this system have never yet been able to devise, or to exhibit in the practical working of colonial government, any means for making so complete an abrogation of political influence palatable to the representative body. . . . Yet such was the system, such literally was the course of events in Lower Canada, and such in character, though not quite in degree, was the spectacle exhibited in Upper Canada, and, at one time or another, in every one of the North American Colonies. To suppose that such a system would work well there, implies a belief that the French Canadians have enjoyed representative institutions for half a century, without acquiring any of the characteristics of a free people; that Englishmen renounce every political opinion and feeling when they enter a colony, or that the spirit of Anglo-Saxon freedom is utterly changed and weakened among those who are transplanted across the Atlantic. . . .

It was an unhappy consequence of the system which I have been describing, that it relieved the popular leaders of all the responsibilities of opposition. A member of opposition in this country acts and speaks with the contingency of becoming a minister constantly before his eyes, and he feels, therefore, the necessity of proposing no course, and of asserting no principles, on which he would not be prepared to conduct the Government, if he were immediately offered it. But the colonial demagogue bids high for popularity without the fear of future exposure. Hopelessly excluded from power, he expresses the wildest opinions, and appeals to the most mischievous passions of the people, without any apprehension of having his sincerity or prudence hereafter tested, by being placed in a position to carry his views into effect; and thus the prominent places in the ranks of opposition are occupied for the most part by men of strong passions, and merely declamatory powers, who think but little of reforming the abuses which serve them as topics for exciting discontent.

The collision with the executive government necessarily brought on one with the Legislative Council. The composition of this body, which has been so much the subject of discussion both here and in the Colony, must certainly be admitted to have been such as could give it no weight with the people, or with the representative body, on which it was meant to be a check. The majority was always composed of members of the party which conducted the executive government . . . the Legislative Council was practically hardly any thing but a veto in the hands of public functionaries on all the acts of that popular branch of the legislature in which they were always in a minority. This veto they used without much scruple. I am far from concurring in the censure which the Assembly and its advocates have attempted to cast on the acts of the Legislative Council. I have no hesitation in saying that many of the Bills which it is most severely blamed for rejecting, were Bills which it could not have passed without a dereliction of its duty to the constitution, the connexion with Great Britain, and the whole English population of the Colony. . . . But the Legislative Council was neither theoretically unobjectionable, nor personally esteemed by the Assembly; its opposition appeared to that body but another form of official hostility, and it was inevitable that the Assembly should, sooner or later, make those assaults on the constitution of the Legislative Council which, by the singular want of judgment and temper with which they were conducted, ended in the destruction of the Provincial Constitution.

From the commencement, therefore, to the end of the disputes which mark the whole Parliamentary history of Lower Canada, I look on the conduct of the Assembly as a constant warfare with the executive, for the purpose of obtaining the powers inherent in a representative body by the very nature of representative government. It was to accomplish this purpose, that it used every means in its power; but it must be censured for having, in pursuit of this object, perverted its powers of legislation, and disturbed the whole working of the constitution. It made the business of legislation, and the practical improvement of the country, subordinate to its struggle for power; and, being denied its legitimate privileges, it endeavoured to extend its authority in modes totally incompatible with the principles of constitutional liberty. . . .

(Lucas, *Lord Durham's Report*, II, 72-84)

~ In a debate on the government of Lower Canada in July, 1839, Buller emphasized the similarity of the constitutional conflict in all the North American colonies, which indicated a fundamental defect in the existing system of colonial government.~

. . . He well knew the difficulty which must be experienced in securing the assent of a Government to so entire a change of its whole policy as that which Lord Durham had proposed in the system of colonial government; but he could not understand how any one could cast his mind over the recent history of our colonies, or advert to their present deplorable state in every thing that respects their government, without coming to the conclusion, that in our whole colonial system there is some radical vice requiring vigorous and searching correction. The system of governing the colonies from home had had a long trial in the North American provinces, and proceeding on the principle of combining an irresponsible executive with a representative legislative, how had it practically worked in them all? He said all: for, in truth, the evils to which he had now to apply a remedy were not to be found in the Canadas alone. In every colony of British North America there was the same constant collision between the Assembly and the Executive Government; and in all the catastrophe of an absolute stoppage of the machine of government either had arrived or was fast approaching. In the case of Lower Canada, the blame was laid on the perverseness of the French . . . he dared say that in the other provinces there were some persons, whom the officials represented as few in numbers, and singularly perverse in purpose, to whose causeless malignity they attributed the constant collision between the different powers of Government. But when they took all those phenomena together − when they saw exhibited in every one of these colonies the same practical difficulties in the working of the present system, were they not forced to conclude, that there must be some common cause for these common ills, and that that cause must exist in the very frame of Government, which was everywhere out of order? . . . This was the error which he would rectify, by establishing an entirely different practice in our colonial government; by proposing it as a rule of government, that the executive of the colony should be kept in entire harmony with the legislature; that the system of constant interference with the details of colonial affairs should be abandoned; and that the colonial government should, in fact, be carried on in the colony, and not in Downing Street. The change proposed was a great one, but it was a simple one; it would, at any rate, render colonial government a much simpler and easier thing than it had yet been. He should like to have it explained to him how, under any other system, it was supposed possible to have any harmony between the different branches of the legislature, or any efficiency in the Government. . . .

(*Hansard*, XLIX, 11 July 1839, 182-4)

2 / THE MEANING OF RESPONSIBLE GOVERNMENT

~ There was considerable debate amongst contemporaries concerning the precise meaning of responsible government and the feasibility of introducing and operating such a system in a colonial dependency where the governor was still considered necessarily accountable for his actions to the authorities in London. It is important to emphasize that the comments of the Reformers show that under a system of responsible government they expected the governor as head of the executive to play

an active role in the colonial politics. He would not only
determine the changing composition of the ministry in accord
with the considered views of the legislature, but would also
act as the leader of the administration and in effect as his own
prime minister. In the event, however, especially with the
development of distinct political parties, a positive role for the
governor was found to be incompatible with the working of
true responsible government, and, like the crown in England,
the colonial governor would have to move out of active politics
and become the nominal head of the executive.

That such a development was not clearly apparent to the
Colonial Reformers or their contemporaries is hardly surprising. Even in the late 1830's Englishmen did not fully realize
the extent to which the crown in Britain itself had already
passed out of party politics and to which its freedom of action
and initiative as head of the executive had been circumscribed
by the politicians. Moreover, insofar as the Reformers may
have foreseen this development in England, it is certain that
they would have been no more prepared than British statesmen
generally to admit the necessity or advisability of encouraging
the same process in the colonies. While the Reformers cannot
be criticized for their failure to predict the drift of events, it
is clear that the misgivings entertained by Lord John Russell
and others concerning the feasibility of responsible government
as a theory of colonial administration were understandable and
not unreasonable. Although the Colonial Reformers were therefore as uncertain about the true nature and practical operation
of responsible government as were its critics, they considered
it perfectly compatible with colonial status and were at pains
to point out how misguided were popular objections to the
system on this score. Again, the debate effectively began with
Lord Durham's *Report*. ~

. . . It is not by weakening, but strengthening the influence
of the people on its Government; by confining within much
narrower bounds than those hitherto allotted to it, and not by
extending the interference of the imperial authorities in the
details of colonial affairs, that I believe that harmony is to be
restored, where dissension has so long prevailed; and a regularity
and vigour hitherto unknown, introduced into the administration of these Provinces. It needs no change in the principles of
government, no invention of a new constitutional theory, to
supply the remedy which would, in my opinion, completely
remove the existing political disorders. It needs but to follow

out consistently the principles of the British constitution, and introduce into the Government of these great Colonies those wise provisions, by which alone the working of the representative system can in any country be rendered harmonious and efficient. We are not now to consider the policy of establishing representative government in the North American Colonies. That has been irrevocably done; and the experiment of depriving the people of their present constitutional power, is not to be thought of. To conduct their Government harmoniously, in accordance with its established principles, is now the business of its rulers; and I know not how it is possible to secure that harmony in any other way, than by administering the Government on those principles which have been found perfectly efficacious in Great Britain. I would not impair a single prerogative of the Crown; on the contrary, I believe that the interests of the people of these Colonies require the protection of prerogatives, which have not hitherto been exercised. But the Crown must, on the other hand, submit to the necessary consequences of representative institutions; and if it has to carry on the Government in unison with a representative body, it must consent to carry it on by means of those in whom that representative body has confidence.

In England, this principle has been so long considered an indisputable and essential part of our constitution, that it has really hardly ever been found necessary to inquire into the means by which its observance is enforced. When a ministry ceases to command a majority in Parliament on great questions of policy, its doom is immediately sealed; and it would appear to us as strange to attempt, for any time, to carry on a Government by means of ministers perpetually in a minority, as it would be to pass laws with a majority of votes against them. The ancient constitutional remedies, by impeachment and a stoppage of the supplies, have never, since the reign of William III, been brought into operation for the purpose of removing a ministry. They have never been called for, because, in fact, it has been the habit of ministers rather to anticipate the occurrence of an absolutely hostile vote, and to retire, when supported only a bare and uncertain majority. If Colonial Legislatures have frequently stopped the supplies, if they have harassed public servants by unjust or harsh impeachments, it was because the removal of an unpopular administration could not be effected in the Colonies by those milder indications of a want of confidence, which have always sufficed to attain the end in the mother country.

. . . Every purpose of popular control might be combine
with every advantage of vesting the immediate choice of advise:
in the Crown, were the Colonial Governor to be instructed t
secure the co-operation of the Assembly in his policy, b;
entrusting its administration to such men as could command a
majority; and if he were given to understand that he need
count on no aid from home in any difference with the Assembly,
that should not directly involve the relations between the mother
country and the Colony. This change might be effected by a
single dispatch containing such instructions; or if any legal
enactment were requisite, it would only be one that would render
it necessary that the official acts of the Governor should be
countersigned by some public functionary. This would induce
responsibility for every act of the Government, and, as a natural
consequence, it would necessitate the substitution of a system
of administration, by means of competent heads of departments,
for the present rude machinery of an executive council. The
Governor, if he wished to retain advisers not possessing the
confidence of the existing Assembly, might rely on the effect of
an appeal to the people, and, if unsuccessful, he might be
coerced by a refusal of supplies, or his advisers might be
terrified by the prospect of impeachment. But there can be no
reason for apprehending that either party would enter on a
contest, when each would find its interest in the maintenance
of harmony; and the abuse of the powers which each would
constitutionally possess, would cease when the struggle for
larger powers became unnecessary. Nor can I conceive that it
would be found impossible or difficult to conduct a Colonial
Government with precisely that limitation of the respective
powers which has been so long and so easily maintained in
Great Britain. . . .

(Lucas, *Lord Durham's Report*, II, 277-80)

~ In December 1839 the *Colonial Gazette* examined the valid-
ity of the objections advanced by the critics of responsible
government for colonies.~

. . . *For what purpose* is representation given? what is it
object? It has no other object, it can have no other, than to give
the people a control over that alone which ultimately affects
them – their executive government. Popular representatives do
not meet for the purpose of merely talking and passing resolutions or bills: they are elected as the organs of the people for
the purpose of rendering the whole of government constantly

greeable to the people. This is the use of an Assembly. We create the power, but forbid its use. The certain consequence is an abuse of the power. The Assembly, prevented from performing the function for which it was created – deprived of control over the ultimate results of government – becomes a revolutionary body, and does little or nothing but violently assail the Executive which it would have found wholesome occupation in directing. The Executive returns blow for blow, until, thoroughly beaten, and then calls out for help from the Mother-country. Such is the history, past, present, and future, of every Colonial Government in which the principles of Representation and Executive Irresponsibility are placed in permanent opposition to each other.

This gross absurdity is acknowledged by some, who nevertheless object to Executive Responsibility, on the ground that it is incompatible with the *dependent* condition of a colony: and the argument deserves examination in two points of view.

First, speaking theoretically, there can be no doubt that a colony which wholly regulates its own affairs is locally independent. The New England Colonies were so, as are Guernsey and Jersey. But if this sort of independence is objectionable, then the principle of representation should not be adopted in the government of colonies. If those affairs of the colony which are strictly of local interest ought not to be regulated by the colonists, this would be a conclusive reason against Colonial Assemblies. But by giving Assemblies we proclaim that the colonists ought to manage their own affairs. What then do we do when we deprive the Assembly of control over the Executive? We convert the gift into a mockery: our second proclamation, as it may be termed, contradicts the first, declaring that the colonies ought not to manage their own affairs. . . .

Practically, in the next place . . . in those colonies which have Representative Assemblies, the government is almost wholly carried on by a colonial body of officials; and the Home Government really determines next to nothing. Take Upper Canada for example. The Family Compact, which rules there, has been at open war with the present Government of this country for years. . . . It has constantly evaded or set at nought whatever orders from the Home Government were at variance with its independent, its almost sovereign pleasure. It has bird-limed and caged successive Governors, and used them for its own purposes. . . .

. . . Let us suppose that the responsibility were real – that it were possible, which it is not, to conduct the local affairs of a colony from so great a distance as Downing Street. To whom would the Government be responsible? . . . If to Parliament, that would be a mere sham, inasmuch as it is quite impossible that Parliament should attend to a hundredth part of the local business of one colony, much more of half a hundred colonies. If to the Crown, that means to the Secretary of State; whom we change once a year . . . whose appointment is nearly always made to suit the convenience of parties at home; who is a Cabinet Minister, perhaps leader of the House of Commons, deeply engaged with the care of his own position and the affairs of his party as an English politician. . . . To whom then would the Colonial Executives be responsible? – to the *permanent* Under-Secretary and his subordinates – to Mr. Stephen and his clerks – to the Family Compact of Downing Street.

We have pushed the argument to its absurdest extreme, and yet have not exaggerated the truth. "King Stephen" is the power to which sticklers for Colonial Responsibility to the Home Government would make the Colonial Executives responsible. His is the crown on which they say that colonies should be kept in a state of dependence. . . .

(*Colonial Gazette*, 4 December 1839)

~ The Colonial Reformers thus exposed the weaknesses in the arguments of their opponents, but it was also necessary to dispel some of the vagueness that surrounded the term "responsible government" in the minds of Englishmen. In his book, *Responsible Government for Colonies*, Buller sought to eliminate this confusion and demonstrate how the principle might be expected to operate in practice.~

Great pains have been taken by those active and influential persons whose emoluments or importance would be lessened by the adoption of a good system of government in the Colonies, to misrepresent the meaning of the demand for Responsible Government. The term "Responsible Government" is certainly general and vague. It may mean various kinds and degrees of responsibility; it may denote a responsibility carried to precisely the same extent and guarded by the same guarantees as that of the Executive of this country; it may mean a responsibility carried to an extent and enforced by means repugnant to the spirit of our constitution. The opponents of the principle take advantage of the vagueness of the term in order to give it the latter of these two characters. Sometimes they content themselves with effecting this purpose by mere vague insinuations. . . . Sometimes they condescend to give a reason for their faith as to the character and tendency of the principle; and that reason is generally an utter and gross misrepresentation of facts. They assert that a "responsible" means an "elective" executive; and that the responsibility proposed is that kind which prevails in the various States of the American Union, where every officer of government is appointed either by the direct vote of the people, or by that of the representative bodies of the State.

It is no wonder that misrepresentations such as these, made with the utmost confidence and repeated with the utmost assiduity, should mislead a great number of persons, on a subject about which so few in this country take the necessary pains to get correct information. Those who make these assertions rely on the indolence of those to whom they address them, and count on their adopting them without examination; for the slightest examination would dispel all misapprehension and even doubt on the subject. Among those who in this country or in the Colonies have made "Responsible Government" their political watchword, there has never been the least difference of opinion as to the object in view: all have confined themselves to demanding that the Crown, while retaining the present unlimited choice of its servants, should nevertheless make a practice of selecting them from among those who possess the confidence of the Legislature. No one has ever proposed a legislative enactment with a view to enforce the principle. It has been seen that the practice of governing by means of those who command the confidence and cooperation of the Legislature, must be established, not by acts of Parliament, but by the good sense of the Crown, impelling it not to make a particular concession at this or any other particular moment, but to adopt a general rule of action as essential to the efficient administration of the government as to the contentment of the people. . . .

. . . The Mother-country should never interfere in the administration of affairs in the colony, either in the legislation on which the Assembly is bent, or in its preference of one Colonial party to the other, but should let the Governor and Assembly get on as they best may, passing such laws, and administering affairs by such parties as they may agree on between themselves. The only exception is, where the course of legislation adopted in the Colony conflicts with the interests of the Mother-country. In these cases, which might be defined, it must oppose itself to the wishes of the Assembly: in all others it should let the business of the Colony be carried on by the powers in which the constitution has vested the government of the Colony; allowing the Governor to use his constitutional powers to influence the legislation of the Assembly, and allowing the Assembly to make use of its constitutional powers to influence the course of the Executive. The Governor would, in fact, stand in the position of the Crown at home; and it is difficult to make out why the prerogative which suffices to maintain the balance of power at home, should not be equally competent to uphold it in a Colony.

This is a division of power of which the maintenance depends upon circumstances and the prudence of the parties. Sometimes the Executive must take the first hint on the part of the representative body, and dismiss its advisers on the first indication of the hostility of a majority. Sometimes, again, it may with perfect safety make a long resistance to the majority, wait for repeated declarations of their will, and not submit even then, unless it finds on trial that they are backed by the people. . . . It is impossible to define the contingency on which the Crown or its representative should be bound to remove a Minister in compliance with the wishes of the Representative body. No law, no precedent, can exactly fix it: it must be settled in Colonies, as in the Mother-country, by the mutual strength, determination, and prudence of the two parties. If left to themselves, their necessities must bring about an arrangement of which harmony will be the result. All that is wanted is, that the authority of the Mother-country should not be interposed in order to retain in office persons who can get *no* Assembly to adopt their course of policy.

Such is the whole aim and object of the Colonial Reformers who seek "Responsible Government." No one will venture to deny its perfect accordance with the spirit and practice of the British constitution. Nor is it possible to show how representative government can harmoniously be carried on without adopting it. If you want the assent of a representative body to the policy of government, there is no other way of insuring harmony between that policy and the feelings of that body, than that of always intrusting the administration of affairs to those who can obtain the concurrence of the majority. This is one of the necessary consequences of representative institutions: it is just as necessary a consequence of representative institutions as the predominance of the majority is. And if, as we hear loudly and confidently asserted, Responsible Government is incompatible with colonial connexion, the only inference is, that representative institutions must be utterly incompatible with colonial connexion. . . .

(Buller, *Responsible Government for Colonies*, pp. 11-21)

~ In reply to comments which appeared in the *Morning Chronicle*, the *Colonial Gazette* explained the role and function of the governor under a system of responsible government more explicitly in 1844, when Sir Charles Metcalfe was experiencing difficulties with the Baldwin-Lafontaine ministry.~

. . . The constitution of Canada is framed on the model of the British. It is exercised by means of a Sovereign, a Representative Legislature, and Ministers interposed between them. The Sovereign must act by his Ministers, and the Ministers must act in accordance with the Representative Assembly. If the representative body refuse its confidence to Ministers, they must resign or be dismissed: the Legislature is entitled to refuse its co-operation until Ministers are appointed in whom it has confidence.

The Sovereign is the British Government; the Ministers are the Council, composed of the Governor and the members of the Legislature, nominated by him to fill certain offices. If the Legislature persist in withholding its confidence from this Ministry, or from any part of it, the Sovereign must ultimately dismiss it, or withdraw the obnoxious parties. But the Sovereign is not obliged to give way at the first or second hostile vote of the Legislature. . . . The Governor is not a temporary Sovereign, but a Prime Minister, with the power of nominating and dismissing his colleagues. In a Ministerial crisis, in Canada, the struggle to retain or dismiss a Ministry is not between the Assembly and the Governor, but between the Assembly and the home Government. The Governor is merely the Prime Minister, the person upon whom devolves the task of making, modifying, or keeping together a Ministry. The home Government, in a struggle to keep or lose a Minister, must ultimately give way, if the Assembly, or, after a dissolution, a new Assembly, stick to its point; but it is for the home Government to try and decide this. The home Government has the same right to support, for a time, its Minister in a minority – to adhere to him against repeated minorities, to choose its own time for dissolving and appealing to the constituencies. . . .

. . . The *Chronicle* would appear to assume that Sir Charles [Metcalfe] is to play the part of a little king – to "reign and not govern," – and that Mr. Lafontaine or Mr. Baldwin or Mr. Baldwin-Lafontaine was a Prime Minister. On the contrary, Sir Charles, as Premier, in filling up his Cabinet, must consult the home Government as well as the Canadian Assembly; and the home Government is not to give him up at the first brush because treacherous subordinates have, for a time, prepossessed the Canadian public against him. Government owes him a chance of having fair play; Government ought not to give him up until experience shows that he and the Canadian Parliament cannot work together. . . .

(*Colonial Gazette*, 29 June 1844)

3 / COLONIAL SELF-GOVERNMENT AND IMPERIAL RELATIONS

~ As part of the structure of colonial government, the Reformers proposed that administrative responsibilities should be divided between the colonial and imperial authorities, and that the areas left under the control of the British government should be restricted to those few matters in which the imperial authorities and the empire at large had an overriding interest. In his *Report* Lord Durham specified these fields of administrative concern as the form of the colonial constitution, the conduct of commercial and foreign relations, and the disposal of public lands. The concept of "responsible government" is usually considered to embrace this division of authority, but the arrangements envisaged by the Colonial Reformers can more accurately be described as internal self-government.~

. . . I know that it has been urged, that the principles which are productive of harmony and good government in the mother country, are by no means applicable to a colonial dependency. It is said that it is necessary that the administration of a colony should be carried on by persons nominated without any reference to the wishes of its people; that they have to carry into effect the policy, not of that people, but of the authorities at home; and that a colony which should name all its own administrative functionaries, would, in fact, cease to be dependent. I admit that the system which I propose would, in fact, place the internal government of the colony in the hands of the colonists themselves; and that we should thus leave to them the execution of the laws, of which we have long entrusted the making solely to them. Perfectly aware of the value of our colonial possessions, and strongly impressed with the necessity of maintaining our connexion with them, I know not in what respect it can be desirable that we should interfere with their internal legislation in matters which do not affect their relations with the mother country. The matters, which so concern us, are very few. The constitution of the form of government, – the regulation of foreign relations, and of trade with the mother country, the other British Colonies, and foreign nations, – and the disposal of the public lands, are the only points on which the mother country requires a control. This control is now sufficiently secured by the authority of the Imperial Legislature; by the protection which the Colony derives from us against foreign enemies; by the beneficial terms which our laws secure to its trade; and by its share of the reciprocal benefits which would be conferred by a wise system of colonization. A perfect subordination, on the part of the Colony, on these points, is secured by the advantages which it finds in the continuance of its connexion with the Empire. It is certainly not strengthened, but greatly weakened, by a vexatious interference on the part of the Home Government, with the enactment of laws for regulating the internal concerns of the Colony, or in the selection of the persons entrusted with their execution. The colonists may not always know what laws are best for them, or which of their countrymen are the fittest for conducting their affairs; but, at least, they have a greater interest in coming to a right judgment on these points, and will take greater pains to do so than those whose welfare is very remotely and slightly affected by the good or bad legislation of these portions of the Empire. . . .

(Lucas, *Lord Durham's Report*, II, 280-3)

~ Many contemporaries asserted that a grant of local self-government would be tantamount to a recognition of colonial independence and could lead only to the disruption of the empire. The Reformers believed, however, that this division of administrative responsibilities offered a means of reconciling the colonists' desire for control over their own affairs with the preservation of imperial unity, and would tend to strengthen rather than undermine the connection between Britain and the North American colonies. Both Durham and Buller were exponents of this sanguine view, but their comments suggest that the Colonial Reformers failed to realize that a permanent line could not be drawn between matters of local and imperial concern, and that the colonists would in time want to extend the range of their self-government to include external as well as internal affairs.~

. . . I am well aware that many persons, both in the Colonies and at home, view the system which I recommend with considerable alarm, because they distrust the ulterior views of those by whom it was originally proposed, and whom they suspect of urging its adoption, with the intent only of enabling them more easily to subvert monarchical institutions, or assert the independence of the Colony. I believe, however, that the extent to which these ulterior views exist, has been greatly overrated. We must not take every rash expression of disappointment as an indication of a settled aversion to the existing constitution; and my own observation convinces me, that the predominant feeling of all the English population of the North American Colonies is that of devoted attachment to the mother country. I believe that neither the interests nor the feelings of the people are incompatible with a Colonial Government, wisely and popularly administered. The proofs, which many who are much dissatisfied with the existing administration of the Government, have given of their loyalty, are not to be denied or overlooked. The attachment constantly exhibited by the people of these Provinces towards the British Crown and Empire, has all the characteristics of a strong national feeling. They value the institutions of their country, not merely from a sense of the practical advantages which they confer, but from sentiments of national pride; and they uphold them the more, because they are accustomed to view them as marks of nationality, which distinguish them from their Republican neighbours. I do not mean to affirm that this is a feeling which no impolicy on the part of the mother country will be unable to impair; but I do most confidently regard it as one which may, if rightly appreciated, be made the link of an enduring and advantageous connexion. The British people of the North American Colonies are a people on whom we may safely rely, and to whom we must not grudge power. For it is not to the individuals who have been loudest in demanding the change, that I propose to concede the responsibility of the Colonial administration, but to the people themselves. Nor can I conceive that any people, or any considerable portion of a people, will view with dissatisfaction a change which would amount simply to this, that the Crown would henceforth consult the wishes of the people in the choice of its servants . . .

(Lucas, *Lord Durham's Report*, II, 284-5)

There seems to be something in the term "Colonial dependence" peculiarly gratifying to national vanity. We assert for ourselves the utmost degree of self-government: we maintain that the rights of Englishmen are so inalienable that we carry them to the remotest regions . . . but when we come to speak of the communities formed by these Englishmen, of whose individual rights we are so tender, we are apt to be far less liberal. When the question is, whether these, like the great community from which they are offsets, shall be allowed to manage their own affairs, and to point out in what spirit and by what kind of persons they wish them to be administered, we are constantly met by this vague term, and these indefinite notions of colonial dependence, and told that in order to preserve the due relations between the empire and its dependencies, Englishmen who settle in the Colonies must be content to be governed in a manner the most repugnant to every notion that education and custom have implanted in their breasts.

Now it is not to be denied, that to a certain extent there is truth in the doctrine that a colony must in some respects be entirely subordinate to the legislature of the mother-country; that there are certain affairs on which the people of the United Kingdom have a voice, but on which those of the colony can have none. There are some questions of frequent occurrence which must be settled for the whole empire by one will; and the will must needs be that of the Imperial Government. A colony of England cannot be at war with a foreign state with which England herself is in peace, or at peace with one which is at war with England. The foreign relations of all parts of the empire must be the same, and must therefore be determined by the same mind. . . . Nor can we allow a colony to have a voice contrary to our own on any question connected with the great interests for the promotion of which Great Britain maintains her Colonies. We cannot allow a colony to interfere with the immigration of British subjects and the disposal of its unoccupied lands, or the trade with Britain. None will dispute the propriety of colonial dependence in these matters. . . .

But again, on the other hand, it must be admitted that there is a large department of Colonial affairs on which the interests of the colony are so entirely distinct from those of the empire at large, that the Imperial Government has very wisely left to the Colonies the sole legislative authority with respect to them. Of course we have an interest in all these matters: it is our interest that every colony in connection with us should be governed by laws which shall secure its prosperity. But it has been held, and wisely held, that in all matters affecting immediately the relations of the colonists with one another – affecting their own internal condition – their stake is so much greater, their attention so much more constantly excited, their means of accurate information so much more complete, and their interest in avoiding error so far more immediate, that the best plan is to leave these matters entirely to the Legislatures which we have established in the Colonies. . . . The division between the two provinces of Imperial and Colonial legislation has been made on a very sound and very simple principle. On all points which immediately affect the empire at large, the Imperial Government retains its legislative authority; on all those which immediately affect the colony alone, it allows the colony to legislate for itself. . . .

This, it will be said, renders the colony in a great measure practically independent of the mother-country. It seems to us very desirable that it should be so. It cannot be alleged that we are inclined to depreciate the importance of colonies, or to recommend the severance of colonial connexions. But nothing seems to us so calculated to weaken the solidity of such connexions as that constant interference with the self-government of our Colonies, which is recommended by some of those who pretend to be warm advocates of our Colonial system. It is in order that our Colonies may long continue connected with the empire, and be the source to us of those advantages which we believe to be the fruit of wise colonization, that we think that their dependence should be held by a very loose rein. . . .

. . . We want colonies in order to have customers for our trade and a field for our surplus capital and labour. These are the sole objects for which we maintain colonies, and for securing which we are obliged to keep up our dominion over them. We are under the necessity of governing them, and of protecting them by our fleets and armies, solely in order that we may be sure of trading with them and sending our emigrants to them. We need interfere with them solely in order to secure an advantageous trade, a ready access to our emigrants, and such a disposal of the lands of the colony as shall promote emigration into it. Practically we see little reason to apprehend collision on these points. Our ancient views of colonial trade are now so completely abandoned, that instead of our maintaining monopolies injurious to the Colonies, we sin against the freedom of trade almost entirely for the purpose of giving our Colonies an injurious monopoly of our own market. The Colonies are not likely therefore to come into collision with us on account of our legislation with respect to their trade. Nor are they likely to quarrel with us for sending emigrants to them, while labour is the great want of a colony, and our authority is exercised with a view of supplying that want. . . .

If we are right in regarding the points in which Imperial interests can be affected by the management of affairs in the Colonies as so few and so simple, we need not be afraid of granting that executive responsibility which is a necessary part of representative government, on the ground of its being a concession incompatible with colonial dependence. The chances of collision between the Imperial authorities and a colony governed on right principles are really so few, that it would be absurd to expose a colony to the certain disturbance of the march of government, which must result from the present system, in order to avoid the remote contingency of a collision on the few points on which the interests of the two parties may be at variance. We do not pretend that the system of colonial government which we think advisable, is free from all liability to be disturbed by the violence and folly of either of the parties. It is doubtless very possible for any one who will reason after Lord John Russell's fashion, to fancy extreme cases, in which a colonial legislature, by extraordinary usurpation, may render any rational system of government impracticable. But it would be difficult for Lord John Russell to point out any form of government which would work well, if we were to suppose all persons who had any thing to do with it so utterly destitute of common sense and common fairness as he is pleased to suppose that colonial legislatures will always be. Nor, of course, are we proposing a form of government, for ordinary times, which would not be liable to great mismanagement in any colony in which the majority of the people should be desirous of severing their connexion with the mother-country. If a colony were bent on severing that connexion, we care not whether the responsibility of the executive might somewhat facilitate the accomplishment of that purpose, since we are quite sure that the continuance of the present system would not prevent the same result. We look to the working of the proposed responsibility of the executive in ordinary times, under the influence of ordinary common sense, and supposing that the feelings of the colony are those of satisfaction with the continuance of its connexion with Great Britain. And in such a state of things we feel assured, that while the responsibility of the executive would render the colony practically independent of the mother-country in the management of its internal affairs, that increase of its independence would not in any way remove the necessary dependence of the colony in those matters in which it is requisite that the interests of the mother-country should be constantly had in view. The increased independence of the colony would rivet its connexion with Great Britain, by removing those numerous causes of collision that constantly arise in the practical working of the present system.

(Buller, *Responsible Government for Colonies*, pp. 23-34)

4 / THE INTRODUCTION
OF RESPONSIBLE GOVERNMENT, 1839-1849

~ Because of the difficulty of reconciling responsible government with a colony's dependent status, imperial statesmen did not initially endorse or implement this important aspect of Lord Durham's recommendations. Since the development in Canada of ministries more in harmony with assemblies was expected to be the result of practical politics in the colonies and not of instructions from London, British statesmen preferred not to commit themselves on the issue beyond a reference to Lord John Russell's Resolutions of 1837 in which parliament had decisively pronounced a judgment on the question. Indeed, ministers refused thereafter to debate the merits of responsible government as a theoretical concept, and, much to the annoyance of the Colonial Reformers, insisted that it was a purely practical question on which no further comment was required. Official silence was considered essential to prevent the whole matter from creating another overtly contentious issue, which only time and experience could satisfactorily resolve.

During the 1840's, therefore, the progress towards the introduction of responsible government in Canada was a gradual one. The fluctuations of party politics in North America were anxiously examined by the Colonial Reformers in London for evidence that steps were being taken towards the practical acceptance of this system of colonial government. The first encouraging sign was Lord John Russell's despatch to Governor-General Poulett Thomson in October 1839 concerning the tenure of crown offices in the colonies. As a means of maintaining harmony between executive and legislative authorities, officials in the colonies would no longer hold office during good behaviour, which in the past has been tantamount to permanent tenure, but at the Queen's pleasure, which would mean that they could be removed from office by the governor when the need arose. Although Russell's comments on responsible government were criticized by the Reformers, the *Colonial Gazette* was prepared to welcome this declaration and the new latitude it would give the governor in maintaining ministries acceptable to the colonial assembly.~

. . . On the publication of Lord Durham's Report, Lord John [Russell] seized the first opportunity of declaring that he did not agree with Lord Durham in his views of Responsible Government. Subsequent consideration appears to have induced him to take the trouble of *understanding* Lord Durham's views, and to refrain from dwelling on theoretical differences of opinion rather than a practical agreement in policy. He now ends the matter by issuing one despatch which takes the only *practical* step which Lord Durham ever proposed, or could have taken were he in Lord John's place, – namely, the substitution of a tenure at pleasure instead of the present permanent tenure of office; and another despatch, in which he declares that he "sees little or no objection to the practical views of Colonial government recommended by Lord Durham, as he understands them." With one who comes to so right a conclusion, we will not quarrel for a few sophistries, by which he tries to make out the consistency of saying "No" and acting "Yes."

Indeed, we are not sure that our present difference of opinion extends to any of the specific arguments used by Lord John Russell in the despatch before us. We do not think him wrong in instructing Mr. Poulett Thomson "to refuse any explanations which may be construed to imply an acquiescence in the petitions and addresses upon the subject of Responsible Government." The adoption of a sound system of executive government must be shown by the acts and not by the answers of the Governor. . . .

In his subsequent remarks, Lord John admits that the advocates of Responsible Government do not extend their doctrines to "questions of foreign war and international relations whether of trade or diplomacy." But he argues that there are "cases of internal government, in which the honour of the Crown, or the faith of Parliament, or the safety of the State, are so seriously involved, that it would not be possible for her Majesty to delegate her authority to a Ministry in a colony." He then puts by way of illustration an extreme case. We readily admit that there are extreme cases. These are met with in every form of government. England has had experience of cases in which it has been found necessary to violate the most sacred principles of her own constitution. But no wise statesmen contemplates these exceptional cases in his general principles of the ordinary government of a country. He makes no provision for them in his constitutional theory: he does not modify the every-day rules of constitutional practice to provide a remedy for these evils, but leaves to the ready wit of the moment the adoption of the resources which unforeseen necessities require. . . .

It is enough for us, however, that Lord John, in spite of these theoretical objections, this repugnance to words, and this susceptibility about extreme cases, admits that he concurs with Lord Durham's practical views of Colonial government; that he "has no desire to thwart the Representative Assemblies of British North America in their measures of reform and improvement"; that he has "no wish to make those provinces the resource of patronage at home"; that he wishes "to open the career of public employment to talent and character in the Colonies, as in the United Kingdom"; and that he "has no desire to maintain any system of policy among her Majesty's North American subjects, which opinion condemns." These declarations are perhaps vague; but they are rendered specific and substantial by the alteration of the present tenure of Colonial offices. When once the moral right to hold office on the tenure of good behaviour is abrogated – when it is established that not only will civil officers "be called upon to retire from the public service, as often as any sufficient motives of public policy may suggest the expediency of that measure, but that a change in the person of the Governor will be considered a sufficient reason for any alterations which his successors may deem it expedient to make in the list of public functionaries" – the principle for which we have contended will virtually be established. To establish it permanently, and render it as available as we desire, we are content to leave to time and – the Parliament of United Canada.

(*Colonial Gazette*, 29 January 1840)

~ In July 1840 Charles Buller wrote to Lord Durham concerning the British government's practical acceptance of the principle of responsible government.~

... You told the British Government that it could never hope to govern the Colonies quietly unless it brought its Executive into harmony with the Colonial Legislatures. From the hour in which you said this, the people in every Colony of G[rea]t Britain took it up as the true & wise principle of Colonial government. The ministers here pretend to differ from you. But what has their whole conduct been but a gradual though unwilling concession to your principles? L[or]d John's Dispatches established while they denied Responsible government. ... And now we have only to wait for 6 months of an United Legislature: and I'll be bound that the principle you have recommended will be so thoroughly adopted in the government of Canada, that men will cry wonder that persons in power were ever foolish enough to imagine they could conduct affairs on any other principle. ...

(Buller to Durham, 20 July 1840, DURHAM PAPERS, vol. 29)

~ Governor Poulett Thomson was sent out to Canada with instructions to carry through the union of the two provinces and meanwhile avoid arousing controversy by declaring the government's support for or opposition to the vague, theoretical principle of responsible government. Nevertheless, Thomson's declarations on his assumption of office suggested to the *Spectator* and the *Colonial Gazette* that he was favourably disposed to the practical implementation of responsible government, even though the authorities refused to avow openly their full acceptance of the principle.~

. . . with respect to the question of Responsible Government, Mr. Thomson is of opinion that no settlement of Canadian affairs can be satisfactory or permanent unless the new Colonial Government be founded on the principle of representation, and also on the principle of admitting the natural *consequence* of representation – namely, the administration of local affairs in constant harmony with the opinions of the majority in the representative body. On this point also, notwithstanding Lord John Russell's declaration against Responsible Government *by that name*, Mr. Thomson adopts the views of Lord Durham as put forth in the High Commissioner's Report. He conceives that representation is a mockery, and a very mischievous mockery too, if the Executive is not made responsible to those in whom the people confide. By what special means he would secure this indispensable condition of peace and order under the representative system, we are not informed; but we have reason to conclude that he intends to be guided upon this point by the opinion of the leading men of the British race in both Canadas. . . .

(*Spectator*, 21 September 1839)

. . . the coquettish *see-sawing* of Governor Thomson on the all-important subject of Responsible Government, in monkey-like imitation of Lord John Russell, renders it the more incumbent on the constituencies of United Canada to make this the question of questions at the approaching election of an Assembly. If the Colonial Minister here and the Governor-General there had unequivocally declared, that the Crown would henceforth govern as at home, both as to persons and things, in agreement with the majority of the Representative body, the question would have been set at rest during their time at least. As it is, the indecision of the organs of the Crown excites suspicions and fears which keep the question alive. . . . It is deeply to be regretted that Canada should still be agitated on this really organic question: but the evil must be borne in order that it may be finally eradicated. The Imperial authorities have not thought fit to *settle the future government* of Canada; and therefore the people of Canada must endeavour to accomplish this object themselves. It is not a very difficult task. The miserable contest of races being over – the national pride of England being no longer irritated by fears of provincial rebellion – United Canada being a British colony – public opinion here will sympathize with public opinion in Canada, and the voice of the colonists as spoken by the majority of their Assembly will have due weight on this side of the Atlantic. If the majority of the Assembly should require that the Executive departments of government be no longer conducted by persons in whom nobody has any confidence, but be intrusted, as at home, to the men who have talent and influence to lead the Representative body, *that* the people of this country will deem a request most fit to be granted . . . there is good reason to believe that Governor Thomson, and even Lord John Russell, howsoever disinclined to admit the "theoretical point" as such, for reasons that will come out in due time, are quite ready to adopt it practically – that is, provided the Assembly should insist on it. . . .

(*Colonial Gazette*, 19 August 1840)

~ Subsequent events suggested that the method chosen by Poulett Thomson, now Lord Sydenham, for governing Canada in harmony with the assembly was to disrupt political factions and conduct the executive as his own prime minister. The Colonial Reformers were to some extent sympathetic to this practice as a means of operating responsible government in a colony, but the *Colonial Gazette* pointed out that the death of the governor-general in 1841 left colonial politics in a state of chaos and uncertainty. ~

. . . It was Lord Sydenham's policy to break up all existing parties, to deal rather with individuals than with parties, and so to get the whole conduct of the executive government into his own hands. He was his own Executive Council and his own Chief Secretary – a sort of Louis Philippe for Canada, whose constant aim, in which he was entirely successful, was to *individualize* the Government, and let no importance, no responsibility exist save only his own. Such a man and such a policy were perhaps required for the occasion. But be that as it may, the result is, that in Lord Sydenham's absence Canadian politics present a chaos of incertitude and indistinctness, of which his successor will for a long while be unable to make head or tail. Just in proportion as the last Governor did every thing and dealt with everybody himself, letting no party nor even any individual gain a prominent position on the stage of politics, so the next Governor, being required to act immediately, must almost of necessity take his chance of the famous Chapter of Accidents. Never for a moment did Lord Sydenham let the reins out of his own hands; and of course, therefore, when he dropped them, nobody was capable of driving as he had done, or indeed any how; and it became necessary for his successor, in the first place to determine on a whole course of policy, and secondly, either to carry it out himself by dint of self-reliance and laboriousness equal to Lord Sydenham's, or instantly to fix on subordinates capable of understanding and giving effect to a whole course of policy. . . .

. . . Lord Sydenham's complete success in what he attempted – in all that, down to the close of the first session of the first united Parliament, he deemed it wise to attempt – was owing to four circumstances in particular. In the first place, his general policy was determined on before he quitted England, and made known to the colonists before his arrival among them. He undertook "to complete what Lord Durham had begun"; and he had the benefit of Lord Durham's best advice and assistance with respect to men as well as measures. Secondly, he really took a pleasure in hard work; and from the time of his arrival to the hour of his death he worked unceasingly. He was thus always master of every subject, and *independent of designing advisers*. Thirdly, he possessed considerable Parliamentary experience, and was thus familiar with the means of managing a representative body. Lastly, and above all, he had a sort of *carte blanche* from the Home Government, with a positive assurance of being supported by Lord John Russell on all occasions. The qualifications which he carried with him were, definite views founded on an extensive knowledge of Canadian affairs, uncommon industry, the most desirable experience, and power to decide as he pleased on the spot. He enjoyed all the means of success, and yet had some hairbreadth 'scapes. Who then can envy Sir Charles Bagot, notwithstanding the assurance, which we have a pleasure in repeating, that his *intentions* with respect to Canada, like those of the present Home Government, are unexceptionable?

(*Colonial Gazette*, 13 October 1841)

~ The Colonial Reformers criticized Sir Charles Bagot for attempting to imitate Lord Sydenham's practice of breaking up hostile parties by inducing their leaders to work together in the executive. They praised the governor, however, when he accepted the necessity of admitting into the ministry Louis Lafontaine, the leader of the French Canadians in the assembly, and Robert Baldwin, the leader of a small section of reformers from Canada West. To Wakefield this reconstitution of the Canadian ministry in 1842 represented the first example of responsible government in operation.~

. . . Sir Charles Bagot, on his arrival in Canada, adopted Lord Sydenham's Ministry as he found it. But shortly before the second meeting of the first United Parliament, it became plain to careful observers, that a majority of the Assembly would oppose the Government as then constituted. Sir Charles Bagot therefore had to choose between making some important change in the composition of his Council, and falling into collision with the Assembly according to custom before the Union. He wisely preferred the former. I am bound to add, that this kind, true, and honourable Governor was shocked at the injustice of the exclusion of the French Canadians from all part in the Government, and is believed to have rejoiced at the opportunity of taking some of their leaders into his Council of advisers. It was much easier, however, to wish this than to do it. . . . After the failure of various negociations in consequence of Mr. Lafontaine's natural suspicion that the Governor General's offer of so large a share of power to his hitherto proscribed countrymen was not sincere, and also in consequence of Mr. Baldwin's wish to oust Lord Sydenham's Ministry *en bloc* with a view of being "sent for" himself and desired to form a new Ministry, an arrangement was made by which about half of Lord Sydenham's Councillors retired, and were replaced by as many members of the Opposition. The Assembly which would have voted against an echo-address in answer to the Governor's speech by about 2 to 1, now warmly expressed its confidence in the Government by a majority of 10 to 1 of the Members present. The working of responsible government had preserved harmony between the Crown and the Representative body. The modification or change of Ministry in 1842 crowned the resolutions of September 1841 [declaratory of responsible government], by giving them full effect in practice.

. . . the Lafontaine-Baldwin Ministry was really formed with no other view than that of doing justice to the French Canadians; and that Mr. Baldwin was brought into power merely as the nominee of the French-Canadian leaders, who thus paid him a debt of gratitude which they had contracted when he resigned office under Lord Sydenham on account of their exclusion from power. When the French Canadians made Mr. Baldwin a Minister under Sir Charles Bagot, he was the leader of a section of the Opposition in the Assembly composed of *four* Upper Canada members. . . .

The Resolutions of September 1841 determined those relations between a Ministry and a Representative body, for which usage is the sole guarantee in this country; but they leave wholly untouched that other part of the machinery of Parliamentary government which consists of the relations between a Ministry and the Crown. In this country, these latter relations are settled like the former, by usage, and depend on the good sense of the parties. They were in no way settled in Canada under Sir Charles Bagot. His Excellency fell into severe illness almost immediately after the formation of the Lafontaine-Baldwin Council, and became incapable of exercising the functions of Governor. The New Council or Ministry, therefore, had in truth no relations with the Governor, but ruled the Province executively without the participation or knowledge of any representative of the Crown. This state of things lasted until the arrival of Sir Charles Metcalfe. . . .

(E. G. Wakefield, *A View of Sir Charles Metcalfe's Government of Canada* [London, 1844], pp. 15-16)

~ Sir Charles Metcalfe at once encountered difficulties with the Lafontaine-Baldwin ministry. Controversy centred around the practical implications of responsible government and the respective authority of governor and ministers in making official appointments. As the comments in the *Colonial Gazette* suggest, the Reformers were strongly in sympathy with Metcalfe's opinions, because they supported a system of government which would leave the power of appointing officials firmly in the hands of the governor and not in those of the colonial executive. In the event, the issue was settled by the dissolution of parliament and an apparent triumph for Metcalfe's views at the subsequent election.~

. . . That is a responsible government in which the rulers cannot for any length of time persist in a course of policy earnestly and conscientiously disapproved of by the people. In England the peculiar relations in which Ministers – the

Executive Government – stand to the Crown on one hand, and to the House of Commons on the other, ensure us a responsible government. Unless by a revolution, no Minister can carry on the operations of Government except through the instrumentality of the House of Commons. As soon, therefore, as a Ministry is found to be decidedly in a minority, it must resign, and the Crown must choose another. By this means the independence of the bench, the preservation or enactment of laws congenial to public opinion, and the rights of private individuals are preserved. Responsible government and its fruits are what we value: the means by which they are obtained we cherish, because we doubt whether more efficacious means could be devised; but still these means – the relations in which Ministers stand to the Crown and the Commons – are only valued as means to the end. Any other method of ensuring responsible government would in reality be equally valuable.

Now, has responsible government been assailed in Canada? Has Sir Charles Metcalfe endeavoured to wrest from the Canadian Parliament its constitutional right to enact laws, to provide "ways and means," to check the accounts of the Executive Government? . . . He has governed Canada by the constitution he found there. He had a right to dismiss his Councillors; he has a right to endeavour to procure new ones; the only limit to the time allowed him for doing this is the necessity of assembling the provincial Parliament as soon as some constitutional function, which it alone is competent to discharge, requires to be discharged. As soon as Sir Charles takes upon him to do alone anything, which by the constitution he can only do legitimately in combination with the provincial Parliament, he will violate the constitution and sin against "responsible government." This he has not done: he is still within his constitutional right.

The ex-Councillors say that Sir Charles made certain official appointments without consulting them, and that in doing this he violated the constitution and subverted responsible government. Assuming, for argument's sake, that their statement is true: where is the law that forbids Sir Charles to make official appointments without the sanction of his Council? . . . The Crown, *de facto*, leaves them to make the appointments, because no Minister will undertake to defend in Parliament appointments made without or against his will. This arrangement is possible and advantageous, for the public business of the empire is settled between Parliament and the Minister for the time being. The necessity of accounting to the satisfaction of Parliament is a necessary check against the ministerial abuse of power. But there is this drawback upon the arrangement: the necessity under which Ministers lie of pleasing Parliament exposes them to the temptation of pleasing Parliament by the appointments – of buying votes.

Now, assuming for a moment that it is the constitution – the law of Canada – that all appointments to office shall in reality be vested in Ministers, how would it work? It would transfer all power from the Governor to his Executive Council . . . the colonial Executive Council, exercising the whole patronage of the colony, would bribe right and left at elections and in the provincial Parliament; it would inevitably grow into a "family compact." And that is what the ex-officials are driving at: they want, by engrossing all patronage, to make themselves as powerful a family compact as that which they have trodden down.

If the Canadians are wise they will insist that the Government shall be conducted, and patronage dispensed by the Governor, with the assistance of an Executive Council, but without the screen of a responsible Executive Council. If the Governor has to deal directly with the provincial Parliament, and to be alone responsible for the acts of Government, it will be his interest to choose able administrators, upright and intelligent men. If he is to deal with the provincial Parliament through the medium of a responsible Executive Council, he is only there to screen the permanent dispensers of colonial patronage by the name and prestige of a Governor appointed by the Crown for a limited time. When a Governor governs directly and visibly, and cannot act in unison with the provincial Parliament, a new governor must be appointed. When he governs through a responsible Council, he and the Colonial-office will leave the Council and the provincial Parliament mutually to obstruct each other.

The ex-officials are misleading their partisans by the use of the word "Ministers." Calling themselves Ministers they assume that they ought to have the same power and privileges as the Imperial Ministers of State. The truth is that they are as much subordinate to the Imperial Cabinet as the Corporation of London or the Town Council of Glasgow. The analogy of their powers and privileges would be more fitly drawn from these bodies. Like theirs, the functions of the Canadian administrative Council are necessarily limited to local legislation. The grand title of "Ministers," as they affect to understand it, is ludicrously inappropriate: that is a trifle; but if they succeed in making the Canadians vain of this title as applied to their

Executive Council, they will make the Canadians pay for the gratification of their vanity, by clapping a family compact on their neck. The pride and privilege of the Canadian is, that he is a free burgher, who has a vote in the constitution of the provincial Parliament, by and through which the Governor must act. To take pride in fancying his Executive Council Ministers, is aping the Cockney who is proud of the Lord Mayor's coach; and to submit to a family compact, in order to obtain this childish gratification, would make him a greater fool than the Cockney still.

(*Colonial Gazette*, 21 September 1844)

~ Nevertheless, the clear acceptance and operation of responsible government in Canada had not yet been fully accomplished. For this reason the subsequent appointment of Lord Elgin as governor-general in 1846 and the presence of Earl Grey at the Colonial Office were decisive for Canadian politics, because both men admitted the necessity of conducting the colony's administration on the basis of responsible government. In February 1848 the *Spectator* surveyed political developments in Canada and concluded that Lord Elgin had no alternative but to accept the defeat of his ministry at the recent election and form a new administration that would enjoy the confidence of the assembly.~

. . . Notwithstanding the ignorance of Colonial matters which generally prevails here, most people are aware that the United Province of Canada possesses representative institutions purporting to resemble those of the Mother-country. The resemblance, indeed, is very far from exact; but at any rate the colonists have a House of Commons (Assembly) and Parliamentary elections. A general election has just taken place. This measure was adopted by the Executive Government as a means of gaining strength in the Assembly, where Lord Metcalfe's sufficient majority had gradually dwindled into a very small one, not to say a minority. The result has totally frustrated the object of Lord Elgin's Government. It appears by the returns . . . that nearly two-thirds of the newly-elected members belong to the Opposition: the Government has been thoroughly beaten. It follows as a matter of course, that there must be a total change in the composition of the Executive Council or Colonial Cabinet. We say "as a matter of course," because we take it for granted that Lord Elgin will not attempt to deprive Canada of that very important British institution which has been termed "responsible government," and which provides that the principal executive offices shall be filled by persons enjoying the confidence of the representative body. A new Provincial Ministry is therefore inevitable. And so far there seems nothing to excite uneasiness, or even to call for remark here. For, apparently, what matters it to this country whether the party of the Smiths or the party of the Johnsons prevail in the Colonial Parliament and Government? And that, indeed, would be a point of total indifference out of Canada, if constitutional government like that of the Mother-country had been long and fully established in the colony: it would be a Colonial question exclusively, about which nobody out of the colony would care any more than people out of these islands care whether we have a Russell, or a Peel, or a Stanley Government. But, unfortunately, constitutional government has not been well established in Canada. The practice, down to a recent period, was representation in Parliament with a mode of carrying it into effect, or rather utterly frustrating it, similar to the means by which Charles the Tenth lost the crown of France: the chief executive officers were persons enjoying the confidence, not of a majority, but of a small minority of the representative body. This strange mode of government produced the rebellions: nobody denies that now. It produced, moreover, (and nothing sufficient has yet been done to destroy the effect,) a revolutionary spirit, hatred of the Imperial state, and leaders of the disaffected, who, by that habit which is a second nature, are demagogues rather than politicians. By the union of the two Canadas into one state, this party acquired a large majority in the representation. Lord Sydenham managed to keep them down by all sorts of unjust and cruel means, which preserved and perhaps strengthened their hostility to British rule. Sir Charles Bagot, choosing between that and another rebellion, disarmed them for a time by investing their leaders with the powers of government. But those leaders, being demagogues and not politicians, had the folly to quarrel with Lord Metcalfe; and they managed by indiscretion and violence to put themselves so much in the wrong, that upon his "appeal to the people" their party fell into a minority; and they have been out of office ever since. The time that has elapsed since Messrs. Baldwin, Lafontaine, and Hincks, broke up their own Government under Lord Metcalfe, was a time which the Imperial power should have most diligently and carefully employed for the purpose of forming a party in Canada, strong enough in numbers and ability to carry on the government by constitutional means and with none but constitutional objects. The task was by no means difficult; but nothing of the sort was attempted. Lord Metcalfe fell ill, and retired; and his successor, Lord Elgin, has hobbled on anyhow till events have taken the cards completely out of his hands. The new House of Assembly, in which he seems to have expected a stronger majority than Lord Metcalfe had against Messrs Baldwin, Lafontaine, and Hincks, contains a large majority of devoted partisans of those gentlemen. It also contains *the* Mr. Papineau, who is to lead the party. The new Ministry – for *United* Canada, observe – must be a Papineau Ministry. Let us repeat, that we take for granted that such a Ministry has ere now been constituted by the Governor-General. Speaking from much private information in addition to what the Canadian newspapers furnish, we cannot doubt that this step has been already taken. No other course was left open to Lord Elgin, supposing him to be in his senses and not trammelled by the Colonial Office: for it is certain that the only alternative was a complete stoppage of ordinary government, and a revolutionary struggle between the Assembly and the Governor-General, with every prospect of humiliating defeat for the representative of the Crown, or of an appeal to arms, with totally inadequate means on the part of the Governor, and with abundance of American "sympathy" on the Popular side.

It does not surely follow, however, that the leaders of the Popular party, *being in office*, will pursue dangerous or inadmissible objects. Being indulged with the enjoyment of that power which necessarily belongs to the trusted chiefs of the majority under really free institutions, they may settle down into diligent administrators of ordinary government, and discreet reformers of the manifold defects and abuses which the ordinary government of Canada still exhibits. May it so turn out: but . . . [Lord Elgin] cannot escape troubles of the most serious nature, except by letting parties in Canada fight it out between themselves, and taking no more share in their contests than the Queen of England does in the rivalry of parties here. Under actual circumstances, there is nothing else left for him to do. And even this, to have a chance of success, must be done very completely; that is, without the least reservation either real or apparent, and with a perfect cordiality towards those, be they who they may, in whom the majority of the Assembly shall choose to place confidence. It is just possible that in this way Lord Elgin might render a Papineau-Baldwin-Lafontaine Ministry tolerable, and even very useful.

(*Spectator*, 19 February 1848)

~ The question of responsible government was decisively and finally settled with the acceptance of the Rebellion Losses Act in 1849. This measure was designed to compensate inhabitants of Lower Canada at the time of the rebellions of 1837 who had suffered losses or damages to property at the hands of British troops or loyalist volunteers. The act was passed as a ministerial measure by a majority in the assembly, and both Elgin and Grey refused to veto the act on the demands of British settlers in Canada who objected to compensating those French inhabitants who had been rebels at heart in 1837. Although both statesmen entertained misgivings about the wisdom or necessity of the act, they accepted it as a matter of purely local concern and as the measure of a ministry enjoying the support of a majority in the assembly. The *Spectator* pointed out that further representations to the British government by opponents of the act would be unavailing: responsible government in Canada was at last a reality.~

Sir Allan M'Nab and Mr. Moffatt, two chiefs of the Opposition in Canada, are coming to England as delegates from their party to protest against the Rebellion-Losses measure, and obtain its disallowance by the Crown or Parliament. They had done better to spare their pains. The Legislature of Canada – the House of Assembly, the Legislative Council, and the Governor – have concurred in making a law. These organs of the Colonial Opposition come to propose that the law shall be unmade. Unmade by whom? By the Crown, say some, under its final power of disallowance. But the Crown has thrice declared its full concurrence in this measure; first, when, through its organ the Governor, it allowed his Ministers to introduce the bill; secondly, when, through the Governor, it assented to the bill as passed by both Houses of Parliament; and thirdly, when the Queen, by Lord Grey's despatch to Lord Elgin, emphatically sanctioned the Governor's proceedings. It is simply impossible, therefore, that the Crown, unless moved by the Imperial Houses of Parliament, should now disallow this Colonial law. The Imperial Houses of Parliament might indeed constitutionally lead the Crown to change its mind, or might themselves annul the Colonial law; but this could not be done without a change of Ministry at home, nor without virtually upsetting the constitution of Canada. And what single reason is there why Parliament should thus interfere with Colonial legislation? It is said that the honour of the Empire is concerned: but in what respect? If the Imperial power represented by the

Crown had originally objected to this measure, then, doubtless, since questions relating to treason and rebellion against the Empire concern the Imperial power, and do not belong exclusively to the Colony, the Crown or Parliament might properly interfere in such manner and to such extent as they should deem fit: but the Imperial power, so far as it is represented by the Crown, has fully approved of the measure, and even been an active party to it. The measure is, to a great extent, that of the Imperial power itself; and it cannot, therefore, by any means be construed into an affront to the honour of the Empire. The Imperial power represented by the Crown – our two Houses of Parliament remaining quite passive from ignorance and indifference – has warmly sanctioned the measure in all its stages: and that which either an individual, or a government, or a nation adopts as its own, cannot by any ingenuity be twisted into an attack upon the honour of the adopting party. But again, it is said, the measure was most impolitic: it has revived the war of races in Canada; it may have the effect, if upheld by the Imperial power, of dismembering the empire. Supposing all this to be true, still the impolicy of overturning the measure now by Imperial authority would be greater than that of the measure itself. The Imperial power could not *now* act on a view of the impolicy of this measure, without stultifying itself, degrading the Crown, depriving Canada of constitutional government, aggravating the conflict of races, and causing the dismemberment of the empire to be more probable than ever. Whether on the ground of Imperial honour or on that of Imperial policy, it is now too late for the Imperial power to interfere without making bad worse. . . . The Rebellion-Losses measure is a *fait accompli*; and all intriguing in this country against the majority which passed it, by the minority which opposed it, will be prevented by prompt and stern rebuff. . . .

(*Spectator*, 2 June 1849)

PART SEVEN:
THE FUTURE OF THE BRITISH EMPIRE IN NORTH AMERICA

1 / THE FORCES OF SEPARATION AND IMPERIAL UNITY

~ Many Englishmen in the 1840's were sceptical of the value of overseas possessions with the movement towards free trade and inclined to believe that the ineluctable tendencies towards separation made colonial independence and the disruption of Britain's empire in North America a mere matter of time. It did not seem likely that settlements enjoying internal self-government would long endure a subordinate and dependent status within a colonial empire. Moreover, since Anglo-Canadian commercial relations were unlikely to be adversely affected by the political independence of the provinces, separation might be mutually advantageous. For Britain it would certainly mean a substantial reduction in expenditure on colonial defence and overseas military establishments, which remained the last major burden of empire.

Though supporters of retrenchment, the Colonial Reformers persistently attempted to counter the argument that the forces of separation in British North America were inexorable. They freely admitted that the preservation of imperial unity necessitated a willing acceptance of the implications of local self-government, and that if essential reforms in British colonial policy were not introduced, it would be better to grant independence than continue to misgovern the colonies. But given a generous and realistic basis for Britain's relations with the self-governing territories, the Reformers maintained that both colonies and mother country stood to benefit from a continuance of the imperial connection. These mutual advantages were elaborated in the *Spectator* in 1848.~

Sir William Molesworth has notified for some day after Easter, a motion, "to call the attention of the House to the subject of the Colonies, and to submit to the consideration of the House a motion with regard to Colonial Government and Expenditure." It is indeed high time that the whole system included in these words should be revised. The actual state of matters is disastrous and fraught with danger. Some colonies, like the great West Indian group, are sinking to ruin under English mismanagement; others, like Canada, have been exasperated by a fast and loose policy, and kept in an intermittent fever of disaffection . . . everywhere there is official injury and popular discontent – to the Mother-country expense, to the Colonies vexation and loss. Meanwhile, the pleas on which the existing Colonial system was based have slipped from under it. . . . Free Trade has annulled the protective part of the Colonial system, and the repeal of the Navigation-laws will abolish its last remnant. The present machinery of administration grew up with that system: yet it is retained after that system is virtually extinct. Mother-country and Colonies are a mutual burden – the Colonies expensive, the Mother-country a hindrance to every kind of development which she ought to foster. . . .

The maintenance of Imperial authority, indeed, is rendered difficult, since it is very difficult to show the *quid pro quo* that the Colonies receive in return for their allegiance. . . .

On the other hand, it is equally difficult to make out what advantage the Mother-country derives from her Colonies still dependent, which she does not derive from her independent colonies, in return for the immense expenditure, civil and military, in their name. It is no longer exclusive trade – it is not waste lands for settlement, since they are barely used; and the United States absorb more emigrants than the whole of our own dependencies together.

"Cast away the useless encumbrances," cries the English economist; and the actual state of the Imperial finances lends force to the appeal. The reflex of the revolution which is spreading over the world as fire over a prairie imparts a new force to the cry of the colonists – "Separation!" . . .

But violent premature dismemberment would be hurtful to all. It would ruin the prestige of England, on which so much of her moral influence depends. It would alienate for ever resources which are still invaluable, though they lie in abeyance. It would cut off the Colonies from the great source of instant prosperity and rapid growth. . . . If a spark of wisdom or public virtue remains in England, none of these results will be hazarded. To that remnant of sense and virtue Sir William Molesworth is to make his timely appeal; and . . . an examination of the principles that bottom the question may prepare our readers for its consideration. . . .

A colony is a domain pertaining to a civilized state, which begins by being a desert and ends by being a copy of the parent state. The rapidity of its growth is determined by the nutritive powers of the parent. So long as there are vacant lands in that colony unsettled, so long does the mother-country retain an interest in the colony as the recipient of its redundant population. The land, at first, manifestly belongs to the parent state: the early settlers and each relay of emigrants owe allegiance to the parent state, and some gratitude for being permitted to appropriate those lands; which they cannot appropriate except under cover of the power and authority of the parent state, or else other great states might also appropriate those lands and subdue the settlers.

The benefit which colonies derive from the colonial relation is the direct nourishment from the parent state, in the shape of organized authority, accumulated capital, and trained labour; all three things of slow growth, if left to mere internal development. The independent colonies, the United States, draw capital and labour from this country; but not so advantageously as colonies still connected might under a good system of colonization; because capital would have its guarantee under a perfect union of laws and authority between metropolitan and provincial states, and the supply of labour would be assorted according to the wants of the colonists, not only according to the expulsive tendencies of overpeopled districts.

This connexion implies the correlatives of authority and protection; but *what* authority, *what* protection?

The authority should secure the due use and development of the colonial resources – the due administration of lands available for settlement; the perfection of every facility for intercourse, political, commercial, and personal, between mother-country and colony, as though the colony were "an integral part of the empire"; the development and training of the colonial community in all the duties of citizenship – self-government, self-support, self-defence. Such an authority would maintain itself, not by limiting or restricting, but by unfolding and strengthening the energies of the colony, so that the connexion would be a manifest source of welfare and strength to the dependency. The colonists would be trained to self-government by the freest institutions, by the appointment of colonists to the highest offices in the local administration, even to the highest of all. No demand would be made on the home government for "civil" expenses. Absentees would cease to be absent, if the colonies became fields of honorary distinction; as indeed they might be made the road to distinction at home. In this way the colony, advanced to maturity, would be an ally bound by every endearing tie of tradition and self-interest to be the close friend of the parent state; "separation" being neither sought nor dreaded, but superseded by equal federal companionship.

No demands would be made for military expenses. The protection accorded to a colony with strength thus developed would consist, mostly, in the latent power of the mother-country. There is not a settlement we have that would not be able and proud, with adequate political institutions, to undertake its own defence against surprise. Against attacks from great states at war with the parent state, it might be protected from home: no force could be directed against even our most distant colony, New Zealand, which might not be counteracted by a force from England. . . .

We have indicated the essentials of a colonial relation neither costly to the mother-country nor oppressive to the dependency – one, in fact, under which the Colonies of Great Britain would not cost the Mother-country a shilling, but would on the contrary swell her strength, reciprocate her commerce, and augment her resources. What hinders us from setting free these essential principles, that they may work truly? The obstacle is *the Colonial Office in Downing Street*: that it is which prevents the proper government of the British Colonies, foments disaffection, and renders them costly encumbrances. It is thus that the Colonial Office costs this country many millions sterling every year, and endangers the integrity of the empire. . . .

(*Spectator*, 29 April 1848)

~ Molesworth developed a similar theme in a parliamentary speech later the same year. Whether or not the Canadians eventually decided to break away from the empire and become independent colonies of Britain like the United States, the imperial value of North America would be most effectively promoted by the recognition of local self-government.~

. . . For what purpose do we keep 9,000 troops in North America? Is it to protect the colonists against the United States? But if they are loyal at heart they are strong enough to protect themselves; if they are disloyal, twice 9,000 men will not keep them down. But suppose they were to separate from us, and to form independent States, or even to join the United States, would they not become more profitable as colonies than they are at present? The United States of America are, in the strict significance of the word, still colonies of Great Britain, as Carthage was a colony of Tyre, and the cities of Ionia and Sicily were colonies of Greece; for the word colony does not necessarily imply dependency, but merely a community composed of persons who have removed from one country and settled in another, for the purpose of cultivating it. Now, our colonies (as I will term them) of the United States are in every point of view more useful to us than all our colonies put together. In 1844, we exported to the United States produce and manufactures to the value of £8,000,000; an amount equal to the whole of our real export trade to all our colonial dominions, which we govern at a cost of £4,000,000 a year; while the United States cost us for consular and diplomatic services not more than £15,000 a year; and not one ship of war is required to protect our trade with the United States; in fact, a British ship of war is very rarely seen off the coasts of the United States. Again, more emigrants go directly from this country to the United States than to all our other colonies put together. In the last ten years, according to the returns of the Emigration Commissioners, 1,042,000 emigrants left this country, of which number 552,000 went directly to the United States; how many went indirectly through Canada, I cannot undertake to say. Last year 251,000 persons emigrated from Great Britain to North America, 142,000 of whom went directly to the United States, the remaining 109,000 to the colonies. At present it is considered that colonies are chiefly useful as affording markets for our produce and outlets for our population. It is evident that in both these respects independent colonies are as useful as dependent ones. I do not, however, propose to abandon the North American colonies; but if we are compelled to choose between the alternative of the continuation of the present vast expenditure and that of abandoning these colonies, it is evident that the latter alternative would be the more profitable one in an economical point of view. But I maintain, that if we govern our North American colonies as we ought to govern them, follow out rigorously the principle of responsible government, and leave them to manage their own affairs, uncontrolled by the Colonial Office, we may with safety diminish our military force and expenditure, and they will willingly continue to be our fellow-subjects. . . .

(*Hansard*, c, 25 July 1848, 832-3)

~ Roebuck extended this line of reasoning when he argued that eventual colonial self-government should be positively anticipated, and appropriate arrangements made to prepare for that welcome event and to establish a firm foundation for continuing friendship between Britain and independent colonies.~

. . . Every colony ought by us to be looked upon as a country destined, at some period of its existence, to govern itself. . . . The colonies which we are founding in America, Australasia, and Africa, will, probably, at some future day, be powerful nations, who will also be unwilling to remain in subjection to any rule but their own. But this withdrawal from our metropolitan rule ought not to offend or wound us as a nation; we should feel in this case as a parent feels when a child has reached unto manhood — becomes his own master, forms his own separate household, and becomes in his turn the master of a family. The ties of affection remain — the separation is not the cause or the effect of hostility. Thus should it be with a mother country and her colonies. Having founded and brought them to a healthy and sturdy maturity, she should be proud to see them honestly glorying in their strength, and wishing for independence. Having looked forward to this time, as sure to come, she should prepare for it; she should make such arrangements in her system as to put all things in order for this coming change in the colony's condition, so that independence may be acquired and friendship retained. The colony would, in such a case, continue to feel towards the mother country with kindness and respect; a close union would exist between them, and all their mutual relations would be so ordered as to conduce to the welfare of both. In the instance of the United States, a very different course was pursued by us; we fiercely resisted, and resented their desire for independence. . . . When, at length, they achieved their independence, years were required before this animosity could be softened. . . . A repetition of this history we ought seriously to guard against; we can best do so by gradually preparing our great colonies for independence, and this can be properly done only by establishing beforehand arrangements which shall be consonant to this new and coming condition. . . .

(Roebuck, *The Colonies of England*, pp. 170-2)

~ The *Spectator* agreed that the existing nature of imperial relations could not remain unaltered. Statesmen had to face up to realities and prepare for the emergence of a self-governing empire.~

. . . Recent occurrences in every section of the Colonial empire make it obvious that the actual, or rather the late relation between England and her dependencies, cannot be maintained; but the change which is inevitable is half made, ready to the hand of the official statesman, by the Colonies themselves. The future relation, whatever it is *called*, if any relation is to exist at all, must be one of federal alliance and reciprocal benefit; the Colonies *wholly* independent of the central administration in their *local* government, but united to the empire by a few broad and simple bonds of mutual interest. Now, towards effecting that sort of independence not much remains to be done. Canada is virtually independent, notwithstanding the large army which this country maintains in that colony, for a show of supremacy . . . with reference to all our colonies proper, we are reverting to the relation which subsisted between England and those settlements that she established on the best *political* footing, the earlier colonies of North America. . . .

The reason why the statesmen who are in office, or waiting outside the portal of office, refuse to recognize and act upon these obvious facts, is that they are blinded by routine and certain conventional tenets, about "the integrity of the empire," the duty of "maintaining its territory intact," and the like. They cannot see the Colonies or their proceedings, for the accumulated heaps of didactic despatches and blue books around themselves. For similar reasons – the fixed contemplation of received ideas, rather than an examination of realities – they cannot discern the utility of colonies municipally independent; and as they cannot bring their minds "to give up the Colonies," they cannot bring their minds to what seems to them equivalent to giving up. If they would simply leave poring over the records and imaginative compositions of Downing Street, and look at the facts open to the broad light of day, these doubting politicians would soon perceive that colonies might be as useful as ever – more so – although they should be municipally independent. The nation that is not continually growing is stationary and about to decline: but if England continue to grow within the compass of the four seas, she will grow too big for her own space . . . colonization affords scope for growth, field for the action of increasing energies. To multiply English settlements, is to multiply English markets for English produce. But there are considerations higher even than commercialism: it is the duty of us all, nations as well as individuals, to do all the good we can, and not to let good be wasted for want of our exertion: it will be the better for the world, if one of the most civilized of nations be extended, rather than one less civilized. Accidental circumstances have conspired to set a lower tone of intellectual, political, and national morality in the great separated colonies of England; and it would be for the benefit of the world if England were able to extend herself, rather than to acquiesce in extension of the United States by absorption of English colonies. It would be better for England to possess allies bound by every tie of blood and undivided interest, rather than rivals prone to contest. Statesmanship worthy of the name deals with realities, and aims at substantial good: true Colonial statesmanship, just now, should consist in confronting the facts and striving after attainable good, not in ignoring the facts and striving to retain obsolete privileges.

(*Spectator*, 29 December 1849)

2 / COLONIAL REPRESENTATION

~ When the Colonial Reformers suggested specific proposals for placing imperial relations on a new and more cordial footing, it is instructive that they should frequently have advocated closer and more formal political ties. Now that direct British control was no longer feasible, the Reformers proposed to secure a necessary degree of continued colonial dependence by some form of representation in London. This did not mean representation in the House of Commons, which would have been unsatisfactory and impracticable, but the appointment of colonial agents or the establishment of a council with delegates from overseas who would discuss prospective British legislation or policy on colonial questions. With the United States in mind, it was even suggested that an imperial federal union might advantageously be formed.

In all these proposals the Reformers assumed that the British government would continue to supervise and legislate for certain areas of colonial administration, and that centralization of authority in matters of imperial concern was essential to the preservation of the empire. Even with local self-government, some degree of colonial dependence was considered desirable, and it was not easy to see what form imperial relations would take or how the benefits of empire might be secured in an era of free trade unless the vague ties of sentiment and self-interest were expressed in concrete political or administrative terms. In actual fact, self-government would prove to be incompatible with centralization, and imperial relations had to be based on a loosening of ties and a more willing acceptance of equality of status than the Reformers were able to envisage. For the moment, however, the *Colonial Gazette* advocated the establishment of a colonial council in London as a means of giving the various parts of the empire a more influential voice in imperial affairs.~

 ... *the Colonists have no Representation in the Parent State*
 ... they have become important branches of the British empire,

and yet have no representative body in the seat of empire. They are large and powerful constituencies without a member – masses of qualified citizens without a vote or voice. Can we wonder at the perpetual jars and jealousies between the Home and the Colonial Legislatures? Can we wonder that every attempt to legislate *for* the Colonies becomes more or less abortive? Can we wonder that where this great safety-valve of our constitution is wanting, every disturbance and irregularity should threaten ruin and overthrow? We most earnestly call attention to this subject, because we are persuaded, that all legislation for our Colonies will ere long become waste parchment, unless they acquire some constitutional channel of expressing their opinions on that legislation, and of influencing it – unless, in short, they are allowed to feel that they are really *members* of the empire, and not mere *subjects* of it. What but the neglect of this really lost us the United States of America? We are not going to enter on the question whether that loss has been detrimental or otherwise to us, but if we wish to preserve the Colonies we now have – if we wish to *govern* them – the time is come when that object can only be accomplished by giving them a representative voice in the Mother-country.

. . . It is not as a measure of favour, or of concession, or of conciliatory policy, or even of justice, that we look at it, but as a measure that has become necessary in order to render any legislation for the Colonies much longer successful, and to realize any hope of preserving them by the natural and peaceable ties of government.

When we speak of Representation for the Colonies, we do not, however, mean that they should be entitled to send Representatives to the Imperial Parliament. This, no doubt, is the first and most obvious idea of Representation, and, as such, is probably the only one that has yet suggested itself to those Colonists who are thinking of the subject. But is this practicable? We much doubt whether, even at the passing of the Reform Bill, it would have been possible for any Minister to have obtained an extension of the elective franchise to the Colonies for this purpose; and *now*, the suggestion of so far unsettling and altering the constitution, if it obtained a hearing from Parliament, would certainly have to struggle its way slowly, and in opposition to many scruples, jealousies, and prejudices. It would really, we believe too, be a very partial benefit to the Colonies, and productive of no trifling inconvenience to the Home Legislature. The House of Commons is too large, and composed of too many discordant elements, as it is, to get on with the business that is yearly before it. What would be the result of throwing into the mêlée forty or fifty more representatives of new interests? And what good, after all, would they effect for the Colonists? If strictly Colonial in their character, they would form a feeble, insulated party – commonly divided on their own peculiar subjects of debate: if, on the other hand, they were to consist of persons involved in Home politics and Home interests, they would be in proportion less of Colonial representatives. . . .

No! There is a more practicable and a more suitable mode of representation for the Colonies – one that is easy, safe, and may at once be adopted, without awakening any constitutional jealousies, or interfering at all with the present machinery of our Home Legislature. We will explain.

We would propose the formation of a *Colonial Board*, to be composed of delegates from the several Colonies, (or agents, as they are now called,) with the Colonial Minister at the head of it. This Board should have the right of discussing all Colonial questions which are to be made the subject of British legislative enactment, *before* any bill should be introduced into Parliament. . . . We would not make it imperative that no measure of Colonial legislation should be introduced into Parliament which had been rejected by this Board: it would give enough representative power to the Board to grant this privilege of *previous discussion and previous decision*, so that the measure, when subsequently brought before Parliament, either by Ministers or by any other Member, may appear with the influence of that previous discussion, and with the light thereby thrown upon it. This, we say, would be sufficient representative power, and exercised in the most convenient way. Any measure introduced into Parliament with the unanimous decision of such a Board in its favour, would, in almost every instance, be sure of receiving the sanction of Parliament. At all events, no measure *negatived* by its unanimous decision could well be carried afterwards. A Board like this would give to the Colonists all that they really want – *a constitutional and public voice in all questions relating to themselves*. With this Board they would feel that they were treated, on all occasions, with respect at least, if not invested with power; and Colonies, like individuals in a lower station in life, in their dealings with the higher powers are sorer under disrespect often than under actual grievance. But it would be *power* – representative power quite enough for all purposes.

To the Colonial Minister also the advantage would be very

great. His power would doubtless be somewhat controlled; but it would be the more easily exercised. And he would become better acquainted with every matter of business which belongs to his department, through the previous public and free discussion at this Board, than is possible by means of *ex parte* statements, or of any of the modes of information now open to him. . . .

(*Colonial Gazette*, 25 September 1839)

~ Wakefield also saw the future of imperial relations as tending towards closer co-operation, but in 1849 he favoured the appointment of colonial agents as the most suitable means of imperial communication.~

. . . Colonists and colonial reformers at home have proposed that every colony should have a representative in the British House of Commons. The object of the suggestion is most desirable, but, I think, not attainable by that means. The object is to bestow on every colony the great advantage of being able to hold legitimate communication with the imperial public and government. It is not supposed that the vote of a colonial member of the House of Commons would serve any good purpose, but . . . might he not be quite as effectually the representative of the colony at home, without being in Parliament? If he might, the whole advantage for the colony would be secured, without having recourse to a measure, which really is open to very serious objections, and still more opposed to some of John Bull's probably unconquerable prejudices.

By recurring to the colonizing wisdom of our ancestors, we shall discover a simple, effectual, and unobjectionable means of attaining the object in view. Under the municipal authority vested in them by our old colonial charters, the old colonies used to appoint "Agents" to reside in England, and to serve as a medium of communication between the colonial and imperial governments. . . . But the valuable institution of colonial representatives at home, has gradually fallen into discredit and practical disuse since the Colonial Office was instituted; and it exists now, for the most part, with no effect but that of adding a few sinecures to the patronage of the Colonial Office. For the Colonial Office, having got to be the real government of the colonies, virtually appoints the colonial agents who purport to be accredited to it by the colonies!

Supposing the government of the colony to be really municipal, it would itself appoint its Agent. If it were the organ of the portion of the colonists having the greatest interest in the colony's well-doing, it would select for Agent or Resident in England one of the most respectable and capable of the colonists. Such a person, so accredited to the imperial government, would be a personage here, and would have weight accordingly with our government and public. He would keep the colony informed of matters at home, with which it behoved the colonists to be acquainted; and he might powerfully forward the interests of both colony and mother-country, by helping to promote the emigration of capital and labour: for in this branch of colonization, there is no more urgent want than some authority residing in the mother-country, but identified with and responsible to the colonists.

The Agents (Representatives seems a better title) would, of course, be appointed and removeable by the governor of the colony on the advice of his responsible council of ministers, and paid by the colony.

If the ancient institution of colonial agency at home were thus revived and improved, as it might easily be, the effect would be to add another powerful tie to the connexion between the colony and the mother-country. To some extent a Representative would have the functions of the representatives of the States of America in the United States Congress. Our system of colonial government, viewed as a whole, would be federative as well as municipal. . . .

(Wakefield, *Art of Colonization*, pp. 309-12)

~ On several occasions when they examined the future of imperial relations in an era of free trade and self-government, the Colonial Reformers advocated the formation of a union or federation. As the *Colonial Gazette* argued in 1846, the various communities that comprised the British empire might advantageously follow the example of the United States and come together in an imperial union. Such an arrangement would offer commercial advantages, but above all, it would stabilize defensive and diplomatic relations, and reinforce Britain's standing as an international power.~

. . . Some of our friends have taken into their heads that, under a system of free-trade, the colonial *nexus* must necessarily be dissolved. *If the colonies are to be governed in future as they have been, this is not unlikely to be the case.* . . . There can be no doubt that a great deal of what has for many years been conventionally called and allowed to pass current for loyalty has been neither more nor less than a sordid spirit of jobbing. The support of one section of colonists to our miserable and unjust system of colonial rule was bought by patronage of "family compacts"; the support of another by the maintenance of exclusive trading privileges. The family compacts have been, most of them, knocked on the head. The vested interests in monopoly are on the eve of undergoing the same fate. Henceforth the stability of Government must be maintained, not by paying court to and bribing individual *cliques* and *coteries,* but by conciliating, through the means of well-intended and efficient measures, the confidence of the mass of the community. No Government will take the trouble to strengthen itself by the laborious method of good and wise administration so long as it can make a shift by the easier method of corrupting knots of influential individuals. The abolition of monopoly, as well as the discountenance of family compacts, is one indispensable prerequisite to the good government of the colonies.

"But what interest have the colonies in remaining subject to the Imperial Government if they are to enjoy no preference over aliens in the trade with the old country?" We will tell our interrogators: – Look to the United States. The Government of Washington is too weak to be a useful domestic Government. . . . Yet is it better for the states composing the Union that they should be conjointly subject to this shadow of a Government, than that each should be entirely independent. A common authority is recognised by all, and thus, in extreme cases, the risk of war among themselves is diminished. The main difficulty in the way of substituting arbitration for war, in the settlement of international disputes, is the want of an arbiter or judge possessing authority over both parties. The Government at Washington is such a judge in the case of controversies between individual states of the Union: the Union is an international system, with a permanent judicial referee at Washington. The union between Great Britain and her colonies must be made something analogous to this. Were the Canadas, West Indies, Australia, the Cape, New Zealand, &c., all to become independent states without any common head, the chances of war among so many proud and energetic communities would be immensely multiplied. Any arrangement which, leaving to these communities a large scope of internal self-government, perpetuates the jurisdiction of the Crown of England over them, diminishes the risk. The time has past when the connexion of colonies with the mother country can be to the extent it has been – one of such entire dependence on the part of the former: henceforth it must be more one of equality in a relation of subjection to one crown. There are elements in the British constitution which admit of its being extended to such a state of relations. It is in our power to make London the central seat of government to a union as much superior in its administration to the United States as its extent is greater, and at the same time its means of intercommunication easier.

Both parties – mother country and colonies – would find their interest in such an arrangement. The defensive and diplomatic establishments of all the communities constituting such a union would be infinitely more efficient and, at the same time, more economical than the multiplied defensive and diplomatic establishments which all of them, if entirely independent, would have to maintain. Their mutual controversies would be more peaceably, economically, and satisfactorily arranged. But England, even more than the others, has an interest in the constitution of such a union. Its colonial empire is no mean element of its strength: stripped of its colonies, England would be a much inferior power to what it is. At this moment the English race is in the process of occupying full two-thirds of the entire globe. The maxims and methods of government applicable to a small island are inapplicable to such an immense space. Already a large section of the Anglican race have erected themselves into an independent and, to a lamentable extent, a hostile empire. If England is desirous of preserving the preponderance among the communities of Englishmen scattered over the globe, which it is, for so many reasons, desirable she should retain, it can only be effected by placing her Government at the head of a greater and better organised Union than the United States.

(*Colonial Gazette*, 18 April 1846)

3 / RELATIONS WITH THE UNITED STATES

~ In common with many of their contemporaries, the Colonial Reformers were apprehensive of the possibility that the Canadian provinces might join the American Union, either voluntarily or by annexation, and of the effects which this would have on Britain's international position and relations with the United States. The Reformers argued that if the provinces remained within the empire, they would provide more accommodating outlets for excess English population and capital, as well as invaluable natural resources to be exploited, and would also continue to buttress Britain's prestige and standing as a world power. Points of friction that arose in Anglo-American and Canadian-American relations were therefore anxiously discussed by the Colonial Reformers.

At the time of the rebellions in 1837 there seemed to Englishmen a real danger that the Americans would intervene on behalf of the Canadian rebels. While the United States government might not instigate such a movement, many Americans living in the border region sympathized with the rebels, and contemporary events in Texas showed how easily and effectively American citizens could take events into their own hands. Lord Durham therefore actively attempted during his mission to allay American passions and the border unrest by emphasizing what he regarded as the true nature of the struggle in the Canadas and by adopting more generous sentiments towards the Americans and their institutions. In August 1838 he explained to Lord Glenelg, the colonial secretary, the causes of friction in Canadian-American relations.~

. . . Satisfied of the disaffected temper of the Canadians as a people, I have naturally taken pains to acquire correct information as to the state of feeling in the United States as respects these Colonies & the Mother-country. All reports concur in assuring me that the present Gov[ernmen]t of the Union, & a vast majority of the American people, are decidedly adverse to a rupture with England . . . but there are points in the state of American feeling towards these colonies & especially near the frontier, of so much moment as to require particular notice.

In the first place, although some persons in the States, & the more so, if they have visited this country, are aware of the true nature of the late rebellion, it is a common opinion in America that the contention in this Province has been between the Executive Gov[ernmen]t, on the one hand, supported by a minority, & the majority of the people without distinction of race, on the other; & that the subject of disagreement has been practical grievances & general principles similar to those which formed the matter of dispute between England & her old Colonies in America. . . . The mistake is easily accounted for. It is only on the spot that one learns how the real subject of strife in Lower Canada has been a question of nationality. Every where else, the false professions & designations employed by both parties, combined with the plain fact that the contest has been between a majority & a minority, is apt to mislead the inquirer by keeping out of view the distinction of races. . . . An ever active sentiment of national pride is perhaps the most remarkable feature in the American character. It might have been foreseen therefore, that the Americans, proudly recollecting the origin & progress of their own revolutionary war with England, should sympathize with the [French] Canadians, or rather with the majority, who happen to be Canadians. Whether they may ever comprehend the false position assumed by both parties in this colony, I will not venture to predict: but so long as their view of the subject shall remain unchanged, they will, I believe, continue to sympathize with that side which has the air of contending for democratic principles & popular objects, & to wish that it may prevail over the other which appears in the light of an oppressive minority.

Secondly, Having regard to the national pride of America, it is certain that the temper & tone of the British party towards that country, tends to stir up angry passions throughout the Union, & especially near the frontier, where articles from the colonial newspapers are generally reprinted. The British cannot but resent that American sympathy with the Canadians which I have just described. . . . Hence their organs of the press abound with false statements, much exaggerated descriptions, perversions of the truth, insulting reflexions, provoking sneers, & low-lived abuse, of which the effect, not to say the aim, is to stimulate & goad the national pride of Americans. . . .

Thirdly, by the existence of a state of things, out of which it is easy to see that war might spring, the American mind becomes more & more familiar with the idea of war. Differing as the Americans do from all other nations in the universal diffusion of an active interest in public affairs, & in a habit which belongs to all ranks, of calculation as to the future, they are led, by the political state of these Provinces to discuss the subject of war hypothetically, if I may use the expression; they are reminded of the events of the last war, & . . . by frequently conversing on such exciting topics, they gradually approach that state of feeling under which the Gov[ernmen]t, necessarily impelled by the people, would find it hard to maintain friendly relations with England. . . .

Fourthly, it is not to be denied that the distracted state of these colonies occasions no little inconvenience to the frontier states, & to the Federal Gov[ernmen]t. It calls for an increase of the army, a sort of military array on the frontier, & the exercise of new powers by the executive which are opposed to the habits if not the institutions, of the American People. All the expense & annoyance are attributed to the British

Gov[ernmen]t. A dispassionate American admits that his Gov[ernmen]t is bound, at whatever cost, to prevent aggressions on the Canadian frontier; & he does not deny that the obligation has been inadequately fulfilled; but when reminded of the inefficiency of the laws for that purpose, & the weakness of the American executive, he answers that the true source of every difficulty is the weakness of the British Gov[ernmen]t in Canada, which has not maintained order amongst its own subjects, nor is able to protect the United States from such a nuisance as arises from the conduct of British refugees within their territory. This retort, without stopping to examine its justice, suffices to show that, until order shall be restored in these Colonies, a great cause of irritation in America will probably continue to operate with increasing force.

Fifthly, the boundary Question, being much mixed, as it unavoidably is in America, with considerations arising out of the state of these colonies, forms a more active element of hostile feeling than would otherwise have been the case.

Lastly, it is certain that amongst the frontier population of the United States, which I should observe has very greatly increased since the last war, there exists a numerous body of men, young, active, energetic, & self-relying, who, from various motives, long for an opportunity of invading Canada. Some of them are moved by an opinion, which it would not be easy to question, that if these colonies were laid open to American enterprize, a great impulse would be given to the industry & trade of that part of the States, which now constitutes the frontier; some are influenced by one or other of the circumstances to which I have already adverted; some by that love of adventure merely, which belongs to the American character; & some by a reasonable calculation of the gain & distinction which, in troubled times, usually fall to the most active & daring. The manner in which these people talk of invading the Canadas, exemplifies the self-reliance of American citizens. They do not expect that the Federal Gov[ernmen]t should open the way for them by military operations; they even avow their belief that, in a contest of troops only, the British would surely prevail; but they reckon upon the friendly disposition towards them of great numbers on this side, & upon swarming over the line in such numbers & at so many places simultaneously, as to get possession of the Country in spite of military obstacles . . . it is well that I should remind H. M.'s Gov[ernmen]t of the invasion of Texas by a body of American citizens, who, without the least aid from their Gov[ernmen]t, have seized an extensive country, defeated armies, got possession of the soil, & established themselves as a nation, with constitutional gov[ernmen]t, a judicial system, & municipal institutions as complete as any in America. There is certainly no immediate danger of an attack upon these colonies; & I have mentioned the subject only for the purpose of indicating the probable character of the contest that would take place here, if all the causes now in operation should finally produce one. It was in consequence of all these important considerations that, during my late residence on the American frontier, I courted the most unreserved communication with all respectable Americans, for the purpose of impressing them with a more sound & accurate conception of the real state of things; with a more just appreciation of our system of gov[ernmen]t and its real objects – & with a due sense of the danger which would arise to themselves, if their gov[ernmen]t remained a passive spectator of all these proceedings, tending, as they did, to destroy all confidence in its executive strength, & all reliance on the national honour.

I am happy to say that my efforts have been successful, that a great change has taken place in public feeling on the American side – & that my exertions to restore tranquillity & good order are encouraged & supported by the most influential portions of the Press & of Society in the United States. . . .

(Lord Durham to Lord Glenelg, 9 August 1838, No. 36, Secret & Confidential, DURHAM PAPERS, vol. 12; or *Report of the Public Archives, 1923*, pp. 320-3)

~ Although British misgovernment in the Canadas had provided a fertile soil for rebels and agitators, the *Colonial Gazette* maintained in 1838 that the activities of American sympathizers along the Canadian border did not reflect responsible opinion in the United States. Provided reforms were speedily introduced, Canada would not be lost to Britain through the attacks of American insurgents.~

We are not among those who are inclined to impugn the good faith of the United States' Government in its late proceedings regarding British America. It may perhaps be true, that some persons connected with the Government have countenanced the sympathizers and insurgents in Canada, but we do not see that the charge can be at all substantiated against the President, or his Administration . . . we know, upon good authority, that the official authorities at Washington were exceedingly anxious for an opportunity of offering to the Queen's Representative the testimony of their desire to perpetuate amicable relations between the two countries.

The *Sympathisers* form a very small proportion of the population of the States, and are a body of persons totally distinct from the capitalists and persons of property, none of whom are disposed to incur the risks of fraternity with the plundering Patriots. The discernment of the mercantile and agricultural interests leads them alike to wish that peace with Great Britain may long continue.

The Americans are, however, keen enough to perceive the unpardonable neglect, to say nothing worse, with which the British Colonies in general have been hitherto ruled. When Colonial discontent arrives at a certain point, it does not require foreign intervention to bring about the natural results of systematic misgovernment. If Canada is lost, as some believe, for all purposes of profit to the mother-country, it is by the Canadians themselves, – either rightly or wrongly, – either justifiably or unjustifiably, – that the connection will have been severed. But we are sanguine enough to hope for better things, and cannot believe that the British Legislature will blindly sacrifice those important Colonies, which offer the means of subsistence, – of comfort, of wealth, – to countless thousands of the suffering population of the mother-country. The approaching session will determine whether the Canadas are irrecoverably lost, or whether we have the wisdom to preserve, by timely, though tardy, good management, one of the richest jewels in the Imperial Crown.

(*Colonial Gazette*, 22 December 1838)

~ Friction in Anglo-American relations was always likely to burst into an open conflict so long as territorial boundaries remained in dispute. Since 1783 the two countries had been unable to agree on a particular stretch of the boundary between New Brunswick and Maine in a region where Britain wanted, for military reasons, to guarantee overland communication between the Atlantic seaboard and Montreal, and where New Brunswick and Maine had conflicting interests over lumbering and navigation of the St. John River. In February 1839 lumbermen and the local authorities in the disputed area clashed in an engagement that came to be known as the "Aroostook War." Although Governor Fairfield of Maine had despatched the state militia into the contested district, and both sides made provocative preparation for open hostilities, the tense situation was soon eased, and the boundary dispute was finally settled in the Webster-Ashburton Treaty of 1842. In 1839, however, the *Colonial Gazette* was apprehensive about the situation and critical of American actions.~

. . . The question of the disputed boundary, between the United States and our Colony of New Brunswick, has, at length, assumed a form which calls for no common share of prudence on the part of the two governments, in order to prevent an open rupture. It is difficult to determine which party is most in fault, for having suffered a question of this nature to remain thus unsettled for fifty-six years, during all which time its importance has been constantly increasing. At the time when the treaty was concluded, by which the independence of the United States was fully recognised by England, the citizens of Maine and Massachusetts on the one hand, and the English Colonists on the other, had ample space for every purpose they could desire, and thought but little about a desert tract, the geography of which was unknown to either party. It is out of this ignorance that the dispute between the two countries has arisen. The negotiators of the Treaty of 1783 took for granted circumstances, which a better knowledge of the facts has shown to have had no existence; but to which one party at least chooses to adhere, with a pertinacity which would be amusing, if it were not for the serious consequences that may possibly grow out of the dispute.

So far as we have at present been made acquainted with the proceedings on both sides, the Governor and legislature of Maine are manifestly in the wrong – so manifestly that we hold it to be impossible for the Government at Washington to countenance their acts. It appears that a party of English lumberers were pursuing their labours in a portion of the disputed territory; and if the Governor of Maine had limited himself to representing the circumstance to the Lieutenant-Governor of New Brunswick, and calling upon him to put a stop to such proceedings, there is no reason whatever to doubt that Sir John Harvey would have done everything in the matter that could reasonably have been required of him. Instead of this, an armed force of about 200 men, with a piece of artillery, are sent against our countrymen; thus verifying the old saying of "a word and a blow, but the blow first."

It would have been wholly incompetent to the general government of the United States, acting according to the laws that govern civilised nations, to have proceeded in this high-handed manner: and *a fortiori* it must be incompetent for an inferior body, having no right of making war, to do so. The act of Governor Fairfield, backed as it is by the Senate and Representatives of Maine, will, in all probability, be disclaimed by President Van Buren; and the matter being, on our part, in the hands of a man of sense and discretion, we trust the whole affair will be speedily and amicably adjusted.

Surely, however, such an occurrence must lead both the English and the American Government to reflect seriously upon the imprudence of leaving so important a question any longer unsettled. For more than half a century, a district containing more than 10,000 square miles, or nearly seven million acres, has been suffered to remain in as wild a state as it was before the discovery of the American continent, while the march of civilization has been proceeding on all sides, and giving a value to these natural forests, which has attracted the attention and excited the cupidity alike of the citizens of Maine, and Massachusetts, and the New Brunswick Colonists.

The legislatures of the two States more directly interested in the question have latterly made no secret of their views and feelings on the subject of this disputed territory. The Legislatures of both have – Maine in 1837, and Massachusetts in 1838 – appointed Committees "to inquire what measures may be necessary in relation to the North Eastern boundary"; and both these Committees have presented reports. That to the Legislature of Maine is violent in the extreme, and threatens, in plain language, that which its Governor has now begun to put into practice. . . .

. . . Massachusetts used a calmer, more dignified, and more constitutional tone in the discussion; but there is reason to fear lest the excitement among the citizens of this last-named State be not almost as great as that avowed in Maine; and lest, in the event of the dispute continuing, and leading to the shedding of blood, the people of Massachusetts may not, either with or against the consent of the Governor and Legislature, make common cause with their neighbours, and thus still further complicate the question.

That in any case this dispute would lead us into war with the United States, we cannot bring ourselves to believe. The advantages of peace between the two countries are so far beyond the advantage to be derived by either party from the most complete measure of success in war, that it would be the height of folly to rush into hostilities; but so long as this territory shall be an object of dispute, there must be a constant likelihood of collision; and, therefore, wisdom and humanity alike call

upon the two governments to apply themselves, without delay, in a spirit of fairness and conciliation, to the adjustment of the difference.
(*Colonial Gazette*, 16 March 1839)

. . . This greediness after additional territory, which, notwithstanding the assertions made to the contrary, has always marked the conduct of America, is an appetite which "grows by what it feeds on"; and it especially behoves England, which is, of all countries, the most exposed to injury from such a disposition, to afford no opportunity for whetting an appetite that must be afterwards gorged at her expense.
(*Colonial Gazette*, 29 June 1839)

~ A further conflict came to a head in 1845 and concerned the territory of Oregon, which had since 1827 been jointly occupied and administered by Britain and the United States. In the intervening years conflicting claims to colonize the area had emerged, and the situation was complicated by a disorderly pattern of settlement. To Englishmen it appeared that America was determined to annex the whole of Oregon, and President Polk's elaboration of the Monroe Doctrine in 1845 advanced the idea of manifest destiny to justify the extension of American colonization and republicanism to the exclusion of further European settlement on the North American continent and of monarchical principles of government. Despite the assertion of American claims and British rejection of them, the issue was settled by partition in 1846 with a boundary running from the Rocky Mountains along the 49th parallel to the west coast. Nevertheless, the *Spectator* was deeply concerned about the course of events in 1845 and critical of American attitudes and ambitions.~

In his message to Congress, Mr. Polk assumes as incontrovertible a doctrine unknown to international law, and utterly untenable, though not entirely new in the mouths of American statesmen. Mr. Monroe asserted it during his Presidency, when he declared that "the American continents, by the free and independent condition which they have assumed and maintain, are henceforth not to be considered as subjects for future colonization by any European Power." Mr. Polk is of opinion, that, in the existing circumstances of the world, the present is a proper occasion to "reiterate and reaffirm the principle avowed by Mr. Monroe." In doing this, he steals a step. "It is due alike to our safety and our interest, that the efficient protection of our laws should be extended over the whole of our territorial limits, and that it should be distinctly announced to the world as our settled policy, that no future European colony or dominion shall, with our consent, be planted or established on any part of the North American continent." From intentional or unintentional looseness of expression, Mr. Polk has here used the phrases "our whole territorial limits," and "any part of the North American continent," so as to give them in a great measure the appearance of being convertible terms.

It is not in words alone that he reaffirms the position of Mr. Monroe. The immediate application of the abstract principle is made to Oregon; and he advises the Legislature to give England notice of the termination of the joint occupancy – to establish an Indian agency in Oregon – to extend the laws and jurisdiction of the United States over its citizens resident there – to make liberal grants of land to "the patriotic pioneers" who may choose to open up "the vast wilderness intervening between our frontier settlements and Oregon" – to connect the North-west territory with those frontier settlements by a chain of stockades and blockhouses and moveable columns of mounted riflemen – and to establish a monthly overland mail between the States and the American squatteries on the Columbia. In the same message which recommends this system of operations, the annexation of Texas is dwelt on with triumph: threats of an aggressive war are held in suspense over the Mexican Republic; and, with a side-glance to the North, it is affirmed that "the people of this continent alone have the right to decide their own destiny" – "should any portion of them, constituting an independent state, propose to unite themselves with our confederacy, this will be a question for them and us to determine, without and foreign interposition" – "the American system of government is entirely different from that of Europe." In short, the President of the United States advises Congress to arm and organize the citizens in order that they may be prepared to avail themselves of any emergency, to receive all communities already settled on the North American continent into the bosom of the Union, and to prevent the colonization of any part of the continent by European nations.

If Congress adopt the principle enunciated by Messrs. Monroe and Polk, they will arrogate to the Government of the United States the sole and exclusive right to colonize the yet unoccupied portions of the North American continent. The mere *ex-parte* declaration of one government cannot make any doctrine part of the law of nations: the common consent of all, or of a majority of governments, is required for that purpose. But the doctrine recognized by the majority of civilized nations on this head is, that all tracts of country inhabited only by savage or nomad tribes not organized into a state, may be colonized by the first government that sees fit to take possession of them; and that a government may, by certain preliminary measures, establish an exclusive right to colonize a more extensive tract of country than it is prepared to do at the moment. The Government at Washington is entitled to insist that all tracts of land to which it has established such an exclusive right shall be colonized either by its own citizens or by individuals who agree to submit to its peculiar laws and institutions; but any other Government, in any part of the world, is entitled to do the same; and Russia and Great Britain have done it.

. . . all denizens of overpeopled countries are entitled to seek for and take possession of new and unoccupied lands. They are entitled to transplant the institutions which habit has made a second nature to them, to their new homes. The European colonist has the same right to plant Monarchical or Aristocratical institutions in the territories to which Russia and Great Britain have established their preferable right of colonization, that the United States colonist has to plant Democratic institutions in the territory on which his Government has laid its hands. In point of equity, the claims of the European colonists are the stronger; for their overpeopled countries leave them no option but to emigrate, while within the settlements of the United States the population is insufficient fully to occupy the soil. The Polk and Monroe policy is the dog-in-the-manger policy, of excluding Europeans from regions which their own countrymen will be unable to occupy for centuries to come. It has its origin in a bigoted political sectarianism, which can see nothing good except in its own political institutions, and would compel all settlers in America to adopt them. It betrays on the part of the Americans a want of faith in the goodness of their own institutions: if sincere and consistent in their belief of their excellence, they would leave them to be voluntarily adopted by the new comers, instead of trying to make submission to them a condition of settlement. The aim of this attempt to prevent European colonization is, to extend the political influence of the American Government, not to promote the individual prosperity of American citizens. The pride of professional politicians may be gratified and their emoluments increased, by widening the sphere within which the authority of the central Government at Washington and the local machinery of Government throughout the Union is paramount; but private citizens can only be benefited by removing every obstacle to the speedy settlement and cultivation of the waste. The imposition of Republican institutions is an obstacle to European colonization. The American citizen who sacrifices real individual interests to gratify the vanity of his Government, is as simple as the European subject who does so to pamper the pride of a Monarch.

(*Spectator*, 27 December 1845)

~ Comments by the Colonial Reformers on American territorial ambitions frequently included some reference to their belief in the superiority of monarchical over republican institutions. The *Colonial Gazette* took the opportunity afforded by Governor Metcalfe's victory in the election of 1844 to expatiate on this theme.~

. . . We have no prejudices against the citizens of the North American Union or their institutions. When we look back on their history, we see that it was impossible that any other form of government could be established among them. But we do not sufficiently admire that form or government to wish to see it spread over the whole of the vast continent of America. We believe that it cheats men with an unreal semblance of freedom, that the personal freedom and impunity of the honest man, which it is the first duty of Government to ensure, is less than in countries where the democratic element is tempered by the aristocratic and monarchic elements. We believe that in the United States each man is a trembling slave to all. We believe that the institutions of the Union are as incompatible with a really free, fearless, and generous spirit as those of Venice of old. We believe, too, that they enthral the minds of men to an absorbing interest in mere material concerns. And we wish to see one portion of the Anglo-Norman occupants of America disenthralled from this delusive semblance of liberty – weaned from feeding on those Dead-sea apples, fair in show without, but choking ashes and bitterness within.

One use of the late victory in Canada ought to be to make that province the citadel of free institutions, tempered by an admixture of monarchy and aristocracy, as in the old country. That victory has put it in the power of the home Government to place our institutions and those of the United States in immediate and startling contrast, so that all the world may see which is best calculated to promote the material and spiritual interests of a people – to make a great a happy state. . . .

. . . Among the British settlers, the Scotch, and descendants of American loyalists, have a similar bias. The majority of the Canadian people are decidedly prepossessed in favour of monarchical and aristocratical institutions; and by favouring and encouraging this predilection the British Government would favour the growth of a Canadian national spirit markedly distinguished from that of the United States. This national spirit would be a common ground on which the population of British and the population of French origin would naturally meet and learn to sympathise with each other. This aristocratico-monarchical feeling would be a bond of sympathy with Britain; would induce the Anglo-Norman population of Canada to effect the British alliance in preference to that of the United States. The development of institutions in harmony with those of the mother country in Canada would moreover impress a more elevated and generous character in the Canadians than that which seems to be gaining the ascendancy in the United States. This would prove an attraction to not a few of the most amiable, accomplished, and wealthy of the American citizens to adopt Canada as their country, and would thus increase the power and prosperity of the country.

(*Colonial Gazette*, 30 November 1844)

4 / AMERICAN ANNEXATION
   OR CANADIAN CONFEDERATION?

~ In their discussions of American ambitions and institutions, the Colonial Reformers constantly referred to the possibility that the Canadian provinces might be annexed or voluntarily drawn into the American Union. Signs of Canadian loyalty or disaffection were anxiously examined, but the likelihood of this unwelcome event was greatly increased by the indifference of British statesmen and their persistently unsympathetic policies towards British North America. The Reformers therefore argued that, unless the remaining defects and abuses in the colonial system were speedily eliminated, there was every chance that the Canadian provinces would not merely separate from the British empire but would join the United States. Admittedly, Canadian loyalty and the advantages of free trade would tend to discourage annexation, as the *Spectator* optimistically pointed out in 1845.~

. . . A more warm and prevalent spirit of loyalty to Great Britain and her institutions animates the Canadas and seaboard provinces at this juncture than in any period since the war of 1812. The wiser policy introduced by Lord Durham has convinced the colonists that there really exists a desire in England to respect their liberties and promote their interests. They are also impressed with a general conviction that it is more advantageous to be born citizens of the British empire than of the American Union; that a wider sphere of action, greater prospects of personal advancement, are open to the British than the American citizen. Conjoined with this is a belief that if old systems of commercial restriction are to survive, British trade is more profitable to them than American; and a surmise that, after all, the exclusive policy is likely to have a shorter tenure of existence in Britain than in the Union. To be drawn into the maelstrom of the American Union, is a thing viewed in Canada with universal distaste; and throughout the whole of British North America, the anxiety to see Oregon rescued from the Republicans is much stronger than in this country. These are facts that cannot be concealed from the Americans; and they tend materially to lessen the numbers of those who dream of one great republic extending from the Isthmus of Panama to the shores of the Icy Ocean. . . . The loyalty of the Canadians will throw cold water on the war fever-heat of the Union: a fact which, it is to be hoped, will not be without influence in our own Foreign Office, whoever is to be its occupant.

(*Spectator*, 20 December 1845)

~ Nevertheless, the *Spectator* argued in 1849 that British policy towards Canada in recent years had been selfish and ill-advised, and that the time for the constructive and successful reform of colonial relations had now apparently passed.~

Fortune favours the Manchester school. As the potato-rot helped them to a repeal of the Corn-laws, so another triumph seems coming to them by means of events in which they have no part. Mr. Cobden no sooner proposes to get rid of our Colonies, than the Colonies set about leaving us of their own accord. . . . England's empire in the West is beginning to dissolve; our Colonial system is falling to pieces; and the British public has not a thought about the matter. Canada is the first to move in this Colonial revolution. . . .

We purposely abstain on this occasion from dwelling on the remote causes of the present disposition of Canada to join the

United States. They have been numerous and various, but would all be described under the general head of wrongs and affronts suffered by the colonists at the hands of Imperial England. Two or three examples will suffice for illustration. England, or rather her Colonial Office acting in her name, prepared and cultivated the antagonism of races in Lower Canada. . . . The government of Upper Canada by England produced the rebellion there, as rebellions in general are occasioned by the governments against which they are directed. England united the two Provinces against the will of a vast majority of the inhabitants; and she did this . . . by means, with regard to a pretended assent by the colonists, which added insult to oppression. The government of Canada by England during the first year of the provincial union closely resembled, in its very worst features, the last year of the government of France by Louis Philippe. England . . . proposed to Canada a great revolution in the commercial policy of the colony: as soon as the suggestion was adopted, and a revolution made which deeply affected every interest in the colony, England suddenly, without a word of notice or apology, overturned the whole proceeding, and half ruined the colony by another revolution of her own sole making. The repeal of the English Corn-laws coming immediately after Lord Stanley's Canada Corn Act, reduced the public revenue of Canada from £506,826 in 1847, to £379,648 in 1848, and threw every farmer and miller and corn-dealer on his back, seven-eighths of the colonists being composed of these classes. England put an end to the Canadian monopolies of timber and corn, but maintained her Navigation-laws after withdrawing the bribe that made those laws tolerable for the colonists. Upon Canada and her other dependencies in North America, as upon her dependencies in the West Indies, England plays fantastic tricks, such as she would do battle with the world in arms rather than allow to be played upon herself. Columns might be filled with a bare catalogue of the provocations to revolt which England has addressed to Canada in the last twenty years. And all this while, but especially during the last ten years, thinkers and writers in England and the Colonies have been hard at work exposing the inherent defects and abuses of our Colonial system. Colonial reform was never a popular subject at home; but in the Colonies a profound impression has been made by the labours of such persons as Mr. Roebuck, Lord Durham, Sir William Molesworth, Mr. Wakefield, Mr. Charles Buller, and Lord Howick, and such journals as the *Spectator* since 1830 and the *Times* and *Morning Chronicle* during the last year or two. The Colonial Reformers have been unable to construct: even Lord Durham's suggestions with regard to Canada were grievously marred in the execution; and in other respects the combined omnipotence and indifference of the British Parliament forbade construction – made the pursuit of reform conducive to destruction only. The old house has been undermined and loosened in all its fastenings; and nothing has been got ready for putting another in its place. There is a time for all things. As respects British North America, and probably the British West Indies, the time for reform has, we believe, passed away for ever. Mr. Roebuck and Sir William Molesworth may promote "inquiry" in Parliament; Mr. Wakefield and Mr. Roebuck may frame plans of colonial government and publish them in volumes: as the Paris revolutionist said of Louis Philippe's abdication in favour of his grandson, "it is too late". . . .

Nevertheless, England may choose to fight everywhere rather than yield her possessions in the West to American annexation. If she did not fight in America, she might have to defend herself in Europe, in Asia, and at home, against France or Russia, or both combined, tempted by her apparent weakness and decline to revenge Waterloo, seize Constantinople, and invade India. The annexation of Canada to the United States is full of awful consequences for England. One of the most probable of them, though not the worst, is a war with the United States: and a war, *that* would be, of infinite fierceness. So, although Fortune appears to favour the Manchester school, she would be fickle as ever before the end. "Financial reform" with an American war on our hands, and perhaps a French one into the bargain! Cobden for ever! – seeing that Russell, and Peel, and Stanley, and John Bull himself, are asleep to the concerns of England in the West.

(*Spectator*, 12 May 1849)

~ The *Spectator* continued to denounce the inaction and indifference that appeared to prevail amongst British statesmen and officials. Positive measures were urgently required if imperial relations were to be placed on a new and more cordial footing, and if separatist tendencies, already much in evidence in British North America, were to be successfully counteracted.~

Tradition says that Queen Mary died of grief for the loss of Calais: how would Queen Victoria take the loss of her Colonies? Such a result is not impossible. On the first blush of the thing it does seem incredible that this mighty empire, "upon which the sun never sets," should go to pieces, and signalize the commencement of its downward career by imitating the dismemberment of the Spanish and Portuguese empires; but such things have been, and England herself has lost one colonial dominion. The idea of independence is becoming familiarized to colonists in various quarters; and several English statesmen, actuated by indifference or the fatalism of official routine, studiously and avowedly contemplate the ultimate separation of the Colonies. The "old English" notion of maintaining the integrity of the empire has succumbed before the philosophy of the Manchester school, which can respect nothing that is not vindicated by the direct profit and loss account in a money value.

Thus there is no influence opposed to the disintegrating process which is at work in the Colonies themselves. It is not to be denied that in all directions the ties are considerably loosened. The Orange party of Canada West is making an organized demand for commercial protection and a federal union of the Provinces as a means of overwhelming the Franco-Canadian majority: but whatever may come of that movement, "annexation" will be the policy of the Opposition in Canada: if federation answer the purpose of the Orangemen, the Franco-Canadians and British Liberals will look to overcome it by annexaton; if federation fail the Orangemen, *they* will look to annexation; material interest points to annexation; the official trifling with the colony converts loyal regard into vexation and dislike; the seclusion of Lord Elgin, apparently in fear of popular outrage, brings the Monarchy which he represents into contempt. The Canadians have poor inducements to loyalty. . . .

In one sense, three alternatives appear to exhaust the prospect of eventualities: to continue as we are; to commence the work of separation by the annexation of Canada to the American Union; to supersede the motives to such annexation by improving the relation of the Colonies to the United Kingdom.

To continue as we are is manifestly impossible. In most of our Colonies there are grievances wholly unsettled, provoking new exasperations, and inflicting a continuance of material injury: it is so with the fast and loose Free-trade policy exercised towards Canada. . . .

Separation, beginning with North American annexation, is not only possible, but highly probable, considering the motives already mentioned, and the official indifferentism. But how it would be possible to maintain the rank of England in the scale of nations when she had been stripped of her Colonies, or how Whig optimists and Manchester economists could reconcile the Sovereign and people of England to the "dismemberment of the empire," we do not foresee.

To improve the Colonial relation, therefore, is the alternative that ought to be earnestly considered. Some broad principles, possessing unity in themselves but capable of diverse application, should be settled. It seems quite possible to do that. To limit and define the matters which must be reserved for the Imperial authority, is the first essential, – sovereignty, foreign relations, ubiquity and inviolability of British citizenship. All other matters may be safely surrendered to the Colonies, to govern according to local knowledge and the varying necessities of varying latitudes. Under the present system, federation can do nothing for the Colonies which they cannot attain separately; but it might greatly facilitate a reformed organization of the Colonial empire. Every group must, in some degree, acquire its own nationality: in character, the West Indian, the North American, and South African, and the Australian, differ as much from each other as they do from the home-keeping Englishman. That distinct nationality ought to be respected in the spirit as well as the letter of the new Colonial constitution. By bringing to bear upon the government of the Colonies grouped into federations all the resources of the empire, it would be possible to excite stronger sympathies than ever, – ambition for official promotion, the more attractive if it were carried through an ascending scale; love of honours, the greater if they were recognized at home; affection for the Monarchy, if that were reciprocally represented in every part of the colony by colonists, and accessible to the colonists by deputy in the metropolis. . . .

(*Spectator*, 25 August 1849)

~ As an effective means of counteracting the influences and ambitions of the United States, the Colonial Reformers advocated a wider union of the British colonies in North America. As Lord Durham argued in his *Report*, a union of the various provinces enjoying the benefits of responsible government would not only offer increased material advantages, but would strengthen imperial ties.~

. . . Such a union would . . . form a great and powerful people, possessing the means of securing good and responsible government for itself, and which, under the protection of the British

Empire, might in some measure counterbalance the preponderant and increasing influence of the United States on the American continent. I do not anticipate that a Colonial Legislature thus strong and thus self-governing, would desire to abandon the connexion with Great Britain. On the contrary, I believe that the practical relief from undue interference, which would be the result of such a change, would strengthen the present bond of feelings and interests; and that the connexion would only become more durable and advantageous, by having more of equality, of freedom, and of local independence. But at any rate, our first duty is to secure the well-being of our colonial countrymen; and if in the hidden decrees of that wisdom by which this world is ruled, it is written, that these countries are not for ever to remain portions of the Empire, we owe it to our honour to take good care that, when they separate from us, they should not be the only countries on the American continent in which the Anglo-Saxon race shall be found unfit to govern itself.

I am, in truth, so far from believing that the increased power and weight that would be given to these Colonies by union would endanger their connexion with the Empire, that I look to it as the only means of fostering such a national feeling throughout them as would effectually counterbalance whatever tendencies may now exist towards separation. No large community of free and intelligent men will long feel contented with a political system which places them, because it places their country, in a position of inferiority to their neighbours. The colonist of Great Britain is linked, it is true, to a mighty Empire; and the glories of its history, the visible signs of its present power, and the civilization of its people, are calculated to raise and gratify his national pride. But he feels, also, that his link to that Empire is one of remote dependence; he catches but passing and inadequate glimpses of its power and prosperity; he knows that in its government he and his own countrymen have no voice. While his neighbour on the other side of the frontier assumes importance, from the notion that his vote exercises some influence on the councils, and that he himself has some share in the onward progress of a mighty nation, the colonist feels the deadening influence of the narrow and subordinate community to which he belongs . . . the influence of the United States surrounds him on every side, and is for ever present. It extends itself as population augments and intercourse increases; it penetrates every portion of the continent into which the restless spirit of American speculation impels the settler or the trader . . . it stamps, on all the habits and opinions of the surrounding countries, the common characteristics of the thoughts, feelings and customs of the American people. Such is necessarily the influence which a great nation exercises on the small communities which surround it. Its thoughts and manners subjugate them, even when nominally independent of its authority. If we wish to prevent the extension of this influence, it can only be done by raising up for the North American colonist some nationality of his own; by elevating these small and unimportant communities into a society having some objects of a national importance; and by thus giving their inhabitants a country which they will be unwilling to see absorbed even into one more powerful. . . .

(Lucas, *Lord Durham's Report*, ɪɪ, 309-12)

~ In the 1840's the Colonial Reformers frequently referred to the question of Canadian union or federation. The theme was fully elaborated by J. A. Roebuck in his book, *The Colonies of England*.~

. . . No one disputes at this time the assertion, that our provinces in North America must soon be independent. A few years since, I was nearly hooted out of the land for stating this disagreeable truth. . . .

. . . The separation of the British North American colonies from England, in itself, never to me appeared a calamity – provided: 1. First, that the separation was *amicable*. 2. And second, that they were not added to the United States, but were formed into one independent federation – governing themselves, and united in bonds of friendship with England.

The extension of the power of the United States to the North Pole I have always considered an event fatal to the maritime superiority of England. Possessed of the St. Lawrence, the United States would, in fact, have no frontier to defend. Her offensive and defensive power would be increased by that acquisition to an extent, that would render her influence dangerous to the general liberty of the world. I seek, therefore, to prevent that acquisition. We cannot do it by doggedly and tenaciously attempting to keep things as they are on the American Continent – but we ought to look forward – and so prepare for the future, as to render the existence of a new confederation not only probable but certain – a confederation which would prove a counterpoise to the gigantic empire and influence of the United States – a confederation, in which there are really no hostile interests. No slavery exists there to separate north from south; – no variety of climate, by producing different commodities, renders necessary different markets, and thus tends to separate interests. The chief products of British North America find their best market in England, or the dependencies of England, and there is, therefore, no jealousy between the separate provinces created by different commercial connexions and necessities. Geographically, they are one people – and may, in despite of their rigorous climate, form by union a really powerful federate community – which, with the friendship and alliance of England, may not only easily maintain itself independent, but constitute a formidable counterpoise to the United States.

If we, however, are determined to consider our colonial dominion immortal; – if we do nothing to relieve the people now living in those provinces from the humiliations of a contrast between their own inferior position and that enjoyed by the citizens of the republic by their side, we shall alienate the now colonists from our rule; – they will seek to obtain independence in the readiest way which offers, and that will then be, by joining the United States as separate and independent states, and becoming members of the republican federation. They will leave us with a hostile feeling – they will leave us probably after a rebellion and a war – they will throw themselves upon the United States for assistance. That assistance will be given, a war with the United States will follow; and whatever may be the valour of our armies, or the skill of our generals, the result is inevitable; the whole continent will be violently wrested from our grasp, and we shall remain shorn of our provinces, seriously injured in our means, gasping and bleeding at every pore, with a world made our bitter foes – and without a friend or ally, either in Europe or America. This language I have always held – and in order to prevent such a fatal catastrophe, I have pressed upon the attention of successive colonial ministers the necessity of preparing the colonies for emancipation and independence, not only with respect to England, but to the United States also. They have either been unable or unwilling to adopt or to frame any scheme for that purpose. . . .

. . . The Colonial Office has been fairly beaten in Canada, and Canada is on the high road to independence. This they who govern in the dark nooks of that favourite resort of tortuous politicians well know; they are perfectly aware of what I am now stating, and they sit with folded hands, content now that

Canada cannot longer be continued as a field of Colonial Office patronage, to let her slip from our dominion, and become an integral portion of the United States. Talk with any of the politicians who, in 1838, would have been well pleased to have indicted me for high treason, and learn what they now say and think: "It is quite clear that independence must come – and soon, though we cannot exactly say when. And, in truth, why should it not?" they inquire. "The parliament of Canada, with responsible government is really independence?" Why she should not be independent in the sense they mean, *I* well know. She should not, because she ought not, for England's sake, to form a portion of the United States. We have seen what American statesmen have done in the south towards an unoffending but weak neighbour. They have stripped Mexico of her fairest provinces – waged with her an unjust war, under all sorts of false pretences, but really, for the sole purpose of extending their territories, and obtaining safe and commodious harbours in the Pacific. They will not be backward to foment disputes between England and her colonies if there be any chance of adding those colonies to the Union. The language which the statesmen of America are accustomed to employ when speaking of Canada, saying, "they have no desire to have any addition made to the Union on that side," is as hollow as that which they employed respecting Texas. *All* politicians now in America are willing, many are intensely anxious to obtain Canada. The large addition to the south, made of territory in which slavery is not prohibited by the constitution, has given to the slave states a chance of increasing their power, by establishing new and slave-holding states, and recovering their preponderance in the Union. The anti-slave party, therefore, seek for more non-slave-holding territory and states. In Canada and all British America, there are territories and communities of this description. The whole northern and abolition parties are eager to add Canada to the Union. In their self-denying protestations I put no faith. They have now precisely the same wishes and feelings as those which influenced their forefathers in 1774 and 1776. . . .

. . . I look, therefore, at the apathy of our own statesmen with alarm – seeing clearly that not only is Canada and all North America lost for England, but that these provinces will be added to the United States, unless the public mind of England is roused by having the real state of things exposed – the difficulties laid bare – and also the mode pointed out by which the impending mischief may be avoided. The time for effecting this great object is not yet passed, though the difficulty is greater, and the benefit likely to result from it not so certain as when, in 1838, I pressed the subject upon Lord Durham's consideration. A bitter feeling of animosity has been created among a large portion of the Canadian population, just that portion upon whom England might have placed her chief reliance – viz., the French Canadians. The population speaking English, have among them many persons coming from the United States, and entertaining the opinions, political and social, of the citizens of that republic. The population of Upper Canada, all by degrees assimilate to that of the United States, and they will be the first to seek a union with the republic. The French Canadians . . . have no sympathy with the active, stirring, go-ahead American. Had we treated them with common justice they would have remained contented under our sway. . . . By care and fairness, the affections of these people, I hope, may be regained; they would form a great item in the federal union I have proposed, and that federal union, by giving dignity and hope to all who form a portion of it, would effectually check the tendency of Upper English Canada to Americanize – would knit Nova Scotia, New Brunswick, Prince Edward's Island, and Newfoundland, into one powerful confederation, which would for centuries be a bulwark for England, and to all time a check and counterpoise to the advancing power of the United States.

Such, then, is my plan for British North America. I contemplate an extension of our dominion across the continent . . . and thus a new life would be inspired into the premature decrepitude of Canada. Let her statesmen feel themselves the rivals of those of Washington, and able to meet them on equal terms; and then in Nova Scotia, in Lower Canada, in Upper Canada, in the new States that might immediately arise on their long frontier line, and also beyond the Rocky Mountains north of the River Columbia – you would soon see them with expanded views and daring conceptions, the really formidable opponents of that encroaching republic which is destined to usurp dominion over the whole continent unless checked and circumscribed by a spirit as bold and free as her own. That spirit we may awake, by calling into existence a great NORTHERN CONFEDERATION OF BRITISH AMERICAN PROVINCES.

(Roebuck, *The Colonies of England*, pp. 188-90, 220-5)

~ Roebuck's comments anticipated the eventual creation of a Canadian confederation, but his advocacy of closer union amongst the provinces of British North America was mainly concerned with the protection of British interests through the formation of an effective bulwark against the territorial ambitions of the United States. Englishmen had long been apprehensive that the Canadian provinces might, singly or jointly, enter the American Union, and the vocal annexationist movement in Canada in 1849 appeared to give substance to this fear. While the Colonial Reformers were correct in emphasizing the increased importance of ties of sentiment as a means of holding together a series of self-governing communities in an era of imperial free trade, Canadian suspicion of and hostility towards the United States was to prove a far stronger force than Englishmen realized.~

SUGGESTIONS FOR FURTHER READING

Amongst primary sources readily available, *Lord Durham's Report*, together with BULLER'S *Report on Public Lands and Emigration*, are crucial. The standard edition of the *Report* is that by C. P. LUCAS (Oxford, 3 vols., 1912), though the edition by R. COUPLAND (Oxford, 1930), contains an excellent introduction. An edition by G. M. CRAIG was published in the Carleton Library in 1963. BULLER'S *Responsible Government for Colonies* was reprinted in E. M. WRONG, *Charles Buller and Responsible Government* (Oxford, 1926). Recently reissued is WAKEFIELD'S *England and America* (New York, 1967).

For the individual Reformers, CHESTER W. NEW, *Lord Durham* (Oxford, 1929) is important (the Canadian portion of this biography, entitled *Lord Durham's Mission to Canada*, is available in the Carleton Library, 1963); useful but unsatisfactory is PAUL BLOOMFIELD, *Edward Gibbon Wakefield* (London, 1961). The ideas and activities of the Colonial Reformers are discussed within the wider imperial context by many authors. Particularly influential, but uncritical and now somewhat outdated, are C. A. BODELSEN, *Studies in Mid-Victorian Imperialism* (Copenhagen, 1924, and London, 1960); ROBERT LIVINGSTON SCHUYLER, *The Fall of the Old Colonial System: A Study in British Free Trade, 1770-1870* (New York, 1945, and Hamden, Conn., 1966); KLAUS E. KNORR, *British Colonial Theories, 1570-1850* (Toronto, 1944, and 1963). A much sounder and more valuable study of imperial policy in the early Victorian period is W. P. MORRELL, *British Colonial Policy in the Age of Peel and Russell* (London, 1930, and 1966).

Canadian developments during these years can be studied in HELEN TAFT MANNING, *The Revolt of French Canada, 1800-1835* (Toronto, 1962); AILEEN DUNHAM, *Political Unrest in Upper Canada, 1815-1836* (London, 1927), reissued in the Carleton Library, 1963; GERALD M. CRAIG, *Upper Canada, The Formative Years, 1784-1841* (Toronto, 1963); J. M. S. CARELESS, *The Union of the Canadas, The Growth of National Institutions, 1841-1857* (Toronto, 1967). Amongst many books on Canadian-American relations, particularly useful are FRED LANDON, *Western Ontario and the American Frontier* (New Haven and Toronto, 1941), reissued in the Carleton Library, 1967; ALBERT B. COREY, *The Crisis of 1830-1842 in Canadian-American Relations* (New Haven and Toronto, 1941).

Index

THE CARLETON LIBRARY